C000017437

Purchasing, Costing and Control in the Hotel and Catering Industry

Frank Wood B.Sc.(Econ.), F.C.A. & *Peter Lightowlers* A.C.I.S.

Purchasing, Costing and Control in the Hotel and Catering Industry

Longman
London and New York

Longman Group Limited
Longman House, Burnt Mill, Harlow
Essex CM20 2JE, England
Associated companies throughout the world

Published in the United States of America
by Longman Inc., New York

First published 1985

British Library Cataloguing in Publication Data

Wood, Frank
Purchasing, costing and control in the hotel and catering industry.
1. Hotels, taverns, etc. Great Britain – Accounting
2. Caterers and catering – Great Britain – Accounting
I. Title II. Lightowlers, Peter
657'.837'00941 HF5686.H75

ISBN 0-582-41341-9

Produced by Longman Group (FE) Ltd
Printed in Hong Kong

Contents

UNIT 3 LEVEL

Preface

This book is intended to help those people who have embarked on a career in the Hotel and Catering Industry, who intend to study, either on a full-time or part-time basis, at Ordinary National Diploma or Certificate Level.

The Diploma requires the study of three Business and Technician Education Council units at levels 1, 2 and 3. in Purchasing, Costing and Control, over a period of two years. This book has been written to cover the three standard units issued by the Business and Technician Education Council in March 1984 (U84/229/236/241).

Students on Certificate programmes will study only the level 1 and 2 units.

Level 1 units are covered by chapters 1 to 5 inclusive, level 2 by chapters 6 to 20 inclusive, and level 3 by chapters 21 to 26 inclusive.

The authors wish to record the held and advice given by the following:

David Chopping, Lecturer in Hotel & Catering Costing, South Devon College of Arts and Technology, who has read some of the chapters and contributed both material and questions.

Michael Bean, Lecturer in Purchasing, South Devon College of Arts and Technology, who devised many of the questions used in the text.

The Hotel, Catering and Institutional Management Association who have given permission to use past examination questions.

PETER LIGHTOWLERS
FRANK WOOD
January 1985

1

Introduction

The study of this unit is intended to bring together the fact that the tasks of Purchasing, of Costing, and of Control in the industry are all inter-related. Purchasing without a real appreciation of the actual costs involved, or purchasing without the ability to control costs, would be extremely ineffective and inefficient. The link between these three aspects must therefore always be borne in mind.

It is important to understand that a hotel or a catering establishment has to make a 'profit' in order to be able to survive. Profit is the very lifeblood of any organisation in the private sector of any industry. Without it the organisation will soon wither away and die. There is not much point in having first-class chefs, or running a hotel so that all the guests are satisfied, unless the business is allowed to carry on and not have to close because of the lack of profits. Even in the public sector organisations have to meet the financial targets set for them. The word 'profit' may not be appropriate for them, but they will have a 'surplus' figure which they will have to meet.

It is also true that profits by themself are not enough. Many a hotel or catering establishment has had to shut down, not because it is not making profits but because it has run out of cash funds, it simply cannot pay its bills as they become due, and it cannot carry on any longer. At this early stage in your studies you may probably not appreciate what the links are between making profits and having enough cash funds to run the business. This will be fully explained to you as you go through this unit.

Such targets of 'profits' and of sufficient 'cash funds' needed to keep the business running efficiently so that the needs of the guests or customers can be met, can only be obtained in the long-term if good methods of purchasing are being used, the costs are known, and proper control is put into effect. A business might be able to exist in the short-term with poor purchasing methods, no knowledge of costs, and therefore obviously no real control, but it would soon start to flounder.

Of course, there are other aspects in the running of a hotel and catering organisation, and these are dealt with in the other units to be studied. A truly successful business has each department of the business running efficiently, all aimed towards the objectives laid down for the whole organisation. A restaurant with the most efficient buying, costing and control systems would not function very well if it employed very poor kitchen staff. One with first-class kitchen staff, but which never bought the right things at the right time would soon be in difficulties, in fact probably the kitchen staff would leave in disgust before too long. A restaurant which offered superb meals, but at too high a price for its customers, would also soon come to an end.

This unit should therefore not be seen in isolation. It is a necessary and vital link between all the other units being studied by you. It should also provide a link in your understanding of how other organisations outside the hotel and catering industry function, because many of the principles involved belong equally as well with them. This should help someone in a hotel, for instance, when dealing with an outside organisation. If the hotel is offering, say, banqueting or exhibition facilities to an engineering organisation, then such a customer will see this as part of its 'purchasing' activity.

The principles they will apply in their 'purchasing', their 'costing' and their 'control' will be the same basically as that applied by your own organisation when purchasing. The appreciation of what it is that you should expect when you are 'purchasing' will help you to satisfy the needs of your own customers/guests when they are 'purchasing'.

2

Principles of Purchasing

Learning Objectives

At the end of this chapter you should be able to:

2A Recognise the contribution of the purchasing function to effective business management.

2B Know the basis on which sources of supply are selected.

2C Know how to use correct ordering procedures.

The need for Purchasing

Buying goods and services is part of our lives. Organisations in the hotel and catering industry also need to buy goods and services. The main reason for buying goods in the industry is to sell them as prepared food and drink to the general public. The role of the hotel and catering industry is to supply food and beverages and/or accommodation to the consumer i.e. the general public.

In normal language usage the words "buying" and "purchasing" usually mean the same thing. Each organisation in the hotel and catering industry will have to perform the "purchasing or buying function". In a small firm this may be only part of one employee's duties, in a larger organisation several employees may be involved.

The buyer will have to obtain the following goods and services:

1. Food and Beverages. In chapter 12 these will be described as "direct materials" and in chapter 18 as "purchases" and "stock".
2. Other goods and services which will be used up i.e. consumed by the firm in the short term. Examples are gas, electricity, wages to employees and cleaning materials. In chapter 4 these will be referred to as "labour and overheads".
3. Goods which will not be consumed or sold. Examples are kitchen equipment, furniture and motor vehicles. In chapter 19 these goods will be called fixed or long term assets and they will last for several years before being replaced.

The Purchasing Function

In order to appreciate how important purchasing is it may be useful to consider what happens when purchasing is not carried out properly. The problems may be summarised as follows:

1. The goods and services may cost more than is necessary, resulting in a poor investment or a reduction in profits.
2. The quality of goods purchased may be inferior or inappropriate, which may result in dissatisfied customers who are unlikely to return, again causing a reduction in profits.
3. Stock required may not be ordered in time. This may result in certain sales items not being available, for example a particular wine on the wine list.

Clearly poor purchasing will cause a reduction in profits, in particular this is true of the buying of food and drink. It is essential not to underestimate the importance of the purchasing function.

The basic principles of Purchasing

Hotel and catering establishments vary enormously in size. A guest house with 10 bedrooms will tackle the buying problem in a different way to an hotel with 500 rooms, which in turn will have a different system to the centralised buying department of a hotel chain or group. Whatever the situation certain basic principles apply. These are:

1. The description and quantity of the goods and services required.
2. The investigation of alternative sources of supply.
3. The rational selection of the best source taking into account:
   - (*a*) The true cost. This will not include Value Added Tax but it will include the benefit of any trade discount. The cost of delivery may or may not be included in quoted prices.
   - (*b*) The quality required.
   - (*c*) The suppliers' reputations and their ability to deliver.
4. The communication of the order to the supplier in a clear and concise way.
5. The correct receipt of deliveries and later payment in the case of credit supplies. The alternative of "cash and carry" by your own organisation should be considered.
6. A correct system of storage and issue for appropriate materials. This will be considered in detail in chapter 3.

Any system of buying or the operation of a purchasing department will have to adopt methods to comply with the above principles.

The Aims of effective Purchasing

The main aims of a buyer may be summarised as follows:

1. To buy the required quality of materials at the lowest possible price. This involves continuous investigation to obtain cheaper and better supplies. To achieve this the buyer will have to be aware of new products and the development of existing products.
2. To standardise stock requirements in order to keep stock levels at a minimum. For example, if a caterer stocked every type of potato which were best for particular dishes, this would be too expensive in terms of both storage space and the holding of stocks of each type. It would be better to stock only a few varieties of potato.
3. To obtain advanced information regarding market price fluctations and also other factors affecting supply in order to ensure continuity of supply.
4. To develop goodwill with the supplier. The buyer needs to be honest and courteous at all times.
5. To use the most appropriate buying system for the variety of goods and services required. This will be discussed later on in the chapter.
6. To devise and maintain an efficient system of documents and records of the work involved in purchasing.
7. To liaise and co-operate with staff in other areas or departments of the organisation.

The Selection of Suppliers

The purchasing process begins with the selection of appropriate sources of supply. Most catering organisations will have numerous suppliers who are prepared to compete for their orders. This makes it more difficult for the buyer because the choice of the correct supplier is vital. The buyer will need to investigate each potential supplier before entrusting any business with a particular firm.

Potential Sources of Supply

In any locality there will be a selection of local suppliers. The easiest reference is Yellow Pages issued by British Telecom. This will provide several suppliers for a particular order and it may be possible to contact other local caterers for advice about a particular supplier. They may be able to suggest a better alternative from their past experience.

It is not always appropriate to use a local supplier. There are national directories aimed at the hotel and catering industry such as The Caterer and Hotelkeeper's Buyer's Guide. This gives company and product information on anything from expensive equipment to cheap food items. For wines and spirits there is Harper's Directory and for food there is the Food Trades Directory and Food Buyers Handbook. There are Trade Exhibitions both at regional and national level. The best known is Hotelympia a bi-annual event in London.

Available Purchasing Systems

There are a number of alternatives available to the caterer:

1. Buying direct from a manufacturer or producer.
2. Buying at a specialized market.
3. Buying through a wholesaler.
4. Buying through a total supplier.
5. Buying at a cash and carry wholesaler.

The buyer may use only one of the above or a combination to meet the firm's requirements. His choice will depend largely on the size of the business and whether he can justify employing specialized buying staff, or whether he performs the buying function entirely by himself. The use of specialists should ensure the "best" price for each commodity by choice of the right system. A firm with only one buyer may use one "total supplier" who delivers all requirements on a daily basis. The following table may be useful to assist the buyer to select the most appropriate system for a particular order:

Purchasing Source	Advantages	Disadvantages
1. Manufacturers/Producers e.g. chocolate, eggs.	Best price, good trade discounts. "Fresh" produce. Credit terms.	Must buy in bulk. Ties up working capital and storage space. Excess paper work.
2. Specialised markets. e.g. fruit, fish, meat.	Good prices. Good range of items. Special offers.	"Middlemen" more costly than 1. Buyer must be present. Own transport required. Possibly no credit.
3. Wholesalers i.e. Middle men who buy from 1 and 2. Provide a warehouse function.	Wide range of products. Good service from wholesalers representatives. Credit terms.	Products not as fresh as 1 & 2. Extra cost for their services.
4. Total suppliers. Special wholesaler stocking all needs of a caterer.	Daily deliveries. Only 1 supplier. Less paper work. Credit terms.	Dependant on one supplier. Extra cost of special service. Out of touch with market prices.
5. Cash and Carry.	Visual display. Emergency only. Less paper work than 1 to 4. Wide range.	Some prices are at retail level, too expensive. Own transport/time. No credit.

The price is probably the biggest factor in deciding the source of supply. In 1, 2 & 3 above the price can be subject to flexibility as follows:

1. Buying in bulk means that the cost price per unit will be less than buying in small quantities. Contracting for large quantities from one supplier over a period of time will also give a price advantage.
2. The buyer's knowledge of prices from alternative suppliers will affect prices. If a buyer is known to compare prices then any supplier wishing to obtain the order will quote the lowest possible price. The common use of daily and weekly quotation sheets (schedules to compare the prices of alternative suppliers for required commodities) is proof of the value of this practice. The quality of the product must be given to the supplier. This is best done by a written specification.

Using Purchasing Specifications

When purchasing commodities the buyer may use "a purchase specification" to obtain comparative quotations from suppliers. The standard specification will include:

1. A definition of the item required.
2. The required grade if a grading system is in common use.
3. The weight if appropriate.
4. The degree of preparation if appropriate.
5. The delivery date.
6. The method of delivery.
7. Any other information relating to quality including variety, development and maturity, age, colour, shape, cleanliness, degree of defects or blemishes acceptable.

The main purpose of the specification is to advise the supplier what is required. There are other advantages including:

1. The comparison of competitive quotations in response to the same purchase specification.
2. Giving advice to the storekeeper regarding standards required before signature of acceptance.
3. Ensuring the same standard for future supplies. This will assist in both costing and control.

The buyer will draw up the specifications with the help of other staff within the organisation. For example the chef may assist with food items. For some products it may be necessary to seek the advice of the suppliers. A copy of the specification will be sent to the suppliers invited to quote, together with an estimate of future quantities required. The returned quotations will be used to select the most suitable supplier. It is important to check that the chosen supplier remains competitive by inviting quotations from other suppliers at regular intervals.

The Correct Ordering Procedure

A catering organisation may be divided into departments. Exhibit 2.1 is an example of an organisation chart of a hotel:

Exhibit 2.1

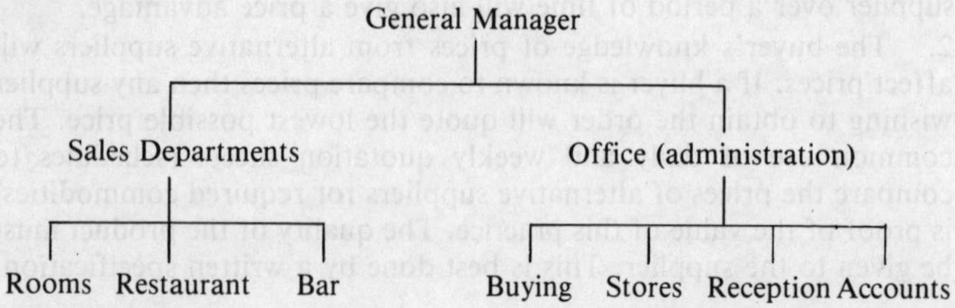

A firm can operate a specialised buying department or allow each departmental manager to do his own buying. Suppose the office manager requires 2 new office desks. We will follow the necessary procedure to obtain the desks assuming a separate buying department.

The office manager will send a PURCHASES REQUISITION to the buying department as in exhibit 2.2.

Exhibit 2.2

PURCHASE REQUISITION

No. 16

Date 1st July 19–4

From Office Dept.

To Purchasing Dept.

Reference/Code	Description	Quantity
	Office Desks	Two

Date for delivery	Signature
August 19–4	P Hewitt

FOR PURCHASING DEPT. USE

ORDERED FROM	ORDER NO.	DATE

This document gives the name of the department ordering the desks, the goods required and any special conditions such as the date by which the goods are required. It must be signed by the head of that department.

Letter of Enquiry

When the Purchasing Officer receives this requisition he will check his sources of information and select possible suppliers. It may be necessary to make enquiries of several firms to ensure that good terms are obtained. This may be done by letter (see Exhibit 2.4), as some firms do, or by a pre-printed form where only blank spaces have to be completed. (see Exhibit 2.3). In the case of goods needed at regular intervals (e.g. stationery, food) a regular supplier will be used so there will be no need to make enquiries for each order.

Exhibit 2.3

ANYFIRM plc
16 The Place
Leeds LS2 6TS

Telephone: 42631
Telex: 62143

OUR REF. YOUR REF.

Date 3rd July 19-4

Messrs. K. Smith & Co.
The Parade
Sheffield

Dear Sirs,

ENQUIRY No : 1620

We should be pleased if you would let us have a quotation for the following items:-

Two office desks (standard)

Delivery to above address within one month of order.

Would you please advise us of any special conditions or terms of sale.

Yours faithfully,
ANYFIRM plc

W Gledhill

W. GLEDHILL
Purchasing Officer

Exhibit 2.4

ANYFIRM plc
16 The Place
Leeds LS2 6TS

TELEPHONE: 42631
TELEX: 62143

DATE 3rd July 19-4

OUR REF. WG/AS
YOUR REF.

Messrs. K. Smith & Co.
The Parade
Sheffield.

Dear Sirs,

Enquiry No :1620

Please advise me of the cost of two standard office desks. We would require delivery to the above address within one month of order date.

Yours faithfully,
ANYFIRM plc

W Gledhill

W. Gledhill
Purchasing Officer

Quotation

The possible suppliers will reply in the form of a quotation. They may also include catalogues of the goods they sell together with price lists and terms of sale (i.e. any discounts and how soon payment is required after the goods have been delivered). In our example the Purchasing Officer receives three replies, each with a very similar price but with the following delivery conditions on receipt of an order.

K. Smith & Co., The Parade, Sheffield	—Delivery immediately from stock
A. Jones Ltd., City Street, Sheffield	—Delivery 2 months
A. Price, High Street, Sheffield	—Delivery 6 weeks

In view of the original enquiry sent out, which quotation do you think the firm should accept?

As the firm required delivery within one month then the quotation of K. Smith & Co. would be the most suitable one. It meets the delivery requirements, and the prices of the three suppliers are similar. If the price had been much higher then the Purchasing Officer would have to decide which was most important — cost or a longer delivery time.

Having chosen a supplier the firm will place an order.

Purchase Order

The order is an offer to buy or, as in this case, an acceptance of a quotation. It is usually on a pre-printed form. Firms will not normally accept delivery of goods unless an official order has previously been sent to the supplier.

Exhibit 2.5

ANYFIRM plc
16 THE PLACE
LEEDS LS2 6TS

Order No. 48231
This number to be quoted in full on all correspondence

To:
K. Smith & Co.
The Parade,
Sheffield.

Date 14th. July 19-4

Dear Sirs
Please supply and deliver the following goods to the above address on or before the specified date: as soon as possible

Quantity	Size	Description	£	p
2	Standard	Office Desks	75 Each	00

Yours faithfully
for and on behalf of
ANYFIRM plc

W. Gledhill

Purchasing Officer

The order will have the following information on it:

(*a*) The name and address of both firms concerned;

(*b*) A reference number;

(*c*) The date the order is made out;

(*d*) The description and quantity of goods required;

(*e*) Any instructions regarding delivery times and dates.

The top copy is sent to the supplier and will be signed by the Purchasing Officer. A copy of the order may be sent to the department requiring the goods and a further copy may be sent to Stores to check the goods on delivery. The Purchasing Department will keep a copy in their files for reference.

The Purchasing Officer will, when looking at the quotations, have considered any possible discounts offered. The discounts usually offered are:

(*a*) Trade Discount — This is a discount allowed to firms in the same trade, or by a manufacturer to a wholesaler, or by a wholesaler to a retailer. The amount of discount can vary from customer to customer. It usually alters according to the quantity ordered to encourage customers to buy in bulk. The price before discount is deducted is called the "gross price", and after discount the "net price" or "trade price".

(*b*) Cash Discount — This is a discount given to customers to encourage them to pay their bills on time and may be in addition to the trade discount. If payment for the goods is made within a specified time then the allowance is deducted from the net price or trade price and the reduced amount is paid, i.e. "2½% 28 days" means 2½% can be deducted from the net invoice total if payment is made within 28 days of date of invoice. The entry is shown in the terms column of an invoice. If a price is shown simply as a "net price" then this means that no cash discount will be allowed.

The Purchasing Officer must be familiar with certain terms and conditions used by a supplier affecting delivery and packing costs. These can include:

(*a*) Ex Works — The price does not include delivery and the purchaser must arrange and pay for transport and delivery.

(*b*) Carriage Paid — The price includes delivery of the goods to the customer's premises.

(*c*) Carriage Forward — The price of the goods quoted does not include delivery. The goods will be delivered but an extra charge for delivery is made.

(*d*) Returnable Empties — Many firms who supply goods in expensive packing, such as wooden crates and drums, make a charge on the containers. This is refunded when the containers are returned to the supplier in good condition.

(*e*) Value Added Tax — VAT is a tax on sales turnover. It is raised at every level of activity starting with the first supplier and ends with the final customer. At each stage VAT is charged to the buyer on the selling price. The government department responsible for collection of VAT is the Customs and Excise. Every firm or individual whose turnover in taxable supplies of goods and/or services exceeds an amount set by the Chancellor of the Exchequer, must register with the Customs and Excise and keep records of all purchases, known as inputs, and all sales, known as outputs. At the end of each tax period (normally three months) a firm completes a form (VAT 100) showing all input tax and total output tax. It is important to firms that detailed records are kept for completion of the VAT form and to enable checks to be made by officials of the Customs and Excise. The actual rate of tax varies from one type of goods to another according to government policy.

Suppliers usually acknowledge orders by postcard and send a delivery note with the goods. This is followed later by an INVOICE which is usually directed to the ACCOUNTS Department, after checking by the buyer. The delivery note and Invoice are illustrated in Chapter 3.

Exercises

Note: **Questions without the suffix 'X' have answers shown at the back of this book. Questions with the suffix 'X' are set without answers in this book so that teachers/lecturers can set the questions for classwork or homework.**

2.1X. (*a*) Name two sources of information available to a purchasing department.

(*b*) Trade discount is given for prompt payment. State whether TRUE or FALSE

(*c*) Who pays the delivery and transport costs on goods purchased "Ex Works"? State whether PURCHASER or SUPPLIER

(*d*) After a quotation has been accepted what document will a Purchasing Officer send to a supplier of goods as confirmation?

(*e*) What is received by a purchaser in reply to a letter of enquiry?

(*f*) Who normally signs an internal requisition?

(*g*) Why do firms allow cash discounts?

(*h*) Who receives the top copy of a Purchase Order?

2.2X. (*a*) How would you install a comprehensive and efficient system of purchasing into any catering business with which you are familiar.
(*b*) What are the advantages of centralised purchasing?

2.3X. What are the relative advantages and disadvantages of using the purchasing system known as 'Cash and Carry'.

2.4X. Describe the procedure and the documentation that a purchasing officer might get involved with when selecting a new supplier for a particular commodity. Describe the above right up to the point when the goods are received into the establishment.

2.5X. Briefly explain (*a*) the work which the Buying Department of a catering enterprise carries out for the management, and (*b*) the duties of the Chief Buyer.

2.6X. (i) List the documents used by the buying department of a large catering organisation when operating their purchasing procedure.
(ii) Name two items which are described as purchases in a catering establishment.

2.7X. List the responsibilities of a buying officer in a large hotel.

2.8X. Why is a purchasing specification necessary?

2.9X. List the aims of purchasing.

2.10X. (i) Name the document a buying officer would use to obtain comparative quotations from different suppliers?
(ii) What information would it include?

3

Effective Storage and Stores Procedures

Learning Objectives

At the end of this chapter you should be able to:

3A **Appreciate the requirements for safe and sound storage of raw materials and equipment.**

3B **Know how to use stores control procedures.**

The person responsible for storage and stores procedures should have a suitable title. It may be Stores Controller or Chief Storekeeper. The controller's main responsibility is to ensure that materials are available when they are required by the other staff in a hotel or catering organisation. This requires the organisation of a system which receives and examines all delivered goods, and stores them under proper conditions until correctly requisitioned.

The controller's duties should not be confined to record keeping, in larger stores the keeping of records can be delegated to a clerk. The main tasks are to develop a sound storekeeping routine and organise a proper system of supervision.

Principles of Storage

Each catering organisation will have its own particular requirements for storage. There is no standard system which will suit all catering firms. Some will have just one central store, others will have several store areas. An hotel may have a food store, a liquor store in the cellar and another store for other consumable materials. Some firms will leave the stores function to each departmental manager.

Situation of the Stores

The stores should be located near to the department concerned if at all possible. For example the food store should be convenient to the food production area. The outside entrance to the store should be suitable for vehicle deliveries. In hotels this is usually at the rear of the building away from the main entrance or reception.

Stores Layout

It is important to utilise the area available and if possible save some space for future expansion. This requires careful planning and the following factors are important:

1. Some materials require special facilities. The following are some examples:

(*a*) Refrigeration for meat, dairy produce and frozen foods.

(*b*) Special racks for wine bottles.

(*c*) Specially designed bins or containers for dry goods, fresh fruit & vegetables etc.

(*d*) Shelving for tinned goods.

(*e*) Drip trays for cooking oils.

2. The bins must be placed so that the room can be divided into aisles. The aisles must provide suitable access for both staff and materials. A wide centre aisle is advisable for the use of trolleys, fork-lift trucks and other handling equipment. The room should be kept clean and tidy and the best use should be made of window light to save electricity.

3. Bins or racks for the most frequently used items must have the most convenient access and heavy goods should be on the floor. Goods should be easy to count and stacked in rows of ten where possible.

4. After delivery and unpacking, if required, materials should flow smoothly through the stores and after requisition into the kitchen or bar. This can be illustrated in a diagram:

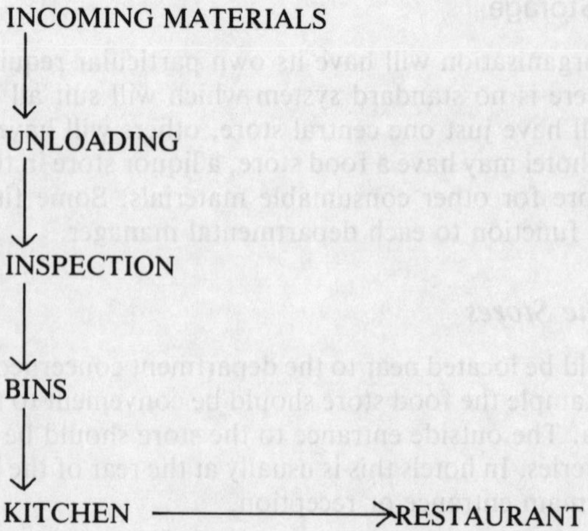

Stores Security

Dishonest staff, especially those handling money or stores, can cause severe losses for a firm. These losses can be due to theft, fraud and carelessness. They can often be avoided by better supervision and record keeping. The following points will improve security:
1. Goods should only be delivered at stated times when the stores staff are on duty and able to receive them.
2. Damaged or opened packages should be recorded on delivery notes before signature of receipt.
3. Delivered goods should be checked against both advice note and order.
4. Valuable stock should be under lock and key, and goods must not be left outside the store.
5. Faulty or missing items should be notified to the buyer or the supplier at once.
6. Authorised persons only should be allowed in the stores. Items should be issued over a counter except where this is inconvenient.
7. Proper stores records should be kept and periodic physical stocktaking should be organised.

Stores Records and Documents

Records are made from the following documents:
1. *Goods Received Notes* – these are written or typed in the stores from delivery notes and sent to the buying office.
2. *Purchase Requisitions* – these are sent by the stores to the buying office when a stores item falls below a given level.
3. *Bin Cards* – these are kept at each bin or container and show quantity receipts and issues. The balance should be the actual quantity in the bin.
4. *Stores Ledgers* – these are kept in either the stores or cost office. They record costs i.e. prices and quantities.
5. *Stores Requisitions* – these should only be signed by authorised persons. Issues should not be made without a signed requisition.
6. *Stores Returns Note* – these are used to record the return of surplus or wrong issues to store.
7. *Stores Transfer Notes* – these may be used to transfer a food item from one dish to another one or a bottle of whisky from the lounge bar to the cocktail bar.

The main documents will be illustrated later in the chapter.

Inspection

All goods received should be checked for quality and quantity as soon as possible. This is not possible for some items delivered in bulk.

A Summary of the Storekeeper's Duties

These duties can be listed:
1. To receive and store all materials until correctly requisitioned.
2. To keep all materials in store in good condition. This means a well organised, clean and tidy store area.
3. To issue materials against authorised requisitions.
4. To keep all unauthorised persons out of the store area.
5. To allow physical stocktaking to take place when ordered by management.
6. To check bin cards or stores ledgers systematically to ensure that re-ordering takes place when minimum stock levels are reached.

Weights and Measures

For the foreseeable future Food & Beverage supplies will continue to be received in either metric or imperial measures. The trend is towards metric therefore stores should adopt metric units and convert imperial supplies to metric.

The following conversions will be useful –

1 pint	=	0.568 litre
1 lb	=	0.4536 kilogram

Hygiene

What is hygiene?

Basically it is preventative medicine, i.e. it is a number of simple rules, most of which are common sense, which reduce your chances of either catching some disease and/or of passing it on to other people. These simple rules will only cost you a few minutes of your time each day, and a little forethought on your part.

Remember – anyone can, in certain circumstances, infect or be the cause of infecting others.

Why is hygiene so important?

(*a*) *Effects on personal health*

Poor attention to elementary hygiene rules can result in yourself and/or others getting food poisoning or dysentry.

The causes of food poisoning are tiny germs which are only visible when viewed through a microscope. These bacteria (germs) can either cause food poisoning or produce toxins (poisons). Germs can be spread in numerous ways: –

(i) by animals – rats, mice, birds;

(ii) by people;
(iii) by dirty premises or equipment;
(iv) by contaminated food or utensils;
(v) by air.

There are many types of food poisoning, some of which may cause only several hours of discomfort e.g. slight nausea (feeling sick) and mild diarrhoea.

In more serious forms, food poisoning results in fever, severe vomiting, diarrhoea, stomach pains and cramps. In some cases it has caused death either directly or indirectly.

Obviously, no one would wish to be the cause of this, either to themselves or to others, when by being careful you can greatly reduce the risk.

(*b*) *Effects on stores*

Poor standards of hygiene in stores operations should not be tolerated.

The local environmental health inspector is likely to call, perhaps the call may be a routine visit or it may be the result of a complaint. The environmental health inspector, who works for the local authority, has the power to: –

(i) require the manager to make small changes e.g. clean things up;
(ii) issue a condemnation notice – which means disposal of food considered unfit for human consumption;
(iii) in extreme cases, close down the business or part of it;
(iv) prosecute, should he decide to do so it would be under either:-
(A) the Food Hygiene (General) Regulations 1970 under which the business can be fined up to £100 for each breach of the regulations. There is also the possibility of up to three months imprisonment for the responsible officials.
(B) the Offices, Shops and Railway Premises Act 1963 which covers a number of areas closely related to hygiene e.g. overcrowding, cleanliness, ventilation and sanitation.

A court appearance is likely to prove time consuming and legal costs can be high. The greatest cost however will be bad publicity – quite possibly a report of the case will appear in the local paper with obvious effects on sales.

As a result of an outbreak of food poisoning which occurred in Winlaton near Gateshead, two men died and ten other people were made seriously ill.

A few years ago, four pensioners were infected by botulism, a severe form of food poisoning, as a result of eating tinned salmon. The deaths of two of the pensioners, and the national publicity given to the incident through the media, resulted, not only in the withdrawal of the affected type of salmon, but most other brands even though there was no question of them being contaminated.

(C) Finally, one of the relevant legal rules which applies here and in other situations is called "vicarious liability". Essentially this means that the law holds the employer liable for many of the mistakes made by his employees. Remember! ignorance of the law is no excuse.

Don't forget that these regulations apply to all people who handle open food at any stage in distribution.

Personal hygiene

(*a*) Some things are obviously desirable, such as washing hands, not spitting and not smoking whilst handling or being near food.

(*b*) Cuts, which may contain harmful bacteria, should be covered with a waterproof dressing. Germs can be passed on, especially by someone who washes food or plates and cutlery which come into contact with the food. Note that washing in warm or hot water does not kill all types of germs.

(*c*) Anyone suffering from certain infections e.g. influenza or a skin disease should stay at home. By going to work they are going to share their germs with others – staff and customers.

Another group of diseases is so serious that the occurrence of them has to be reported to the medical officer of health, e.g. Typhoid.

(*d*) Toilets and washing facilities must be provided, and notices requesting staff to wash their hands after using them.

(*e*) Personal clothing and overalls must be kept clean.

Premises

It is no use having hygienic, well-scrubbed staff if the equipment and premises are dirty and unhygienic. They may be so for a variety of reasons. e.g.

(*a*) dirty or greasy floors and walls;

(*b*) dirty or greasy equipment;

(*c*) the presence of rats, mice and cockroaches which carry germs;

(*d*) badly heated and ventilated premises – this can encourage germs to multiply.

Under suitable conditions, germs multiply by dividing into two every 20-30 minutes. So one germ can become over 2 million in 7 hours. If your doubt the correctness of the arithmetic, try asking your lecturer in Business Calculations. He will be interested in this form of progression. After 12 hours continuous growth there may be 7 billion.

If the premises and equipment are dirty or greasy, even though relatively germ free, flies will be attracted, these are often carriers of infection.

Food handling and storage

(*a*) Special facilities may be necessary for storing food e.g. fridges, refrigerated counters and ultra violet insect killers;

(*b*) Open food, e.g. cooked meats, should not be handled directly. Many caterers provide special utensils in appropriate cases, e.g. tongs for cakes;

(*c*) As has already been mentioned, the preparation and storage of food is covered by the Food Hygiene (General) Regulations 1970 which are part of the Food and Drugs Act 1955. This will be discussed in detail in Chapter 10.

Benefits of hygiene consciousness

(*a*) Unwashed floors, dirty cutlery, staff wearing grubby overalls may not in themselves result in food poisoning. However such obvious disregard indicates that the possibility exists.

(*b*) The benefits to business of hygiene precautions include: –

(i) extra custom;

(ii) reduction in the likelihood of customers, staff and others (e.g. deliverymen and representatives) contracting food poisoning;

(iii) reducing the possibility of prosecution and losses resulting from (ii) above;

(iv) reduction in losses due to spoiled food and beverages.

It thus makes good business sense to be hygiene conscious.

Safety

Why should we be safety conscious?

There are three reasons why each of us, no matter who we are, should try to make our surroundings – at home, work or elsewhere, as safe as possible.

(*a*) *Ethical* – Any reasonable person would think we owed it to others not to do anything or fail to do anything reasonable in order to reduce accidents. 'Do unto others as you would wish they would do unto you'.

(*b*) *Legal* – the law, both criminal and civil, also states that you should take care to reduce safety hazards. It penalises those who fail to do so, when injury occurs. This is discussed in more detail later.

(*c*) *Financial* – The high money costs of accidents, in addition to the pain and discomfort, cannot be overlooked.

What accidents cost

(*a*) *Cost to Society* – The costs of medical treatment, hospitals, ambulances and medicines resulting from accidents are paid by society in general, but chiefly by a group of which you are a member, that is of wage or salary earners. These costs are met from income tax and other form of taxation. Each pay day among the deductions from your wage or salary is one for National Health Contributions.

There is also the far greater cost of lost work. Someone off sick for a week obviously cannot do his job.

The state pays sickness and other related benefits to those who have have accidents. The cost of these is ultimately met by the taxpayer – you!

Under the National Insurance (Industrial Injuries) Act 1965, all persons in insurable employment are insured against:

(i) Personal injury caused by accident arising out of and in the course of their employment.

(ii) Certain diseases and personal injuries not caused by accident but which are due to the nature of the person's employment.

(*b*) *Costs to the Business* – As well as losing the benefit of the injured person's work, the business may also have to pay him. If the injury resulted from the negligence of the employer then the injured person, whether employee, customer or anyone else, can sue. This may mean heavy legal costs and compensation, which can be thousands of pounds in a case where someone is seriously injured.

This incidentally is why businesses are compelled by law to have insurance to cover these possibilities, known as employers' liability insurance. Otherwise they may not be in a position to pay compensation to the injured.

(*c*) *Costs to the Individual* – No-one can put a price on the suffering and loss of enjoyment resulting from an accident. Certain results can be costed, e.g. loss of earnings and damage to clothes and to other personal possessions.

Who is at risk?

(*a*) *The staff* – can be at risk in a variety of situations, such as using dangerous equipment, e.g. food slicing machines.

(*b*) *Others* – such as representatives and deliverymen, who may be put at risk by lack of care in the stockrooms and delivery bays due to poor lighting, unauthorised use of equipment by untrained personnel and uneven and/or slippery floors.

In addition inadequate fire equipment and precautions, lack of emergency exits, poor lighting, lack or appropriate training and first aid facilities, affect the safety of all.

The Law

The law protects people from safety hazards and in some cases even from themselves. If it were not for the law many people would probably ignore safety considerations and the number of accidents and deaths would be higher than it is.

(*a*) *Civil Law* – The civil law is concerned with the rights of the individual and the actions of others who affect these rights. If as an individual you do something or fail to do something which interferes with another person's rights, then you may have committed a 'tort' (a Civil Law wrong).

Everyone has a legal right to expect others to take reasonable care in their business and other activities so that people are not put at risk.

Anyone who behaves carelessly may be breaking this duty of care rule. This tort is called 'negligence' and anyone taken to court in such circumstances and who is found guilty may have to pay a great deal of compensation.

(*b*) *Criminal Law* – Basically a criminal act is one which can harm any individual citizen, in certain circumstances negligence may be a criminal offence.

The principal laws concerned with safety are:

(i) The Offices, Shops and Railway Premises Act 1963
(ii) The Health and Safety at Work Act 1974.

The Offices, Shops and Railway Premises Act 1963 regulates working conditions in premises covered by this Act. Many of the provisions of this act relate directly or indirectly to safety such as:

(i) A room in which people work must not be so overcrowded as to cause risk of injury to health.
(ii) Lighting should be suitable and sufficient.
(iii) Floors, passages and stairs should be kept as free as is reasonably practicable from obstruction and from slippery substances. Stairs must have handrails.
(iv) Guards are required on dangerous parts of machinery.
(v) Only those over 18 and suitably trained may clean certain machinery.
(vi) Restrictions on lifting or moving heavy weights.
(vii) Providing adequate first aid facilities.
(viii) Imposing penalties for dangerous acts and interference with equipment.
(ix) Fire precautions.

The Health and Safety at Work Act 1974 relates to any type of workplace and requires that the employer ensures, so far as is reasonably practicable, that the health, safety and welfare of employees and others is looked after.

"Reasonably practicable" means what a reasonable man would do to limit hazards, e.g. a reasonable man would make sure that there were enough fire doors fitted. This does not mean that it would be reasonably practicable to expect him to replace all doors with fire doors.

The employer's duties under this act are to: –

(i) Draw up and publish a safety policy statement;
(ii) Ensure that safety procedures are carried out;
(iii) Keep and publish safety records;
(iv) Advise staff and others of their responsibilities; in other words to promote and maintain safe working conditions.

Employees are also held responsible by law if they do not follow safe methods of working.

The Health and Safety Executive or enforcing authority, i.e. local inspector of the Environmental Health Department may prohibit the use of unsafe machinery or premises, and may institute criminal proceedings against those who break the law.

Under the Act either the employer or employee may be fined an unlimited amount. Additionally a gaol sentence of up to two years can be imposed in extreme cases. The Act will be considered in more detail in Chapter 10.

Stores Documents and Records

The George Hotel Ltd. has ordered ten ladies wristwatches for sale in the hotel kiosk from Brown & Co. Ltd.

The first document is the delivery note. (Exhibit 3.1)

The hotel then makes out a goods received note. (Exhibit 3.2)

The store keeper enters the receipt on a stock card (Exhibit 3.3) or a bin card (Exhibit 3.4). Some firms use both documents.

A further supply is received on the 1st March and on the 1st April the kiosk withdraws eight from store using a stores requisition (Exhibit 3.5). A physical check on the stock in hand is carried out on the 30th April (Exhibit 3.6).

Brown & Co. Ltd. may post an advice note to the George Hotel Ltd. stating that the goods are about to be delivered. Some firms operate a system of separate advice notes and delivery notes. Others issue a combined document (see exhibit 3.1). Strictly speaking, a delivery note should be sent with the goods and an advice note sent separately by post, stating the goods have or will leave the premises of the supplier. This will be followed by an Invoice (Exhibit 3.7).

Let us imagine that one of the watches was faulty. The watch would be returned with a request for a Credit Note. There are several circumstances where a purchaser would request a credit note. This is just one example.

At the end of the month the supplier Brown & Co. Ltd. will send a Statement of Account to the George Hotel Ltd. (Exhibit 3.8).

Exhibit 3.1

DELIVERY NOTE/ADVICE NOTE No. 483

from

BROWN & CO. LTD.
The Parade
Sheffield
S15 2RS

Date: 22 January 19-3

Your Order no. 1234

Telephone: 0284-2342

Telex: JKBN 19873

To:

George Hotel Ltd.
The Place
LEEDS
L62 6TS

Please receive

10	Watch W3	one parcel

Received by: T. Green

Exhibit 3.2

GOODS RECEIVED NOTE No. 148

Supplier: BROWN & CO. LTD.

Date Received: 22/1/19-3

Delivery/Advice Note No. 483

Received per: firm's van

Order No.	Description	Quantity Received
1234	W3	10

Received by	Date	Entered in Stock by	Date
T. Green	22/1/-3	F. Briggs	23/1/-3
Inspected by	S. Black	Date	22/1/-3

Shortages/
Damage recorded:

Exhibit 3.3

Article WATCH 3 Minimum Stock 5

DATE	RECEIPTS	ISSUES	BALANCE
22/1/-3	10		10
1/3	10		20
1/4		8	12

Stock Card

Exhibit 3.4

ARTICLE WATCH 3

MINIMUM STOCK 5 BIN No. 4

DATE	RECEIVED	ISSUED	BALANCE
22/1/-3	10		10
1/3	10		20
1/4		8	12

Bin Card

Exhibit 3.5

GEORGE HOTEL LTD.

STORES REQUISITION

No.: 15

Date: 1/4/-3 Dept.: KIOSK

	QUANTITY
WATCH 3	8

Signed J. Smith

Exhibit 3.6

GEORGE HOTEL LTD.

STOCK SHEET No.

Date: 30/4 19-3

ARTICLE	QUANTITY IN STOCK	UNIT	£		ARTICLE	QUANTITY IN STOCK	UNIT	£	
W3	12	2×8 10×9	16 90						

Exhibit 3.7

This is a business document prepared whenever one person sells to another on credit. The invoice lists the goods purchased one person sells to another on credit. The invoice lists the goods purchased and tells the purchaser how much he owes the supplier.

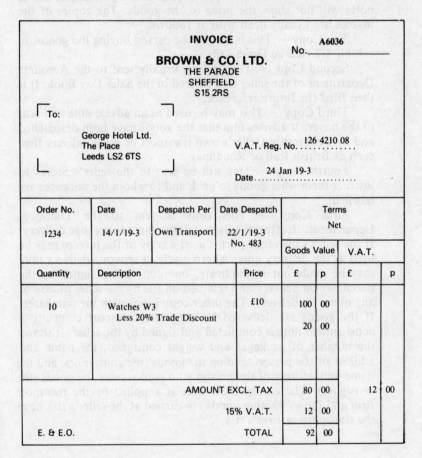

INVOICE

No. A6036

BROWN & CO. LTD.
THE PARADE
SHEFFIELD
S15 2RS

To:

George Hotel Ltd.
The Place
Leeds LS2 6TS

V.A.T. Reg. No. 126 4210 08

Date 24 Jan 19-3

Order No.	Date	Despatch Per	Date Despatch	Terms
1234	14/1/19-3	Own Transport	22/1/19-3 No. 483	Net

Quantity	Description	Price	Goods Value £	p	V.A.T. £	p
10	Watches W3	£10	100	00		
	Less 20% Trade Discount		20	00		
	AMOUNT EXCL. TAX		80	00	12	00
	15% V.A.T.		12	00		
E. & E.O.	TOTAL		92	00		

It also tells the purchaser:

(*a*) Invoice number and date;
(*b*) VAT Registration Number of the supplier;
(*c*) Original order number and date;
(*d*) Method of delivery – firm's own transport or other carrier;
(*e*) Terms of payment – cash discount if any offered;
(*f*) Quantity and description of goods supplied;

(*g*) The letters E & O E are printed on the invoice meaning "errors and omissions excepted". This allows for any errors in calculation or omissions from the invoice.

The invoice is a printed form, usually in a "document set", i.e. a number of copies fastened together. The number of copies varies from firm to firm. Copies used as delivery notes and advice notes will not show the price of the goods. The copies of the invoice are usually dealt with as follows:

Top Copy – This is sent to the person buying the goods, in exhibit 3.7 George Hotel Ltd.

Second Copy – This copy is usually sent to the Accounts Department of the seller and entered in the Sales Day Book. It is then filed for future reference.

Third Copy – This may be used as an advice note and sent to the buyer. It advises him that the goods have been despatched and by what means (seller's own transport or other delivery firm such as British Rail or Roadline).

Fourth Copy – This will be sent to the seller's Stores to instruct them what goods to pack and to whom the packages are labelled.

Fifth Copy – This copy is sent to the Transport Department. In effect it tells that department to arrange delivery. If the seller's own transport is used a copy of the invoice may be used as the delivery note. Alternatively, a separate delivery note may be made out in duplicate, one copy being signed by the purchaser on delivery and retained on file by the seller in case of any query on delivery. The other copy is left with the purchaser. If the goods are delivered by a private transport company a consignment note is completed and signed by the seller. It shows the number of packages and weight consigned, the name and address of the person sending the goods (the consignor), and the name and address of the person who is to receive the goods (the consignee). The consignment note is supplied by the transport firm and shows whether goods are carried at the seller's risk or at the transporting firm's risk.

Pro-forma invoice

A pro-forma invoice is similar to a quotation and is used as follows:

(*a*) When goods are sent on approval. If a quotation has to show a number of items with discounts, it will probably be more convenient to make it out in the form of an invoice showing the purchaser how the invoice will be made out if he decides to purchase the goods.

(*b*) When goods are sent on a Sale or Return basis, i.e. only goods sold are paid for. It is necessary to show the person receiving the goods the price that will eventually be charged.

(*c*) Where payment is required before the goods can be sent or goods are sold cash on delivery.

Debit Note

This is similar to the invoice and is used to make adjustments to an invoice. Some firms use a further invoice instead of a separate debit note. If, for instance, a supplier has made an undercharge on the original invoice he will use the debit note for the difference. In the supplier's Accounts Department the debit note will be treated in the same way as an invoice.

Credit Note

As its name implies, the credit note is issued to the purchaser by the seller when money is owed to the purchaser. This can occur when there is an overcharge for goods delivered or as the refund of a deposit on packing materials returned. A credit note is also used when, for any reason, goods are returned to the supplier, e.g. too many goods delivered. The credit note is usually printed and typed in red. It should, whenever possible, show the original invoice number and date. It is usually issued before payment of an invoice is made so that the purchaser can deduct the amount of credit from the invoice total. Some firms use an invoice form typed in red instead of a separate document but practice varies from firm to firm.

In the case of the faulty watch the credit note calculation would be:

	£ p
1 Watch K3 faulty	10.00
Less 20% Trade Discount	2.00
	8.00
15% VAT	1.20
TOTAL	9.20

Statement of Account

Sales made to each customer are recorded in a personal ledger account. At regular intervals, usually the end of a month, these entries are transferred to a statement of account which is then sent to the customers concerned. With the greater use of accounting machines, many firms make entries in the ledgers and on the statements of account at the same time.

Exhibit 3.8

Accounts Department:
VAT Registered Number 126/4210/08

BROWN & CO. LTD.
THE PARADE
SHEFFIELD

STATEMENT

GEORGE HOTEL LTD.
THE PLACE
LEEDS
LS2 6TS

Account Number 01/542
Jan. 19-3

Notes on Payment:
All invoices are due for payment 28 days from the date of invoice.
All cheques should be made payable to Brown & Co. Ltd.
Please return this statement with your remittance. Cash received after the end of the month is not shown.

Date	Detail	Debit	VAT	Credit	Balance due
24.1.19-3	A 6036	80.00	12.00		92.00
26.1.19-3	C/N 41		(1.20)	8.00	82.80

Transaction Code:
CH Cash or Cheque
DS Discount
DD Direct Deb
CR Credit

Terms: Net

E. & O.E.

The Statement of Account shows:

(*a*) The balance brought forward from the previous period;
(*b*) Details of net amount on each invoice issued during the current period;
(*c*) Any payments made by the customer or credit notes issued to the customer during the period;
(*d*) The balance owing at the end of the month.

The Statement of Account is not only a record of goods supplied but a reminder to the purchaser of the amount owing.

The business transaction involves a number of documents, some issued by he purchaser and some by the seller. Each document is a response to action requested. Although the design and layout of the forms varies from firm to firm the basic information given or requested is common to all. The sequence can be summarised:

Document	Completed by	Purpose
Internal purchase requisition ↓	A department in a firm	To request goods
Letter of enquiry ↓	Purchasing Department of firm wishing to buy goods	For information from possible suppliers
Quotation ↓	Sales Department of firm wishing to sell goods	Giving information of prices, terms of sale and delivery dates
Purchase Order ↓	Purchasing Department of firm buying goods	Forms a legal contract for supply of goods
Invoice ↓	Sales Department of seller	To advise buyer of cost of goods and amount to be paid. Copies can be used as advice note, packing note, delivery note
Debit Note ↓	Sales Department of seller	To make adjustments to an invoice. It increases amount owed
Credit Note ↓	Sales Department of seller	To make adjustments to an invoice. It decreases amount owed
Statement of Account	Accounts Deparment of seller	A record of all transactions between seller and a customer for a certain period. Acts as a reminder to pay and shows final balance owing.

The Return of Empties and Faulty Goods

Empty Containers

These are returned to the supplier if there is a charge on delivery. If they are valuable they should be carefully stored to avoid damage until they are returned at the time of the next delivery. A copy of the document showing the return should be available to check against the Credit Note issued by the supplier in due course. These copies are often sent to both the buyer and the accounts section. Cheap non-returnable containers should be disposed of and not left in the store causing untidiness and a waste of space.

Faulty Goods

Incorrect or damaged goods should be notified as soon as possible to the supplier, possibly by telephone. Documents showing the fault should follow. The supplier will have the option of replacing the goods or issuing a Credit Note.

Pricing Stores Issues

Material costs are calculated by multiplying the quantity of stores issued (Q) by the cost price (P). Costs = Q × P.

The cost office will have details of Q from copies of stores requisitions. Cost prices are obtained from invoices:

10 watches W3	× list price £10	100.00
	less 20% trade discount	20.00
	Cost Price	80.00
	add VAT 15%	12.00
		£92.00

As value added tax (VAT) is recoverable, except in the very smallest of businesses, that will not be taken as part of the cost. The cost of one watch is therefore £80 ÷ 10 = £8. It must be remembered that trade discount is simply a means of arriving at the cost price.

Goods Received Book

This is an alternative to Goods Received Notes entered on Stock Cards or Bin Cards. It may include some of the following:

(*a*) date;
(*b*) supplier;
(*c*) consignment number;
(*d*) order number;
(*e*) number of packages;
(*f*) carriers;
(*g*) condition.

Personnel receiving goods should remember at all times when signing for goods received to ensure that they correspond with the documentation. When in doubt they should sign for them as 'damaged', 'short delivered' or 'unchecked'.

Exhibit 3.9 is one example of a Goods Received Book: –

Exhibit 3.9

GOODS RECEIVED BOOK

DATE	SUPPLIER	Order No.	DESCRIPTION	Quantity	REMARKS

Computerised stock control

It is important for organisations to keep correct stock records. The computer enables an organisation to maintain effective stock levels. What should be in stock at any time can also be checked. If a VDU (Visual Display Unit) is available in the stores, by entering the stock code number – the quantity and location of the particular item in stock can be shown on the screen.

Exercises

Note: **Questions without the suffix 'X' have answers shown at the back of this book. Questions with the suffix 'X' are set without answers in this book so that teachers/lecturers can set the questions for classwork or homework.**

3.1. The following is a requisition sent by Stores to the Buying Department. Indicate which lettered spaces should be filled in by:

(*a*) The Buying Department.

(*b*) The Storekeeper.

A.B. CATERING LTD.

PURCHASE REQUISITION. No. 1

TO BUYING DEPARTMENT.

ALLOCATION.

............Date ....19............

Symbol or Code No.	Quantity Required	Description of Material	Delivery Requirements
E	F	G	H

Purchase Order No.	Date	Supplier	Authorised by: –
A	B	C	D

3.2. Draw up a bin card and show the balance after each entry:

	19-2	
1 June	Balance	30 tins of salmon
2 June	Issued to kitchen	15 tins of salmon
6 June	Issued to kitchen	10 tins of salmon
13 June	Received from suppliers	85 tins of salmon
20 June	Issued to kitchen	15 tins of salmon
25 June	Issued to kitchen	20 tins of salmon

3.3X. List the points which should be taken into consideration when planning the storeroom of a catering organisation.

3.4. Fill in the blank spaces.

When goods are delivered by a supplier the storekeeper should sign a document known as a (i) ________. The goods should be checked against this document to make sure they are correct. The goods are then entered onto the relevant (ii) ________ ________ and the document entered into a (iii) ________ ________ book and a document known as the (iv) ________ ________ ________ is completed and copies sent to various departments.

3.5X. (i) State five considerations which you would have when deciding on the physical location of a store within a building.

(ii) List five different major items of equipment that would be required in a new storage area.

(iii) In arranging the layout of equipment in a store, give 9 factors which will affect your decisions of the eventual layout.

4

Basic Food Costing and Pricing

Learning Objectives

At the end of this chapter you should be able to:

4A Cost simple dishes and items using a costing sheet and calculate selling price for a given profit percentage.

4B Calculate percentages and ratios which can be ascertained from related flows of revenues and costs and understand the systems of VAT and Service Charges.

It was explained in Chapter 1 of this book that businesses needed to make profits, and to avoid running out of cash funds, if they wanted to continue operating at all in the long-term. Such desirable objectives simply cannot be undertaken if the hotel or catering organisation does not know what its costs are, or what they should be.

The Elements of Cost

Costs are divided up as follows:

1. MATERIALS : These consist of food and beverages.
2. LABOUR : These are the costs of employing labour. It consists of wages, salaries, staff meals provided, national insurance contributions, sick pay and so on.
3. OVERHEADS : These are all the other expenses used up in the period being considered.

Obviously, costs cannot be used for control purposes if accurate cost information has not been recorded. In real life the amount of control exercised may vary from very little to full cost control. The lack of control where it *should* and *could* exist would be a condemnation of the efficiency of the organisation. In general most catering firms have, as a minimum, cost control related to food and beverage operations.

An organisation with an effective stores system will be able to undertake dish costing which is likely to be used as the basis for pricing. It is generally accepted that an average of 60% gross profit is adequate to cover labour and overheads and leave a satisfactory net profit in hotel and restaurant food operations. In other food operations, e.g. industrial canteens, take-away food etc. the gross profit will be lower.

The gross profit can be expressed in terms of either the Margin or of the Mark-up. Margin is the gross profit expressed as a percentage (or fraction) of the selling price. Mark-up is the gross profit expressed as a percentage (or fraction) or the cost price. The following is an example (service charge and VAT are ignored in this example):

	Food Cost +	Gross Profit	= Selling Price
	£4	£6	£10
Expressed as % of selling price	40%	+ 60% (margin) =	100%
Expressed as % of cost price	100%	+ 150% (mark-up) =	250%

It may be useful to convert margin percentages into mark-up percentages. In the case of the margin the *selling price percentage* will always be 100%. For the mark-up the *cost price percentage* will always be stated as 100%. This is because for the margin the profit is as a percentage of *selling price,* therefore selling price has to be given as 100%, whereas mark-up is based on *cost* and therefore for this cost always has to be 100%.

The mark-up can now be found when the margin is 50%. In the table we will complete the margin line, and will insert 100% under cost in the mark-up line, as cost is always 100% for cost when calculating mark-up.

	Cost %		Gross Profit %		Selling Price %
Margin	50	+	50	=	100
Mark-up	100	+	?	=	?

Now the relationship between Cost and Gross Profit when calculating the Margin line can be seen. Gross Profit *in this case* is exactly once times the Cost Price %. In the Mark-up line the *relationship* should remain the same, in that the Gross Profit % should *also* be once times the Cost Price %. The table can therefore be completed.

	Cost %		Gross Profit %		= Selling Price %
Margin	50	+	50	=	100
Mark-up	100	+	100	=	200

This can be tested out where there is a margin of 80% to be converted to a mark-up percentage.

	Cost %	+	Gross Profit %		= Selling Price %
Margin	20	+	80	=	100
Mark-up	100	+	$(\frac{80}{20} \times 100)$ 400	=	500

If figures of £2 for cost and £10 for selling price are taken, then the last example can be tested, try it for yourself.

Most caterers will have to charge Value Added Tax (VAT) on sales, and many include a Service Charge which also attracts VAT.

Value Added Tax – VAT is a tax on sales turnover. It is raised at every level of activity starting with the first supplier and ends with the final customer. At each stage VAT is charged to the buyer on the selling price. The government department responsible for collection of VAT is H.M. Customs and Excise. Every firm or individual whose turnover in taxable supplies of goods and/or services exceeds an amount set by the Chancellor of the Exchequer must register with H.M. Customs and Excise and keep records of all purchases known as inputs and all sales known as outputs.

At the time of writing the rate of Value Added Tax is 15%, so to find the correct fully inclusive price a series of calculations will be necessary. These are shown in exhibit 4.1.

Exhibit 4.1

The food costs are £4. Margin is to be 60%. To this cost a 10% service charge is added, and all this is subject to 15% VAT.

	£	
Food Cost (C)	4.00	
+ Gross Profit Margin	6.00	*1
= Exclusive Sales Price S(Ex.)	10.00	
+ Service Charge 10% SC	1.00	*2
	11.00	
+ VAT 15% of £11.00	1.65	*3
= Sales Price Fully Inclusive S (inc.)	12.65	

*1 Margin given as 60%. Mark-up could then be calculated as 150%, giving £4 × 150% = £6.
*2 The Service Charge is calculated on Exclusive Sales Price, 10% of £10.00 = £1.00.
*3 VAT is calculated on total of Exclusive Sales Price + Service Charge = £10.00 + £1.00 = £11.00 × 15% = £1.65.

Dish Costing

A suitable detailed example will now be illustrated in Exhibit 4.2.

Exhibit 4.2

DISH COSTING SHEET

Leek and Potato Soup – 4 portions — Date 4.1.19-3
(Potage de poireaux et pommes)

Quantity	**Ingredient**	£ **Price**	£ **Cost***
400g	LEEKS	0.70 per kg	0.280
25g	BUTTER	2.00 ” ”	0.050
200g	POTATO	0.18 ” ”	0.036
750ml	WHITE STOCK	10% of total	
	SALT, PEPPER etc.	of other costs	0.037
	DISH COST		0.403
	Portion Cost ¼ × 0.403		
	Rounded off figure (say)		0.10
	Kitchen Profit (60% margin)		0.15**
	Selling Price		0.25

*Correct to 3 decimal places of £1.
**Kitchen profit means gross profit margin 60% or mark-up 150%.

If a restaurant included 10% service + 15% VAT, the inclusive menu price would be £0.25 × 1.1 × 1.15 = £0.31625 say 32p.

The above example is only one recipe for leek and potato soup. Some chefs would not agree with either the ingredients or the quantities.

Generally it is in the interests of a catering firm to have a consistent standard for each dish both in quality and portion size. This is best achieved by a system of portion control. This will be discussed in Chapter 5.

Table d'Hôte costing

Table d'hôte menus are common in most restaurants. This is really a limited menu when the customer can choose from say 3 starters, 5 main courses and 4 sweet courses, with tea or coffee an extra.

Some catering firms will not operate individual dish costs. The chef or food and beverage manager will decide on the number of each dish to be prepared for the table d'hôte operation and list the weights and measures of the ingredients to be used. The cost prices of each ingredient can then be obtained to calculate the 'total' cost of the food prepared for service in the restaurant.

The restaurant sales obtained, less this 'total' food cost, will give the gross profit for say a lunch-time operation. e.g. Number of covers served at £4 excluding VAT 100 × £4 = £400 less total food cost (say) £160 = Gross profit £240 i.e. 60% margin.

Sales and Costs Relationships

At the start of this chapter the elements of cost were stated as materials, labour and overheads. The relationship between costs and sales can be expressed as percentages.

Let us imagine the trading results of a restaurant for a year to be: Sales £200,000, Cost of Food and Beverages £80,000, Wages and Salaries £50,000, Other costs or Overheads £40,000, giving a profit of £30,000.

The above may be expressed as follows:

PROFIT & LOSS STATEMENT FOR YEAR ENDED 31/12/19-4

			£	%	
	Sales		200,000		100
less	Food & Beverage Costs	80,000		40	
,,	Labour Costs	50,000		25	
,,	Overhead Costs	40,000	170,000	20	85
	Profit		30,000		15

If in the above example Food & Beverages Sales were recorded separately the relationship between the two sales figures could be expressed as a ratio. If Food sales were £150,000 and beverages £50,000 the ratio would be:

Food	:	Beverages
£150,000	:	£50,000
3	:	1

Exercises

Note: **Questions without the suffix 'X' have answers shown at the back of this book. Questions with the suffix 'X' are set without answers in this book so that teachers/lecturers can set the questions for classwork or homework.**

4.1. For the business of J. James, classify the following between 'Capital' and 'Revenue' expenditure. (Capital Expenditure means buying Fixed Assets. Revenue Expenditure means buying Materials, Labour and Overheads.)

(*a*) Purchase of an extra motor van.
(*b*) Cost of rebuilding storehouse wall which had fallen down.
(*c*) Building extension to the stores.
(*d*) Painting extension to stores when it is first built.
(*e*) Repainting extension to stores three years later than that done in (*d*).
(*f*) Carriage costs on bricks for new store extension.
(*g*) Carriage costs on purchases.
(*h*) Carriage costs on sales.
(*i*) Legal costs of collecting debts.
(*j*) Legal charges on acquiring new premises for office.
(*k*) Fire insurance premium.
(*l*) Costs of erecting new machine in the kitchen.

4.2X. For the business of H. Potter, classify the following between 'Capital' and 'Revenue' expenditure:

(*a*) Repairs to meat slicer.
(*b*) New tyre for van.
(*c*) Additional restaurant furniture.
(*d*) Renewing signwriting on restaurant.
(*e*) Fitting partitions in restaurant.
(*f*) Roof repairs.
(*g*) Cost of extra attachment to blending machine.
(*h*) Cost of electronic till.
(*i*) Repairs to restaurant furniture.
(*j*) Menu cards.
(*k*) Cost of electricity.
(*l*) Advertising.

4.3. A restaurant expects to sell 500 three course meals per week. The food cost is £1.20 per meal and labour and overhead costs are £300 per week. The net profit target is £100 per week.

(*a*) Calculate the selling price per meal.
(*b*) The food cost as a percentage of sales.

4.4X. A high class restaurant wishes to introduce business lunches in a city centre at a competitive price of £3 per lunch. The food and beverage cost is an average 40% of sales and the other costs are £1 per lunch.

(*a*) Calculate the net profit per lunch.
(*b*) The other costs as a percentage of sales.

4.5. A first class Restaurant has both table d'hôte and à la carte menus. The pricing policy is 60% margin. The menu prices include 10% service charge + 15% VAT.

(*a*) Find the Food Cost of a Table D' Hôte price of £2.30. (Work to nearest pence).
(*b*) Find à la carte menu price of a cover costing £1.00.

4.6. The following ingredients are required to produce 10 portions of Poussin rôti au lard: –

10 single poussins	@	£1.00 each
200 g. lard	@	48p per kg.
400 g. streaky bacon	@	£1.04 per kg.
½ kg. potatoes	@	7p per kg.
2 bunches watercress	@	15p each
100 g. bread	@	42p per kg.
1 button onion	say	1p
1 litre brown stock	costing	10p
¼ litre of milk	@	26p per litre

Calculate: –

(*a*) The food cost per cover.
(*b*) The selling price per cover, inclusive of VAT at 15%, to produce a gross profit of 60%. There is no service charge.
(*c*) The gross profit percentage achieved if the selling price (inclusive of VAT at 15%) is £4.00 per portion.

Note: All calculations can be made to the nearest penny.

4.7X. The total of a restaurant bill is £60.72. It includes V.A.T. at 15% and a 10% service charge.

(i) Calculate the amount of V.A.T. charged.

(ii) Calculate the service charge.

4.8. The food cost for a meal is £1.30 and the selling price is £4.00 (excluding V.A.T.):

(i) Calculate the gross profit percentage (there is no service charge).

(ii) The management policy is to achieve a 66% gross profit. Has this target been met or not?

4.9X (*a*) The recipe for carbonnade of beef is as follows:

40 kg lean beef	@ £4.15 per kg.
1500 g castor sugar	@ £0.46 per kg.
20 kg sliced onion	@ £0.26 per kg.
25 litres beer	@ £1.35 per litre

(i) Calculate the total cost of the ingredients to two places of decimals.

(ii) If the cost per portion is £0.5141 how many portions could be served from the above ingredients.

(*b*) If the management of a catering establishment requires a 60% gross profit on the selling price for the carbonnade of beef.

(i) Calculate the total gross profit for all the beef sold (to two places of decimals).

(ii) Calculate the selling price per portion (to three places of decimals).

4.10. From the recipe, quantity and costs detailed below: –

(*a*) Transfer the standard recipe to a Costing Sheet

(*b*) Calculate the cost of each ingredient to three decimal places of a £.

(*c*) Calculate the total cost of the dish

(*d*) Calculate the cost per portion of the dish

(*e*) Calculate the selling price (including V.A.T.) assuming the required Gross Profit percentage to be 65%, rounded up to the nearest 5p.

Recipe for 12 portions of Paupiettes de Boeuf

1 kg 350gms of Lean Beef	@ £5.28 per Kg
360 gms of Carrots	@ £0.11 per Kg
125 gms of Dripping	@ £0.70 per Kg
1.8 litres of Brown Stock	@ £0.25 per Litre
1 Bouquet Garni	@ £0.08
120 gms of Stuffing	@ £2.00 per Kg
360 gms of Onion	@ £0.11 per Kg
90 gms of Flour	@ £0.29 per Kg
45 gms of Tomato Puree	@ £0.47 per Kg.

4.11X. Complete the costing sheet below by inserting the missing numbers. Then calculate the alternative selling prices per person (include VAT at 15%). If gross profit percentages of either 45%, 50% or 60% are to be used.

Dish Name: CREME CARAMEL Number of Portions: 40

Quantity	Unit	Description	Unit Cost	Quantity Cost
4	Litre	Milk		1.200
	Dozen	Large eggs	0.90	1.800
	kilo	Gran. Sugar	0.28	0.168
2	single	Vanilla Sticks	0.15	
			Total Cost	
			Portion Cost	

5

Control Procedures

Learning Objectives

At the end of this chapter you should be able to:

5A **Understand the importance of portion control.**

5B **Know how to show the relationships between cost and revenue elements by graphical means.**

5C **Understand the importance of the control of cash receipts.**

Portion Control

Suitable equipment is needed to regulate portion size. Such equipment will include:

1. Scales
2. Graded scoops and ladles
3. Measuring jugs
4. Slicing machines
5. Standard-size baking tins
6. Standard-size cups, glasses, soup bowls
7. Bar optics (Drink measures)

Pre-packed portions may be included in the above list. This would be the ultimate in portion control and the practice is likely to increase because of improved freezing methods etc.

Scales are used for dry weights and also for carved meat. However the expert chef can estimate the weight of a portion of meat when carving without weighing every slice. Scoops will be used for vegetables and ladles for soups. Baking tins are designed for an exact number of portions and there are various sizes e.g. a tin to make exactly eight portions of a flan.

Portion Control will not be successful without:

1. *Standard recipes* – the dish produced must consist of the same ingredients every time if portions are to be consistent in weight and quality.
2. *Portion charts* – employees must know the portions. Charts can be displayed in the kitchen. The expression of portion size must be easy for the server e.g. 2 slices of meat, 1 scoop of carrots.

3. *Regular checking* – supervision is essential. The portion sizes must consistently be the same as the portions costed. Portion control does not mean serving small portions.

Portion control may assist the buyer if YIELD TESTING takes place.

This is to discover the respective yields of the whole range of dishes produced and therefore assist with revision of standard recipes and standard dish costs. The results of yield testing should be used to compile purchases specifications and requisitions sent to the Buying office.

Advantages of Portion Control

A good system of Portion Control will enable the food and beverage department to achieve its objectives by ensuring the target gross profit percentage and customer satisfaction. (all customers receive the same portions) This should result in the budgeted or expected sales in terms of numbers of covers being served in the restaurant.

Graphs and Charts

Graphs and charts are used to display costs and profit details so that this information may be seen "at a glance".

If you are going on holiday to a sunnier climate you will often find that the travel firm's brochure has a chart showing how the amount of sunshine per month, or the temperature per month, compares with the U.K. In fact you will find that these charts are based on averages.

Graphs

It is often better to present information in a visual way rather than a page full of facts and figures. A graph or a chart presents information which is easily interpreted and understood.

To show this information graphs and charts must be drawn *NEATLY* and *ACCURATELY*.

Some matters which should be observed are

1. The horizontal axis should represent the fixed amount and the vertical axis should be the variable information.
2. The scale should be as large as possible so that the graph covers the whole sheet and is not squashed in one area.
3. The points on the chart should be positioned very carefully.
4. The lines joining these points should be drawn carefully.
5. Both the horizontal axis and vertical axis should be clearly labelled.

(Look at exhibit 5.1 where these are illustrated.)

Exhibit 5.1

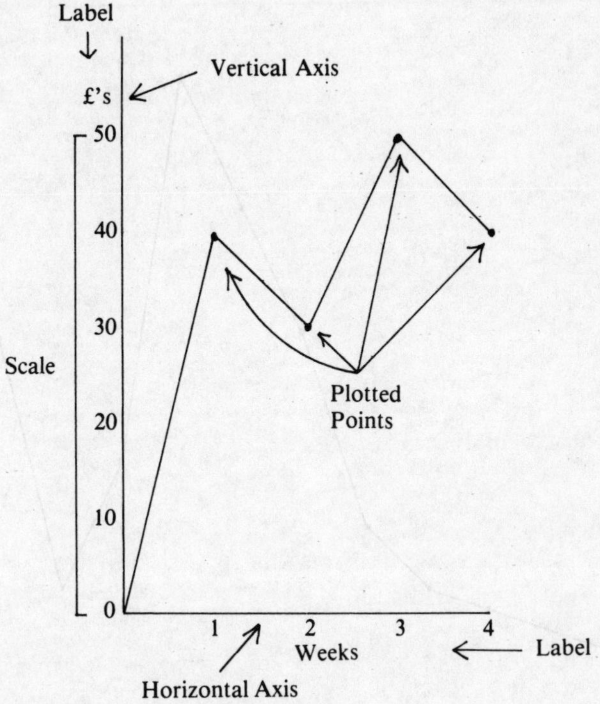

To illustrate the difference between reading figures and reading a graph let us look at this illustration. The following are Number of Covers sold by a restaurant in a year.

Month	No.	Month	No.
Jan.	1500	July	5000
Feb.	1600	Aug.	6000
March	1700	Sept.	3000
April	2000	Oct.	2000
May	2500	Nov.	4000
June	4000	Dec.	5000

I think you will agree that exhibit 5.2 is far easier to understand than looking through the list of numbers.

You can identify the busiest month more easily than if you studied the statistics, You will also note quickly that there are two busy times of the year and two relatively slack times.

Slack times – January to March; September and October.

Busy times – June to August; November and December.

Exhibit 5.2

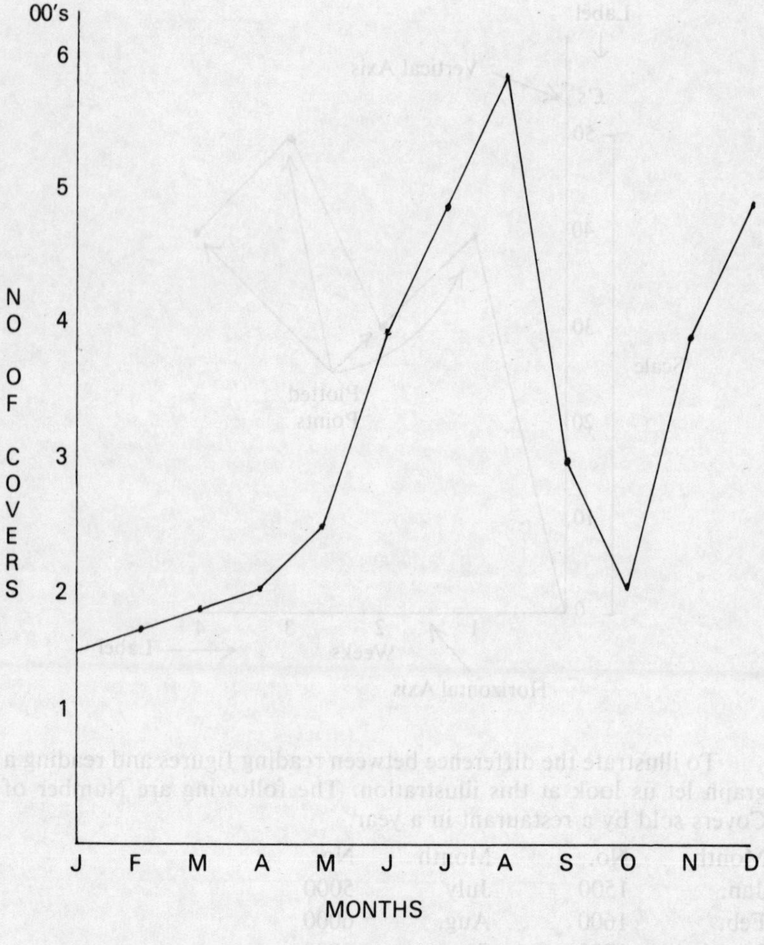

Other information may also be obtained from graphs by *INTERPOLATION*. This is the process of reading information from the graph by obtaining values between those you have plotted.

A catering firm sells an item at £2 each and in a year sells 60,000 items. See Exhibit 5.3.

60,000 × £2 = £120,000 Sales Value.
From the graph
if 40,000 are sold Sales = £80,000 (A on the graph)
if Sales are £50,000 No. of articles = 25,000 (B on the graph)

Exhibit 5.3

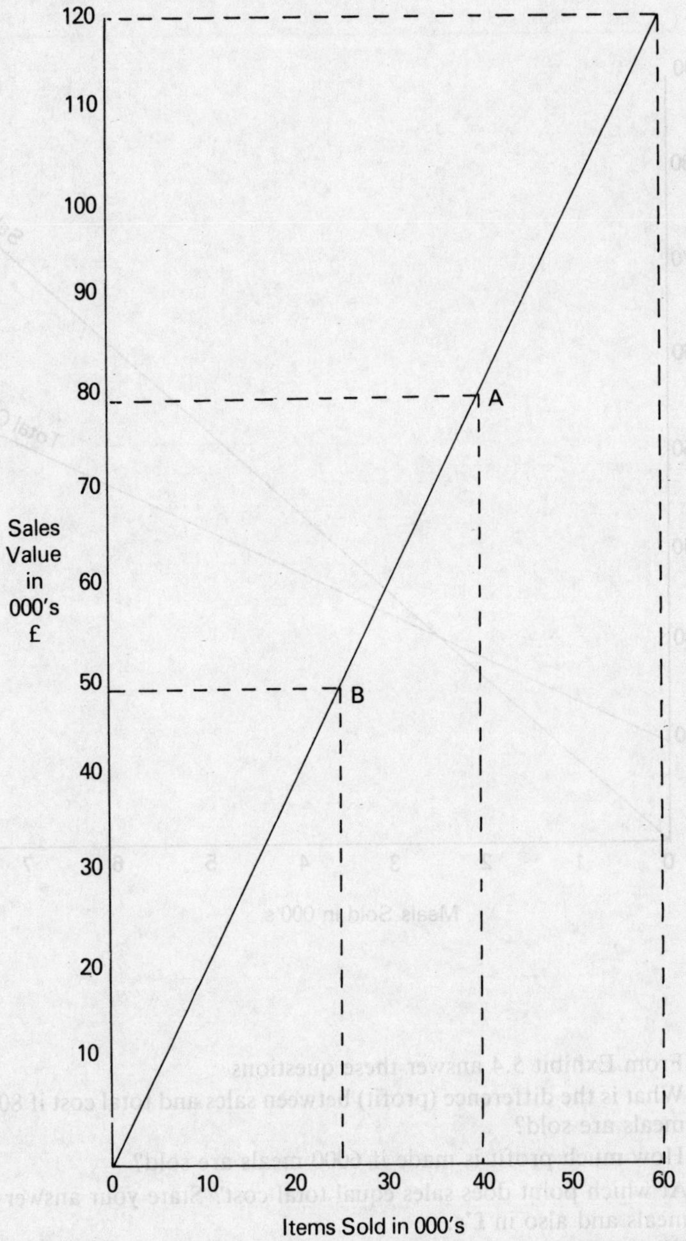

120
110
100
90
80
70
60
50
40
30
20
10
Sales
Value
in
000's
£
A
B
0
10
20
30
40
50
60
Items Sold in 000's

Exhibit 5.4

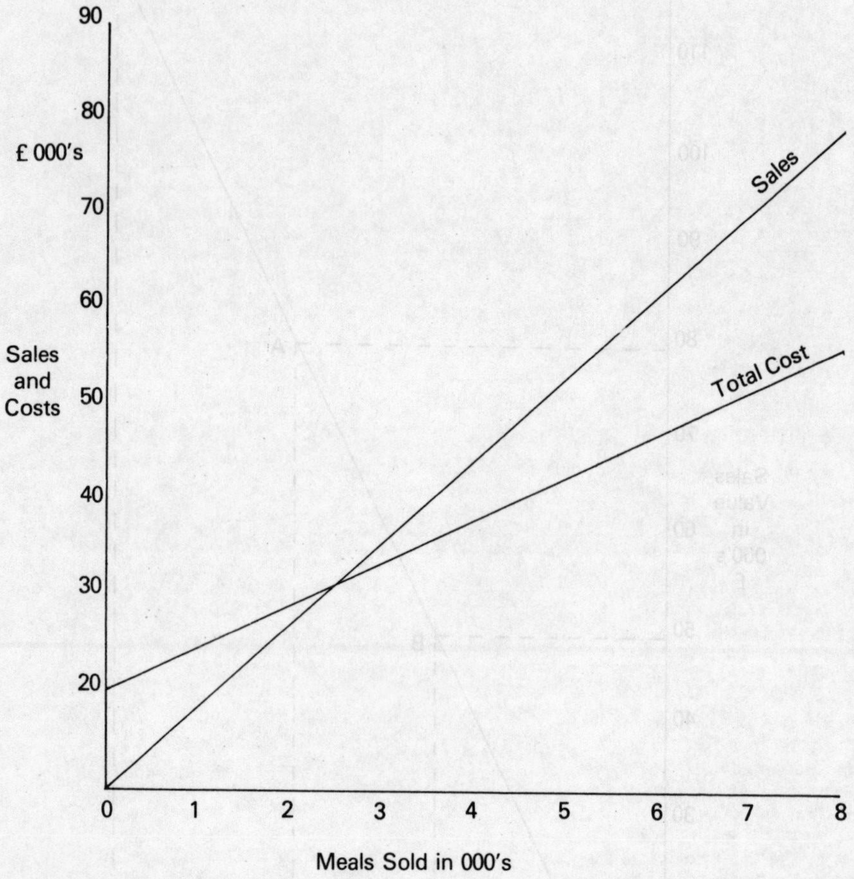

From Exhibit 5.4 answer these questions

(*a*) What is the difference (profit) between sales and total cost if 8000 meals are sold?

(*b*) How much profit is made if 6000 meals are sold?

(*c*) At which point does sales equal total cost? State your answer in meals and also in £'s.

(*d*) What happens if only 1000 meals are sold?

Compare your answers with those of other students.

Charts

If you look in newspapers and magazines you will find that information is presented in other ways than by graphs. There are many ways of presenting information but the two kinds that we are going to look at are known as pie charts and bar charts.

The pie chart is based on a circle and when constructed looks like a pie which has been divided into different portions.

Let us construct a pie chart from this information from an Hotel.

Type of service	Sales Value in £'s
Rooms	360,000
Bar	72,000
Other	72,000
Restaurant	216,000

Before we follow the steps to construct a pie chart we must bear in mind that the angle at the centre of a circle is 360 degrees.

We are going to relate the 360 degrees to the sales value.

Step 1. Total the sales of all products

£360,000 + £72,000 + £72,000 + £216,000 = £720,000

Step 2. Write 360 degrees = £720,000 (the total)

$$1 \text{ degree} = \frac{720{,}000}{360}$$

1 degree = £2000

Step 3. Divide each sales category by £2000 to calculate the number of degrees that each is to occupy

$$\text{Rooms} \quad \frac{360{,}000}{2000} = 180 \text{ degrees}$$

$$\text{Bar} \quad \frac{72{,}000}{2000} = 36 \text{ degrees}$$

$$\text{Other} \quad \frac{72{,}000}{2000} = 36 \text{ degrees}$$

$$\text{Restaurant} \quad \frac{216{,}000}{2000} = 108 \text{ degrees}$$

Step 4. Check that the degrees calculated adds up to 360 degrees.

Step 5. Draw a circle, a convenient size for the paper you are using and then using a protractor measure the degrees, for each product, from the centre of the circle. The answer is shown in Exhibit 5.5.

Exhibit 5.5

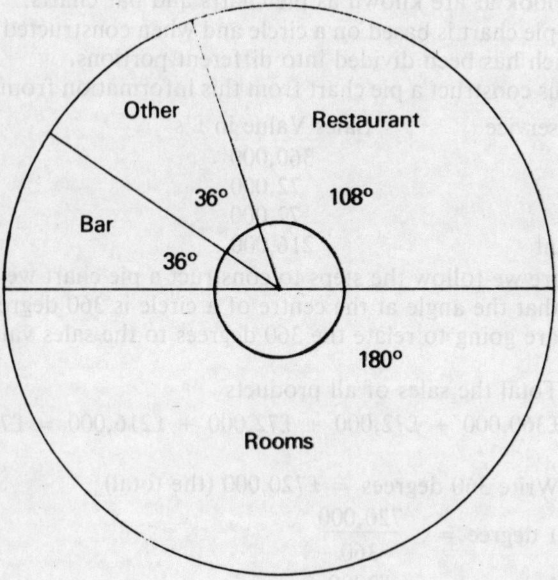

Exhibit 5.5 is the finished pie chart and shows the proportion of total sales of each department more easily than looking at lists of figures. Remember the circle equals, in this case, the total sales.

If you know the total, which is represented by the circle, you can calculate what each "slice" of the pie represents.

Exhibit 5.6 represents the total sales of a catering firm with five departments.

Department A
Department B
Department C
Department D
Department E

If the total sales are £353,520 how much does each department sell?

Exhibit 5.6

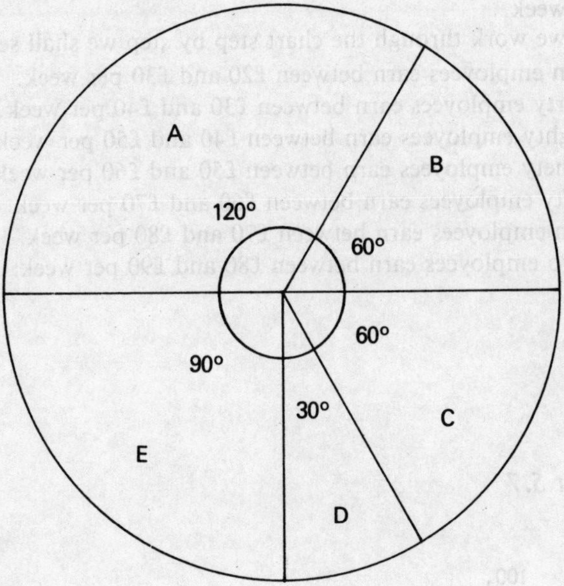

To calculate

Step 1. Measure the number of degrees occupied by each slice of the "pie".

Step 2. Write each angle over 360 degrees

Step 3. Multiply this by £353,520

Department	Calculation		Answer
A	$\frac{120}{360} \times 353,520$	=	£117,840
B	$\frac{60}{360} \times 353,520$	=	£ 58,920
C	$\frac{60}{360} \times 353,520$	=	£ 58,920
D	$\frac{30}{360} \times 353,520$	=	£ 29,460
E	$\frac{90}{360} \times 353,520$	=	£ 88,380

Step 4. Add the answers to make sure that they equal the total, in this case £353,520 — £353,520

Bar Charts

Exhibit 5.7 shows the number of employees and the amount they earn in one week.

If we work through the chart step by step we shall see that

(*a*) Ten employees earn between £20 and £30 per week.
(*b*) Forty employees earn between £30 and £40 per week.
(*c*) Eighty employees earn between £40 and £50 per week.
(*d*) Ninety employees earn between £50 and £60 per week.
(*e*) Fifty employees earn between £60 and £70 per week.
(*f*) Ten employees earn between £70 and £80 per week.
(*g*) Two employees earn between £80 and £90 per week.

Exhibit 5.7

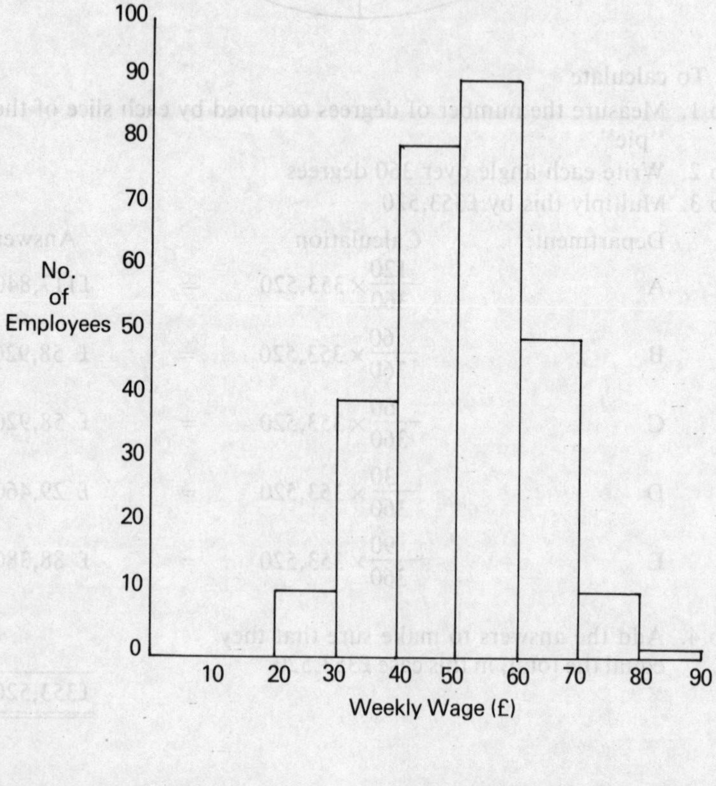

A few employees earn less than £30 per week (in fact 10) and a few earn over £70 per week (in fact 12) whereas the greatest number of employees earn between £50 and £60 per week.

As an aid to construction you will see that the number of employees are plotted on the vertical axis and their earnings grouped in tens of £'s are plotted on the horizontal axis. In exhibit 5.7 the wages per week are grouped in intervals of ten. If you wanted greater accuracy the wages could have been plotted in intervals of five.
e.g. Exhibit 5.7 shows that 10 employees earn between £20 and £30 per week but with further analysis this may reveal that

2 employees earn between £20 and £25 per week
and 8 employees earn between £25 and £30 per week.

Histogram

This is a graph drawn from a frequency distribution. The following example relates to the staff of an hotel:

AGE DISTRIBUTION OF STAFF IN AN HOTEL

Age Group			**Number of Staff**
15	but less than	20	10
20	”	25	17
25	”	30	28
30	”	35	42
35	”	40	38
40	”	45	30
45	”	50	25
50	”	55	20
55	”	60	10
TOTAL			220

The resulting graph is shown in exhibit 5.8:

Exhibit 5.8

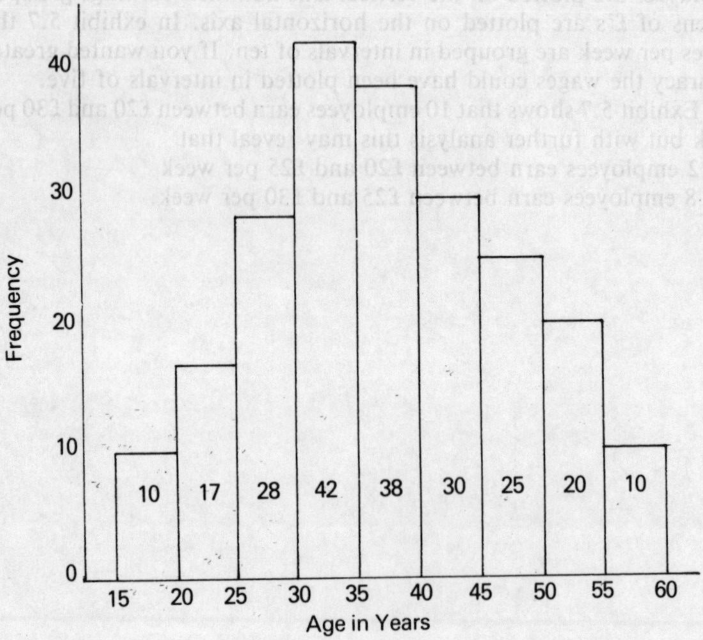

The frequency of each group is shown by a rectangle in the histogram. It is the area of the rectangle not its height which shows the frequency of each age group (class interval).

If the age groups were all the same then height could be used to draw the graph. This is the case in the above example. Let us imagine the same frequency distribution but staff over 50 are in one group instead of two. This group (50+) will have a different interval to the other age groups.

If heights were used an incorrect graph would result as in exhibit 5.9.

Exhibit 5.9

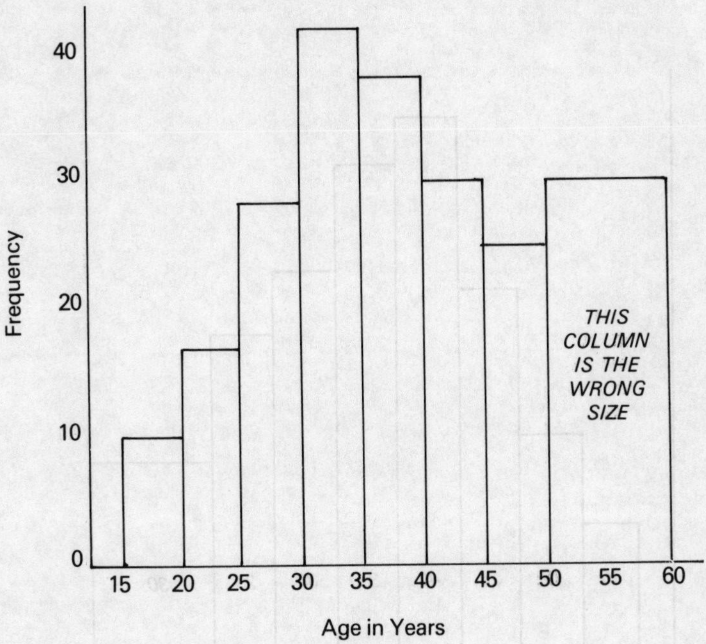

The area showing the fifty to sixty age group is double the area it should be.

The correct histogram is shown in exhibit 5.10.

Exhibit 5.10

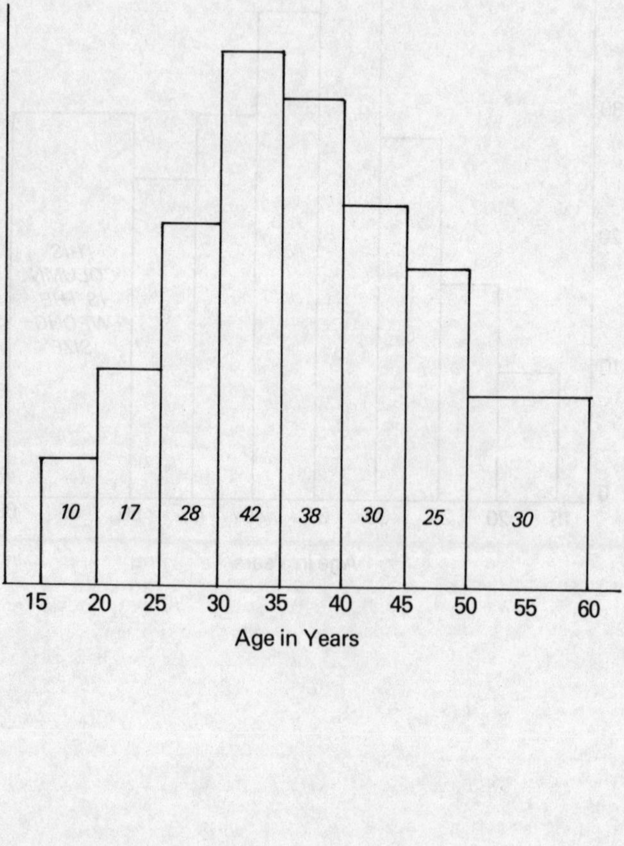

Histograms can be used to show elements of costs and revenues: see Exhibit 5.11.

Of each £1 spent by customers in a restaurant in a year?

£
0.43 was used for food and beverages
0.26 was used for labour costs
0.20 was used for overheads
0.11 was NET PROFIT

Exhibit 5.11

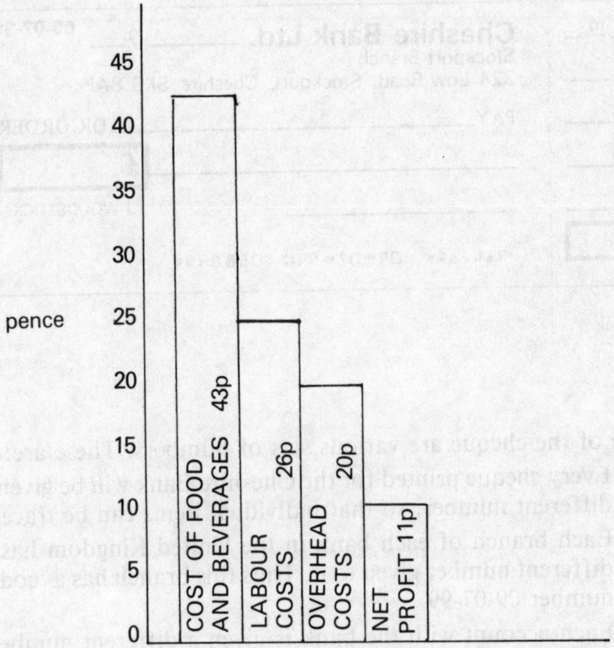

Control of Cash

Cash receipts (i.e. sales for notes and coins) are the rule in restaurants, bars, public houses, cafés and works canteens. There is an increasing amount of receipts in the form of cheques, (used with a cheque card) Visa and Access cards etc. and also travellers' cheques. Cashiers should be trained to handle these non-cash receipts carefully. The main features of cheques and cheque cards are now given.

Cheques can be used to make payments out of the account. Normally we must ensure that we have banked more in the account than the amount paid out. if we wish to pay out more money than we have banked, we will have to see the bank manager. We will then discuss the reasons for this with him, and if he agrees he will give his permission for us to 'overdraw' our account. This is known as a 'bank overdraft'.

The person filling in the cheque and using it for payment, is known as the *drawer*.

The person to whom the cheque is paid is known as the *payee*.

We can now look at Exhibit 5.12, which is a blank cheque form before it is filled in.

Exhibit 5.12

19
PAYEE
£
914234
This part is the counterfoil
Cheshire Bank Ltd.
19
09-07-99
Stockport Branch
324 Low Road, Stockport, Cheshire SK6 8AP
PAY
OR ORDER
£
J WOODSTOCK
⑈914234⑈ 09⑆07⑆99⑆ 058899⑈

On the face of the cheque are various sets of numbers. These are:

914234 Every cheque printed for the Cheshire Bank will be given a different number, so that individual items can be traced.

09-07-99 Each branch of each bank in the United Kingdom has a different number given to it. Thus this branch has a 'code' number 09-07-99.

058899 Each account with the bank is given a different number. This particular number is kept only for the account of J. Woodstock at the Stockport branch.

When we fill in the cheque we copy the details on the counterfoil which we then detach and keep for our records.

We can now look at the completion of a cheque. Let us assume that we are paying seventy-two pounds and eighty-five pence to K. Marsh on 22 May 19-5. Exhibit 5.13 shows the completed cheque.

Exhibit 5.13

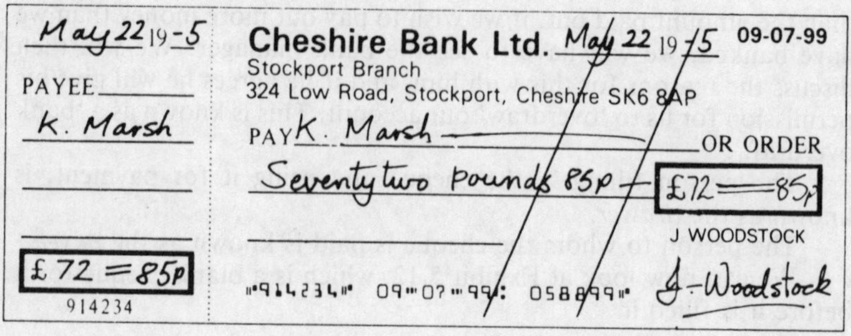
May 22 19-5
PAYEE
K. Marsh
£72 = 85p
914234
Cheshire Bank Ltd.
May 22 19-5
09-07-99
Stockport Branch
324 Low Road, Stockport, Cheshire SK6 8AP
PAY K. Marsh
OR ORDER
Seventy two pounds 85p
£72 = 85p
J WOODSTOCK
J. Woodstock
⑈914234⑈ 09⑆07⑆99⑆ 058899⑈

In Exhibit 5.13:
The drawer is: J. Woodstock
The payee is: K. Marsh

The two parallel lines across the face of the cheque are drawn as a safeguard. If we had not done this the cheque would have been an 'uncrossed cheque'. If someone had stolen a signed uncrossed cheque he could havé gone to the Stockport branch of the Cheshire Bank and obtained cash in exchange for the cheque. When the cheque is crossed it means it *must* be paid into a bank account, Post Office Giro bank or Savings Bank.

Cheques can be further safeguarded by using specific crossings, i.e. writing a form of instruction within the crossing on the cheques as shown in Exhibit 5.14.

Exhibit 5.14

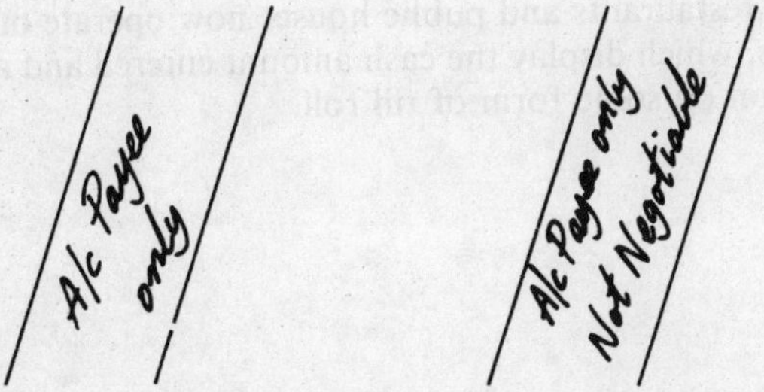

These are specific instructions to the banks about the use of the cheque. The use of 'Account Payee only' means the cheques should be paid only into the account of the payee named. If cheques are lost or stolen the drawer must advise his bank immediately and confirm by letter. These cheques will be 'stopped', i.e. payment will not be made on these cheques, provided you act swiftly. The safest crossing is that of 'A/c Payee only, Not Negotiable'. If the cheque is lost or stolen it will be of no use to the thief or finder. This is because it is impossible for this cheque to be paid into any bank account other than that of the named payee.

Cheque card

A Bank Cheque Card is an assurance that the bank will pay anyone accepting any cheque you sign (up to £50 at the time this book was written). It means you can pay by cheque anywhere with no questions or delays. It can also be used to withdraw cash up to £50 at any of the branches of the banks taking part in the scheme. In addition, through the Eurocheque scheme a holder can cash two cheques per day up to £50 each at banks in most European countries. The ready acceptance of cheques backed by a cheque card considerably improves the use of payment by cheque and reduces the need to carry large sums of cash. It is necessary, however, for the cheque card to be produced at the time of signing the cheque. The signature on the cheque card must correspond with the signature on the cheque. The person receiving the cheque writes the number of the cheque card on the reverse of the cheque. There will be no difficulty in making payment in shops or restaurants with a cheque card as payment is ensured providing the conditions on the back of the cheque card are observed.

Cash Registers (Tills)

Most hotels, restaurants and public houses now operate one or more cash registers, which display the cash amount entered and also record the transaction on some form of till roll.

Till Rolls

Till rolls show the values of transactions which have taken place.

They vary in the information given, but it is usual for them to record at least each transaction and provide a total whenever the till is cashed up.

It is very important that the total cash takings from every till are properly recorded every day, because the total amount of cash in the tills must be exactly equal to the total cash sales.

Till rolls are also used to check that the correct amount of cash is in the till. Some tills rolls have two or three copies. A modern till is usually designed so that the customer is issued with a receipt from one copy of the till roll and the other copy is fed into a locked compartment. The assistant can obtain a total (often known as a 'Z' reading) on the till by reading the till roll through an aperture (that is a hole) on the machine. The manager or the staff from the control office can unlock the sealed compartment on the till, remove the till roll and check it against the amount of cash which has been removed from the till.

If there is a regular shortage in the till, it is a sign that bar or restaurant staff (cashiers) are being either careless or dishonest and steps should be taken by the management to correct this fault.

Cashing Off Slips

The cashier usually cashes up the till at the end of each day.

Where a good system for security exists, the cashier can obtain a total reading through the aperture on the till but can not remove the till roll from the locked compartment.

It is also necessary to carry a "float" in a till. A float is an amount of change with which to start the day. A cashing off slip is usually designed to show the value of the float to start the day, the value of the float which is left in at the end of the day, and details of the actual notes and coins which are taken from the till.

A cashing off slip should be designed so that it is simple to read and so that the opening float can be deducted from the total amount in the till.

Exhibit 5.15 shows a cashing off slip showing that the total amount in the till is £42.67, the float is £3.47, therefore the total sales for the day are £39.20 (£42.67 − £3.47).

Exhibit 5.15

Cashing Off Slip | **Date** 12th Sept 19-2

	£ p
Notes	30.00
Coins, £1 & Silver	3.30
Copper	22
Total cash	33.52
POs & Cheques	9.15
Total	42.67
Deduct Float brought forward	3.47
Sales	39.20

Float retained for next day
£ p
3.52

It is important to have a safe place to keep cash when the business is closed for sales. A secure safe is an expensive item for the smaller business and therefore the amount of cash kept on the premises should be kept to an absolute minimum. Excess cash takings should be banked at least daily, using a 'Bank Giro Credit'.

Paying-in Slips

When we want to pay money into our current accounts, either cash or cheques, or both, we use a paying-in slip. One of these is shown as Exhibit 5.16.

J. Woodstock has banked the following items:

Four	£5 notes	
Three	£1 coins	
One	50p coin	
Other silver	30p	
Bronze coins	12p	
Cheques received from:		Code numbers:
E. Kane & Son	£184.15	02-58-76
J. Gale	£ 65.44	05-77-85

Exhibit 5.16

Face of paying in-slip

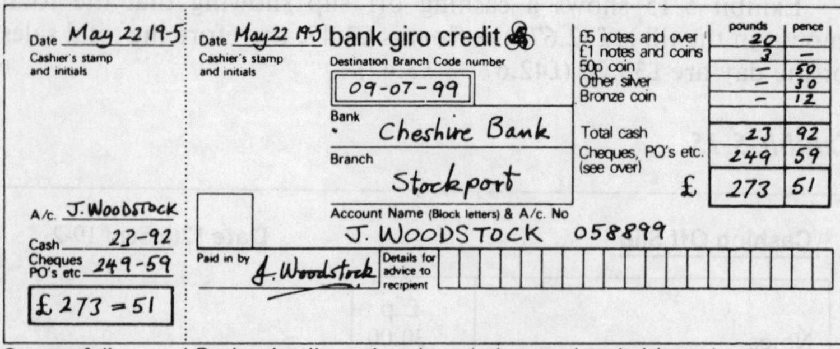

Date May 22 19-5
Cashier's stamp and initials
A/c. J. WOODSTOCK
Cash 23-92
Cheques PO's etc 249-59
£273 = 51

Date May 22 19-5
Cashier's stamp and initials
bank giro credit
Destination Branch Code number 09-07-99
Bank Cheshire Bank
Branch Stockport
Account Name (Block letters) & A/c. No J. WOODSTOCK 058899
Paid in by J. Woodstock
Details for advice to recipient

	pounds	pence
£5 notes and over	20	—
£1 notes and coins	3	—
50p coin	—	50
Other silver	—	30
Bronze coin	—	12
Total cash	23	92
Cheques, PO's etc. (see over)	249	59
£	273	51

Counterfoil retained by Woodstock

Paying-in slip and cash and cheques handed in to bank

Reverse side of paying-in slip

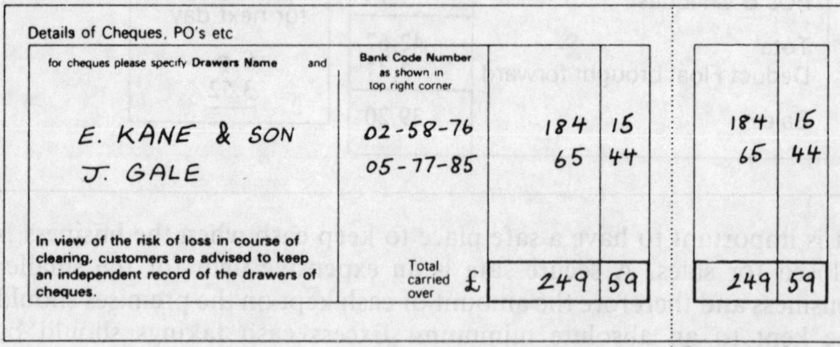

Details of Cheques, PO's etc

for cheques please specify Drawers Name and	Bank Code Number as shown in top right corner				
E. KANE & SON	02-58-76	184	15	184	15
J. GALE	05-77-85	65	44	65	44
	Total carried over £	249	59	249	59

In view of the risk of loss in course of clearing, customers are advised to keep an independent record of the drawers of cheques.

Reverse of counterfoil

Restaurant Sales

Most restaurants use some form of billing and/or triplicate checking system. Examples are given in exhibits 5.17, 5.18 and 5.19.

Each waiter has a numbered check book (some systems are not in book form but are still numbered). The numbering provides a system of control and it is important not to destroy a numbered check when a mistake has been made.

The top copy is sent to the kitchen where it is used to order the meal. The second copy is taken to the cashier, who uses it to prepare the customer's bill. The third copy is retained by the waiter.

The customer's bill is in duplicate, the top copy is the customer's receipt (or in a hotel it may be sent to reception to charge against a guest's room). The cashier keeps the copy. There are, of course, many variations of the above system.

After the restaurant service the top copies of the waiters' checks are sent by the kitchen to the control office, where they are checked against the duplicate bills sent in by the restaurant cashier.

Exhibit 5.17

The Duplicate Check Pad

TABLE No. ________________ COUVERTS ________________

DATE ________________ INITIALS ________________

02085-41

Exhibit 5.18

009750

M

VAT REG. No.		DATE	
	COUVERT		
	CAFE		
	WINES		
	SPIRITS		
	LIQUEURS		
	BEER		
	MINERALS		
	CIGARS AND CIGARETTES		

TABLE No.	No. OF PERSONS

V.A.T. @ %		
TOTAL £		

WOOD'S RESTAURANT

DINNER

TABLE No. .... COVERS ....

DATE .... INITIALS ....

00508-11

Exhibit 5.19

TOWNSLEY'S RESTAURANT
11 HIGH STREET,
STOPFORD
Tel: 061-483 7936

Table No. | Date ....

Starters	Covers
☐	
Main Course	
☐	
Sweets	
☐	
Wines/Spirits	
Coffee	
010938 ☐	All prices include VAT VAT Registration No. 332 1457 87

Cash Payments

Most catering firms will pay by cheque or bank giro rather than in cash. However, some cash payments will be necessary and the best control is to operate a Petty Cash Book, using the Imprest System.

The Analytical Petty Cash Book and the Imprest System

It is obvious that in almost any firm there will be small cash payments to be made. It would be an advantage if the records of these payments could be kept separately. Where a separate book is kept it is known as a Petty Cash Book.

The task of handling and recording the small cash payments could be delegated to one junior member of staff who would then be known as the petty cashier. In hotels, the receptionist usually deals with Petty Cash.

When the petty cashier makes a payment to someone, then that person will have to fill in a voucher showing exactly what the expense was. He may well have to attach bills obtained by him – e.g. bills for petrol – to the petty cash voucher. He would sign the voucher to certify that his expenses had been paid to him by the petty cashier.

The Imprest System

The basic idea of this system is that the cashier gives the petty cashier an adequate amount of cash to meet his needs for the ensuing period. At the end of the period the cashier ascertains the amount spent by the petty cashiers, and gives him an amount equal to that spent. The Petty Cash in hand should then be equal to the original amount with which the period was started.

Exhibit 5.20 shows an example of this procedure:

Exhibit 5.20

		£
Period 1	The cashier gives the petty cashier	100
	The petty cashier pays out in the period	78
	Petty cash now in hand	22
	The cashier now reimburses the petty cashier the amount spent	78
	Petty cash in hand end of period 1	100
Period 2	The petty cashier pays out in the period	84
	Petty cash now in hand	16
	The cashier now reimburses the petty cashier the amount spent	84
	Petty cash in hand end of period 2	100

Of course, it may sometimes be necessary to increase the fixed sum, often called the cash 'float', to be held at the start of each period. In the above case if it had been desired to increase the 'float' at the end of the second period to £120, then the cashier would have given the petty cashier an extra £20, i.e. £84 + £20 = £104.

Illustration of an Analytical Cash Book

An analytical Petty Cash Book is often used. One of these is shown as Exhibit 5.21.

The receipts column represents the debit side of the petty cash book. On giving £50 to the petty cashier on 1 September the debit entry is made in the petty cash book. A similar entry is made on 30 September for the £44 reimbursement.

Then entries on the credit side or payments side of the petty cash book are first of all made in the totals column, and then are extended into the relevant expense column. At the end of the period, in this case a month, the payments are totalled, it being made sure that the total of the totals column equals the sum of the other payments totals, in this case £44. The expense columns have been headed with the type of expense.

Exhibit 5.21

19-4			
Sept	1	The cashier gives £50 as float to the petty cashier	£
		Payments out of petty cash during September:	
,,	2	Petrol	6
,,	3	J. Green – travelling expenses	3
,,	3	Postages	2
,,	4	D. Davies – taxi Room 2	2*
,,	7	Cleaning expenses	1
,,	9	Petrol	1
,,	12	K. Jones – show tickets Room 7	3*
,,	14	Petrol	3
,,	15	L. Black – travelling expenses	5
,,	16	Cleaning expenses	1
,,	18	Petrol	2
,,	20	Postages	2
,,	22	Cleaning expenses	1
,,	24	G. Wood – travelling expenses	7
,,	27	Settlement of C. Brown's account – a supplier	3
,,	29	Postages	2
,,	30	The cashier reimburses the petty cashier the amount spent in the month.	

*Visitors Paid Out (V.P.O.). This means the hotel petty cashier pays on behalf of a guest and charges a Room number. This will be discussed later in the Hotel Tabular Ledger. (Chapter 20).

Exhibit 5.21

Petty Cash Book

Receipts	Folio	Date	Details	Voucher No.	Total	Motor & Travelling Expenses	Visitors Paid Out	Postages	Cleaning	Ledger Folio	Ledger Accounts
£					£	£	£	£	£		£
50	CB 19	Sept 1	Cash								
		,, 2	Petrol	1	6	6					
		,, 3	J. Green	2	3	3					
		,, 3	Postages	3	2			2			
		,, 4	D. Davies	4	2		2				
		,, 7	Cleaning	5	1				1		
		,, 9	Petrol	6	1	1					
		,, 12	K. Jones	7	3		3				
		,, 14	Petrol	8	3	3					
		,, 15	L. Black	9	5	5					
		,, 16	Cleaning	10	1				1		
		,, 18	Petrol	11	2	2					
		,, 20	Postages	12	2			2			
		,, 22	Cleaning	13	1				1		
		,, 24	G. Wood	14	7	7					
		,, 27	C. Brown	15	3					PL 18	3
		,, 29	Postages	16	2			2			
					44	27	5	6	3		3
44	CB 22	,, 30	Cash			GL 17	GL 20	GL 44	G 64		
		,, 30	Balance	c/d	50						
94					94						
50		Oct 1	Balance	b/d							

Exercises

5.1X. (i) Why is portion control essential in a food and beverage control system in a catering establishment.

(ii) Why is it essential for staff to know what size of portions they are to serve to customers.

5.2X. (*a*) List the different types of cash control to be found in the Hotel and Catering Industry.

(*b*) Selecting *ONE* type answered in (*a*) above, itemize the key aspects of control applicable.

(*c*) Utilizing your selection in (*b*) above, outline the problems likely to be caused in designing a specific procedure.

5.3. From the information given below write up a Petty Cash Book. Include column headings, viz. "TOTAL", "STATIONERY", "POSTAGE", "SUNDRY EXPENSES", "TRAVELLING EXPENSES", and "LEDGER". The amount of the imprest is £35.

May 1 Balance in hand, £10.04.
" 4 Received cash to make up the imprest.
" 5 Bought postage stamps, £7.55.
" 7 Paid electricity account in cash, £3.78. (There is a Heating and Lighting Account in the Ledger).
" 11 Paid window cleaner, £1.45.
" 12 Paid travelling expenses to Clitheroe, £3.25.
" 13 Bought carbon ribbons, £1.34.
" 14 Bought postage stamps, £12.25.
" 15 Bought cleaning fluid, 47p.
" 16 Total and bring down the balance.

5.4X. (*a*) Write down what you understand by the words 'portion control'.

(*b*) State 9 different methods or pieces of equipment which facilitate control over portion size.

5.5. Calculate, showing workings, the following percentages:

(*a*) The food cost percentage (as a fraction of selling price) if a product costing £5.20 is sold for £8.30 inclusive of VAT.

(*b*) The gross profit as a percentage of sales, if a product costing £3.00 is sold for £15.00 exclusive of VAT.

(*c*) The 'mark-up' percentage on cost, if a gross profit of £0.50 is made on a dish selling at £1.80 exclusive of VAT.

5.6. A cafe manageress aimed to make a gross profit of 60% on sales. The figures for the week were Food Cost £253.40, and Sales (inclusive of VAT) £700.00.

(*a*) What was the actual Gross Profit achieved as a percentage of sales?

(*b*) By how much cash did the estimated Gross Profit differ from the actual Gross Profit.

5.7X. A restaurant proprietor forecasts that his table d'hote menu will attract 300 customers. His prediction of their selection, together with his calculation of portion costs, is shown below. Calculate an average cost per customer on the basis of his forecasts and a selling price for the menu based on a 45% gross profit. Include in the price to the customer a service charge of 5% and VAT at 15%.

Menu Choice	Portion Cost	Numbers Anticipated	Total Cost
Grapefruit	£0.135	80	
Avocado Cocktail	£0.216	220	
Filet de Sole Bercy	£0.38	140	
Dindonneaux Rotis A L'Anglaise	£0.43	160	
Choux de Bruxelles Au Beurre	£0.10	100	
Pommes Parisienne	£0.07	300	
Charlotte Russe	£0.17	203	
Creme Caramel	£0.14	97	
Cafe	£0.09	300	
		Total Cost	£
		Portion Cost	£

5.8X. Calculate the 'selling price' (exclusive of VAT and Service Charge or cover charge) from the following inclusive customer prices:

(*a*) £8.99 inclusive of service charge of 10% and VAT at 12%.

(*b*) £3.21 inclusive of VAT at 17½%.

(*c*) £0.96 inclusive of cover charge 10p and VAT 15%.

5.9X. Draw a graph which represents the following data. The sales of an hotel per month for a year were:

Month	Sales £	Month	Sales £
Jan.	3600	July	5200
Feb.	4000	Aug.	4800
March	4200	Sept.	2000
April	4400	Oct.	4200
May	4500	Nov.	4400
Jun.	5000	Dec.	3600

5.10. From the graph you have constructed for 5.9 answer these questions:

(*a*) Which month had the highest sales.

(*b*) How many and which months had sales equal to or exceeding £4500?

(*c*) In which month do you think repairs took place.

5.11X. Now try this

An hotel's annual sales are: –

	£
Rooms	99,858
Restaurant	68,085
Public Bar	54,568
Cocktail Bar	22,695
Kiosk	27,234

Draw a pie chart which represents the above sales.

5.12X. Construct a bar chart from the following information.

As a result of a survey of individuals spending in an hotel during a period it was found that:

Amount spent £	No. of Customers
5 – 10	100
10 – 20	150
20 – 30	180
30 – 40	200
40 – 50	220
50 – 60	190
60 – 70	80
70 – 80	60
80 – 90	40
90 – 100	20

6

The Law of Contract: Part 1

Learning Objectives

At the end of this chapter you should be able to:

6A **Define the essentials of a valid contract.**

Introduction

Everyone is involved daily in the making of contracts. Contracts have become an essential part of everyday life, e.g. purchase of food, catching a bus, enrolment on a course at college, all involve the making of a contract.

Contracts are even more important to business organisations. The transaction of business is the inherent reason for their very existence, and the transaction of business is normally done by the making of contracts. If an organisation sells goods or services to another then there will exist a contract for the sale of those goods, or for the provision of those services. Similarly, if an organisation purchases goods or services from another, then again a contractual relationship will be formed.

Over the years, legal rules have evolved in order to facilitate the conducting of these business transactions. Almost all such transactions with other persons, be they employees, customers or suppliers, will be governed by these legal rules. Therefore, where problems or disputes arise, the rules can be applied and a decision and subsequent settlement can be made, e.g. if a seller refuses to deliver the agreed quantity of goods to the buyer (perhaps because he can sell them at a higher price to someone else) then the rules can be applied to decide whether the seller should be compelled to deliver to the buyer, or, if not, whether the buyer should receive compensation from the seller.

The rules regulating these business transactions are known collectively as the 'Law of Contract'. In the first part of the chapter we shall examine the general rules that apply to contracts in English law. However, it must also be noted that there are, in addition, specific rules which may apply only to specific types of contracts, e.g. Sale of Goods Act 1979, contains special rules relating to contracts for the sale of goods; the Companies Acts, contains special rules relating to contracts made by companies.

Procedure For Solving A Dispute

Most contractual disputes are settled out of court, and the legal rules may not be strictly enforced. A businessman may, for example, think it prudent not to jeopardize any potential future transactions by immediately insisting upon the enforcement of his strict legal rights. However, many disputes *are* solved by an application of the legal rules. In such cases we must ask four questions in order to produce a solution: –

(i) Does a binding contract exist?

(ii) What are the terms of the contract?

(iii) Is there a breach of the contract?

(iv) What remedy should be available for the breach?

We will now examine these questions in detail.

Does a binding contract exist?

A contract is an *agreement* between two or more persons by which they intend to be *legally bound,* and which is enforceable by law.

Thus, if a dispute arises between two parties, we must first establish that they have made a definite agreement. If this is so, it must then be shown that they both intended to be bound by the agreement. (As one would expect, this intention is normally presumed to be present in business agreements).

Finally, English law, unlike many other legal systems requires that the parties provide 'consideration' under the agreement in order to make it enforceable. This means, simply, that each must pay a price for the other's obligation.

Thus we can see that a legally enforceable agreement, a contract, must contain certain basic essentials: –

1. AGREEMENT – between the parties,
2. INTENTION TO BE LEGALLY BOUND – by both parties,
3. CONSIDERATION – given by both parties.

However, even if these essentials are present, other factors may render the contract defective and perhaps unenforceable at law.

It would be unjust, for example, to enforce a contract against a party who had been totally misled, perhaps fraudulently, into entering into it. Similarly, as certain persons have only a limited mental ability to realise the implications of their actions, the law restricts their liability if they enter into a contract. This particularly applies to insane or drunken persons, and to minors (persons under the age of eighteen). Further, if a fundamental mistake has been made in relation to the contract e.g. as to the identity of the person being dealt with, then the contract may be defective. Finally, it would be against the interest of society generally to enforce certain contracts e.g. contracts to commit crimes. Such agreements, therefore, will be illegal and will not be enforceable. Thus the following factors may render the contract defective or unenforceable: –

1. MISREPRESENTATION – misleading the other party;
2. MISTAKE – if fundamental;
3. CAPACITY – lack thereof;
4. ILLEGALITY – contrary to public policy.

(We will refer to these as *Vitiating* Factors).

Therefore, to prove the existence of a contract, we must establish that all the essential requirements are present, and that there are no vitiating factors.

What are the terms of the contract?

Once we have established that the parties have made a legally binding agreement then, in order to solve any dispute between them, we must discover the exact bargain made, i.e. What are the terms of the contract agreed by the parties?

The terms are normally to be found in a written document drawn up by the parties or in verbal statements made by the parties while negotiating the contract.

Do contracts have to be in writing?

You will have noted that we did not include writing as an essential element of a legally binding contract, and that the terms of a contract can be found in verbal statements.

A contract does *NOT* have to be in writing to be legally binding. Contracts may be made orally or may even be implied from the conduct of the parties, e.g. the purchase of goods from a market trader creates a binding contract even though there is nothing put into writing.

However, it must be noted that a small number of contracts *do* require something in writing, e.g. Hire purchase contracts; contracts for the sale of land.

Is there a breach of the contract?

Once we know exactly what the terms of the agreement are, we can discover whether the parties have performed their obligations under the agreement. If a party has performed exactly what he agreed to perform, then his obligation will cease and he will not be liable for any breach. However, if a party does not perform his obligation, or only partly performs it, then he may well be in breach and may be liable for the breach.

Once we have established whether or not there was a breach of the contract, we are much nearer to solving the dispute.

What remedy should be available for the breach

Once we have established that there is a breach, we must decide what remedy, if any, should be available to the injured party. In many circumstances, a sum of money paid as compensation for loss suffered will be sufficient. This sum is usually called 'damages'. In some exceptional circumstances it may be fairer to compel the party in breach to actually perform his obligation under the contract, or to order him not to break the contract. Such remedies are called 'specific performance', and 'injunction'.

Conclusion

Thus, to solve a dispute which arises between the parties to a contract, we must answer the four questions referred to above.

We shall now examine the detailed legal rules which have evolved over the last few hundred years (mainly in business disputes) to regulate contractual agreements. This should help us to answer the questions in most given situations.

These rules are collectively called the 'LAW OF CONTRACT'.

Terms of the Contract

Having established that a contract does exist because all the essential ingredients are present, we must next establish just what the terms of the agreement are. Only then can we move on to decide whether there is a breach of the contract.

We have seen earlier that a contract can be created orally, in writing, or may perhaps be implied from the conduct of the parties. In order to discover exactly what the terms are therefore, we must look at what the parties have expressly agreed, either by word of mouth or in writing, and also consider whether any terms may be implied into the contract from the conduct of the parties or from elsewhere.

The terms can thus be divided into EXPRESS terms and IMPLIED terms.

Express Terms

The express terms of the contract will have been agreed by the parties either orally or in writing.

Oral Terms

If the agreement is made only by word of mouth then it is necessary to assess the validity of the evidence given by the parties as to what they said. This obviously can cause problems, and therefore business contracts will usually be made in writing.

Written Terms

When the parties have made the contract in writing then it is easy to discover the terms. They are to be found in the written document. However, some problems may arise as to their interpretation. If vague words or phrases are used then it is the task of the court to interpret their true meaning, e.g. would a contract for the purchase of "ten British-made Triumph cars" be fulfilled by the delivery of ten Triumph Acclaims?

Once a written contract has been created it is presumed that *ALL* the terms are included in the document. Thus, oral evidence of the agreement will be inadmissable as the parties are presumed to have included every term that they intended to be bound by, in the document. This 'parol evidence' rule would operate harshly in some circumstances, and therefore certain exceptions have been developed. e.g. if there is evidence to show that the parties did *not* intend the terms to *only* be contained in the document, then oral evidence may be admissable.

QUICKMAID RENTAL SERVICES LTD. v REECE (1970)

The plaintiffs persuaded Reece to install a vending machine at his garage. The salesman promised not to install any similar machine in the immediate vicinity. Reece signed a written contract for the installation of the machine. The salesman's promise was *not* included in the written document. Subsequently, another salesman from the company installed another machine nearby. Reece refused to pay any further instalments. The oral statement made by the salesman *WAS* **held** to be a term of the contract. Consequently, the company was in breach of the agreement and Reece's refusal to pay was justified.

However, it must be stressed that oral evidence will *NOT* be admissable if its effect would be to contradict or vary the written terms.

Standard Form Contracts

Businessmen prefer to contract in writing. It is often very convenient for them to use a standard printed document in numerous different transactions, rather than to negotiate different terms on each occasion. Such standard documents are commonly known as 'standard form contracts', e.g. much building work is done under a J.C.T. standard form. This is a model form of contract, designed by the Royal Institute of British Architects and the National Federation of Building Trades Employers, for builders generally to use.

In addition to such industry – wide standard forms which have been negotiated and agreed by the respective interested parties over many years, individual businesses may adopt their own standard forms e.g. insurance companies and finance companies. These latter standard forms present a 'take it or leave it' situation to the other party, who is often in a weaker bargaining position (e.g. consumers generally). Therefore, the law has intervened in many situations in order to protect these weaker parties, and various rules have been introduced to provide this protection. Examples include the Unfair Contract Terms Act 1977, and the Consumer Credit Act 1974, which will be examined in detail later.

Terms and Representations

Finally, having established exactly what the parties have said or put into writing, we must decide whether all the statements made were intended to be binding. Some statements will obviously have been intended to be terms of the contract, but others may have merely been made as part of the negotiations leading up to the making of the contract. The former will be binding, as terms, whereas the latter may not, as they may be merely representations.

In order to decide whether a statement is a representation or a term we must determine the intention of the parties. This decision is frequently very difficult to make, but some basic rules have been developed in order to help.

(i) **When was the statement made?**
The nearer the statement was made to the time of the making of the contract, then the more likely it is that it is a term, and vice-versa. Obviously, parties will normally emphasise the important aspects of the negotiations at the time that the contract is made.

ROUTLEDGE v McKAY (1954)

The plaintiff was negotiating the purchase of the defendant's motor bike. On 23rd October the defendant, reading from the registration document, said that the bike was a 1942 model. A written contract was signed on 30th October which did not refer to the date of the model. It was in fact a 1930 model. When he discovered this the plaintiff sued for breach of contract. It was **held** that the statement as to the date of the model was NOT a term of the contract. The contract was made a full week after the statement AND the oral statement was not included in the written contract, though it could quite easily have been.

(ii) **Does one of the parties have special knowledge or skill as compared with the other?**
The greater the knowledge of the person making the statement, the more likely it is that the statement is a binding term. However, the less knowledge the person making the statement possesses as compared with the other, then the less likely it is that the statement is binding.

DICK BENTLEY (PRODUCTIONS) LTD v HAROLD SMITH (MOTORS) LTD (1965)

The plaintiff purchased a Bentley car from the defendants, who assured the plaintiff that the car had only done 20,000 miles since having a new engine and gearbox fitted. The defendant honestly believed the statement to be true, but in fact the car had done a much greater mileage since the work had been done on it. The plaintiff sued for breach of contract when he discovered this. The statement was **held** to be a term of the contract because the defendant was a car dealer who could or should have known the car's history. Thus it was easy to infer that the statement was intended to be legally binding.

Although the above factors *may* be taken into account, they are by no means conclusive. The *intention* of the parties is paramount.

IMPLIED TERMS

In addition to the express terms, a contract may contain terms implied by custom or by statute.

Terms implied by custom

Such terms may be implied by the customary dealings between the parties, or by the custom or usage of a particular trade or industry.

BRITISH CRANE HIRE CORPORATION LTD v IPSWICH PLANT HIRE LTD (1974)

Both parties were in the heavy plant hire business. The defendants urgently needed a crane for their own use. They agreed by telephone, to hire one from the plaintiffs at a certain price. No conditions were agreed orally but the plaintiffs, as per usual practice, later sent a printed form to the defendants. Before this was signed the crane sank in marshy ground, with nobody at fault. A condition set down in the printed form provided that the defendants were liable to indemnify the plaintiffs. This was a standard condition used throughout the industry by all firms, including the defendants. The court **held** that although the form was not signed, the defendants were bound by the condition. Both parties knew that such conditions were always to be found in such contracts within that industry.

Terms implied by statute

Over a long period of time certain terms have become impliedly incorporated into special types of contract by trade and customary usage. In order to consolidate this process, many of these terms are now implied into these contracts by statute. By far the most common example is the Sale of Goods Act 1979 which implies terms into contracts for the sales of goods.

CONDITIONS AND WARRANTIES

The terms of a contract can normally be divided into CONDITIONS and WARRANTIES. A condition is an important term which forms the very basis of the contract. A warranty is a less important term which is ancillary to the main part of the contract. e.g. if a newly purchased car is delivered without an engine and gearbox there is a breach of *condition;* whereas if only the wheel trims are missing then there is only a breach of *warranty.*

The difference between the two becomes very important when we examine the consequences of a breach of a condition or a warranty. A breach of a condition is so serious that the innocent party may treat the contract as repudiated and thus be no longer bound by it. A breach of warranty however is much less serious, and the innocent party will remain bound by the contract but will be able to claim damages. The following two cases effectively illustrate this.

POUSSARD v SPIERS AND POND (1876)

The plaintiff agreed to sing in an opera from 28th November, the first day of its run. She was taken ill on 23rd November and could not appear until 4th December. The defendants had to employ a substitute and they refused the plaintiff's services when she finally arrived. The plaintiff sued for breach of contract. It was **held** that by missing the first week of the run the plaintiff was in breach of an important term of the contract. This breach of condition therefore entitled the defendants to treat the contract as repudiated, as they had done, and to hire a substitute.

BETTINI v GYE (1876)

The plaintiff agreed to sing on a tour commencing 30th March, and to attend at rehearsals for six days before that date. The plaintiff fell ill and did not arrive until 28th March. The defendant refused to accept the plaintiff's services. The rehearsal clause was **held** to be subsidiary to the main part of the contract which was to sing on the tour. The plaintiff was available for the actual tour and was therefore only in breach of warranty. The defendant could not treat the contract as repudiated and was himself in breach by refusing to accept the plaintiff's services. Therefore he had to compensate the plaintiff.

Although these two cases seem to illustrate the difference between conditions and warrantees it is often very difficult to decide into which category a term fits. In a Bettini v Gye type case for example, someone who was risking a large sum of money on the success of a show would be distinctly unhappy if a star performer was to miss a large proportion of rehearsal time. Thus one might argue that the plaintiff's action in that case was a breach of condition.

In many cases, therefore, the court will take particular note of any express statement by the parties as to the categories into which the terms fall. A typical example would be a contract which was to be performed by a specific date. If the performance was completed one day late, this would probably be a breach of warranty. However, if one of the parties had stressed that the date of performance was vital, i.e. that time was of the essence in the contract, then the late performance would be a breach of condition. Thus, again, the *intention* of the parties may be of paramount importance.

Exercises (no answers given at back of book)

6.1. Draw up a list of *ten* different contracts entered into as part of everyday life.

6.2. Explain why contracts are important to business organizations.

6.3. Explain why we need a 'law of contract'.

6.4. List *four* 'special' types of contract to which 'special' rules apply.

6.5. Explain why a contract is different in law from a mere agreement.

6.6. Explain, in your own words, the basic essentials of a contract.

6.7. List, and illustrate, vitiating factors which may affect the enforceability of a contract.

6.8. Give examples of everyday contracts which are not made in writing.

6.9. Explain the remedies available for a breach of contract.

7

The Law of Contract: Part II

Learning Objectives

At the end of this chapter you should be able to:

7A **Describe the effects of exclusion of liability by (a) the purchaser, (b) the seller.**

Terms Which Exclude or Limit Liability

Because the parties to a contract are free to negotiate their own terms, it is possible for a term excluding or limiting liability for the breach of the contract to be included. Such a term is legally binding if agreed by both parties. However, in many instances it is illusory to say that the parties are 'freely' negotiating the terms of the contract, e.g. if one attempts to park a car in a city centre on a Saturday morning, one is compelled to use a car-park and in turn, to accept the conditions imposed by the owner of the car-park. A similar 'take it or leave it' situation is created by the use of a standard form contract, whereby it is extremely difficult for one party to negotiate a variation of the conditions contained in the standard form.

In order to remedy the harsh effects of the enforceability of exclusion clauses, both the judiciary (under common law) and Parliament (by statute) have introduced rules to limit their validity. We must now examine these rules.

1. Common Law Limitations

The judiciary will not enforce an exclusion clause if it is not a term of the contract or if it does not (on its wording) cover the damage. Sometimes also, if there has been a fundamental breach of the contract by the party who wishes to rely on the exclusion clause, then the clause will not be enforced.

(i) **Is the exclusion clause a term of the contract?**
The exclusion clause will be a term of the contract if it is incorporated within it. To be incorporated, notice of its existence must be given to the other party before or at the time the contract is made. Obviously, fresh terms cannot be imposed on a party after the contract has been made.

OLLEY v MARLBOROUGH COURT HOTEL (1949)

The plaintiff entered the hotel, paid for a room for a week in advance at the reception desk, and then went up to the room. A notice on the wall of the room exempted the hotel from liability for loss or theft of property. The hotel staff were negligent and the plaintiff's fur coat was stolen from the room. The court **held** that the hotel was not protected by the exclusion clause because it was communicated *AFTER* the contract had been made at the reception desk.

NOTE – if she had stayed at the hotel before, the clause might have been valid. A previous consistent course of dealings between the parties can result in the clause being implied into the contract.

SPURLING LTD v BRADSHAW (1956)

The two parties had dealt with each other for many years. The defendant delivered some barrels of orange juice to the plaintiffs' warehouse for storage and they were accepted. He subsequently received a notice of receipt which had certain conditions printed on the back. One of these exempted the plaintiffs from liability for loss or damage. When the defendant collected his barrels they were empty. He therefore refused to pay the storage charge. The exclusion clause was **held** to be valid. It was incorporated into the contract by the previous course of dealings between the parties (as that document had been sent on each occasion). Thus, the defendant had to pay.

NOTE – there must have been a CONSISTENT course of dealings. Exactly how many previous deals will be necessary will vary from case to case.

Obviously, if the exclusion clause is contained in a written contractual document which has been signed, then it will be incorporated into the contract. Thus the clause will be binding even if the person signing has not read it.

L'ESTRANGE v GRAUCOB (1934)

The plaintiff signed a 'Sales Agreement' for the purchase of a machine. She did not read certain clauses which were in 'legible, but regrettably small, print'. It was **held** that because she had signed the written agreement she was bound by all the clauses therein.

If the exclusion clause is not contained in a signed contractual document, then the general rule is that it is only valid if it is REASONABLY brought to the attention of the other party. Thus, if the clause is on a notice, the size and position of the notice would be important factors. The test is, 'would a reasonable person have discovered the existence of the exclusion clause?'

THORNTON v SHOE LANE PARKING LTD. (1971)

The plaintiff approached the defendants' car park. At the entrance a notice said, "All cars parked at owner's risk." He drove up to the barrier. A ticket popped out of the machine. He took it, the barrier was raised, and he entered. Words printed on the ticket said that it was issued subject to conditions displayed on the premises, but the plaintiff did not read these words. A condition printed, along with many others, on a notice board inside the car park excluded the defendants from liability for injury to customers, howsoever caused. The plaintiff was physically injured when he returned to collect his car. In the circumstances it was **held** that insufficient notice of the existence of the exclusion clause had been given. The defendants should have made a greater effort to communicate the clause to customers in order that it be binding. Lord Denning said that the reference on the ticket to the conditions displayed inside was made *after* the contract had been made with the machine. Thus the existence of the clause was communicated too late.

NOTE ALSO –

(i) the actual notice inside communicated the clause too late, and

(ii) the wording on the notice at the entrance was interpreted as only applying to damage to cars, and not to damage to customers.

There are a number of cases in which it has been held that a *ticket* can be an effective communication of the existence of an exclusion clause PROVIDED that it is handed over before or at the time of the making of the contract, and that it is a contractual document and not, for example, a mere receipt.

CHAPELTON v BARRY U.D.C. (1940)

The plaintiff hired two deck-chairs and was given two tickets in return. He put them in his pocket without looking at them. Words printed on the tickets excluded the defendants from liability arising from the hire of a chair. When the plaintiff sat on his chair it collapsed and he was injured. It was **held** that no reasonable person would have expected to find contractual terms on such tickets. Consequently, they were not contractual documents but were mere receipts for money paid. The exclusion clause was not valid and thus the plaintiff was awarded compensation.

Finally, whether a ticket is a contractual document very much depends on the type of ticket or on the circumstances in which it is issued. The more detailed the information printed on the ticket, the more likely it is that it is a contractual document, e.g. airline tickets and train tickets.

–

(ii) **Does the exclusion clause cover the damage?**

The court will examine an exclusion clause very closely in order to ensure that it applies to the actual damage suffered. A very strict interpretation is given, and any ambiguity or vagueness in the clause will be interpreted to the detriment of the person who inserted the clause and who seeks to rely on it. Thus, in Thornton v Shoe Lane Parking (above) the notice at the entrance which said 'all cars parked at owner's risk' was interpreted only to apply to damage to cars and

NOT to damage to customers. Similarly, a clause which proposes to exempt a party from liability for 'breach of any warranty' will *NOT* exclude liability for breach of a condition.

(iii) **Has there been a fundamental breach?**
It would seem unfair to allow a person to exclude liability for a *fundamental breach* of a contract (i.e. a complete failure to perform the contract as agreed), particularly where the other party has unequal bargaining power. Thus, in some cases the party seeking to rely on the exclusion clause could not do so if there was a fundamental breach of the contract on his part.

KARSALES (HARROW) LTD. v WALLIS (1956)
The defendant inspected a car and, finding it in good order, agreed to buy it. He signed a written contract which contained a term that said, "no condition or warranty that the vehicle is roadworthy or as to its condition or fitness for any purpose is given by the owner, or implied." The car was subsequently left outside the defendant's premises by the plaintiff. The car was not the same as before. The cylinder head was broken. The car would not go, and the defendant refused to pay for it. The plaintiff sued for the price, relying on the exclusion clause to cover the defects in the car. It was **held** that because the plaintiffs had not delivered the thing contracted for then they could not rely on the clause, which was not enforceable. Therefore the defendant could treat the contract as repudiated and did not have to pay.

For a time it was thought that a fundamental breach would automatically render an exclusion clause ineffective. However the House of Lords has established that, depending on the intentions of the parties, an exclusion clause *CAN* exempt a party from liability for a fundamental breach.

PHOTO PRODUCTION LTD. v SECURICOR LTD. 1980
The defendants agreed to protect the plaintiff's factory at night time by making periodic visits. An employee of the defendant started a small fire on one of his visits. The fire got out of control and destroyed the entire factory and its contents, worth about £615,000. The plaintiffs sued and the defendants relied on an exclusion clause in the contract which said that there was to be no liability for injurious acts or defaults by employees unless these acts could have been foreseen and avoided by the exercise of due diligence by the defendants. The court **held** the exclusion clause was clear in its meaning and adquately covered the defendant in these circumstances. Thus the defendant was not liable.

NOTE – this was certainly a fundamental breach! However, the parties were of equal bargaining power and had freely negotiated the whole of the agreement. Also, from an insurance point of view, it was more convenient for the owners of the property to insure against fire than for the employers of the guards to insure against the negligent acts of employees, i.e. it is easier to quantify the damage from the possible loss of the property than the possible damage from the guard's negligence, and it is therefore easier to fix the premium.

In cases where the parties are not bargaining on equal terms the doctrine of fundamental breach has become much less important. This is because the provisions of the Unfair Contract Terms Act 1977 have restricted the use of exclusion clauses in such cases.

2. Statutory Limitations

The most important statute relating to exclusion clauses is the Unfair Contract Terms Act 1977. This Act did not come into force until February 1978 and does not apply to contracts made before that date. (Thus it was not applicable in Photo Productions Ltd. v Securicor). Despite its title it does not apply to unfair terms generally, but only to *unfair exclusion clauses* in contracts made in the course of a business. Some such clauses are rendered totally ineffective and others are subject to a test of reasonableness.

(i) **Clauses rendered totally ineffective**

1. Exclusion of liability for death or personal injury caused by negligence.

S2(1) renders ineffective any clause which purports to exclude liability for death or personal injury caused by negligence. This would now apply to cases similar to Thornton v Shoe Lane Parking Ltd. and Chapelton v Barry U.D.C.; (above).

2. Exclusion or restriction of liability for breach of a contract for the sale or supply of goods.

This part of the Act is discussed in detail later.

(ii) **Clauses subject to a test of reasonableness**

1. Exclusion of liability for damage *other than* death or personal injury caused by negligence.

S2(2) provides that a clause excluding liability for 'other loss or damage' caused by negligence is only valid if it satisfies the test of reasonableness. This provision would cover financial loss caused by negligence.

2. Exclusion of liability for breach of contract where one party deals as a consumer, or on the other party's standard terms of business.

S.3 provides that an exclusion clause which purports to exclude liability for breach of contract in a business contract *CANNOT* be enforced by the businessman against the person dealing as a consumer *UNLESS* it satisfies the test of REASONABLENESS. This provision would now apply in cases similar to Olley v Marlborough Court Hotel; and Karsales Ltd V Wallis (above).

Similarly, S.3 applies to *ANY* standard form contracts, even between two businessmen. The party on whose standard form the contract is made cannot enforce a clause excluding liability for breach of contract contained therein, *UNLESS* it satisfies the test of REASONABLENESS. This provision would now apply in cases similar to Photo Productions Ltd. v Securicor; and L'Estrage v Graucob (above).

3. Exclusion or restriction of liability for breach of a contract for the sale or supply of goods made between businessmen.

Test of Reasonableness

No detailed test of reasonableness is set out in the Act. However, in Schedule 2 are to be found certain 'guidelines' which a court should consider. These guidelines are not conclusive, and other factors may influence the court's decision in some cases. Schedule 2 refers particularly to: – the relative strength of bargaining position of the parties; whether the party had the opportunity to enter into a similar contract with some other person WITHOUT having to accept a similar exclusion clause; and whether the party ought reasonably to have known of the existence *and the extent* of the exclusion clause.

This latter guideline overlaps with the common law rules relating to exclusion clauses which we looked at earlier. It must be stressed however that the Act has not superseded these rules and thus they remain of great importance.

Contracts for the sale of goods

The law relating to contracts for the sale of goods is found in the Sale of Goods Act 1979. The law of contract applies equally to the sale of goods but has been supplemented by statute to cover important aspects of contracts for the sale of goods such as transfer of ownership, implied terms, title and the remedies of the parties for breach.

However, S.55(1) of the 1979 Act provides that the parties to a contract for the sale of goods are free to vary or exclude any of the provisions of the Act except in so far as the Unfair Contract Terms Act 1977 may otherwise provide. These important provisions will be dealt with later.

All section numbers refer to the Sale of Goods Act 1979 unless otherwise stated.

Definition

S.2(1) defines a contract for the sale of goods as "A contract by which the seller transfers or agrees to transfer the property in goods to the buyer for a money consideration called the price". This definition will now be examined more closely.

"Goods" is defined by S.61 as "all personal chattels other than things in action and money and . . . includes emblements, industrial growing crops, and things attached to or forming part of the land which are agreed to be severed before sale or under the contract of sale".

"Personal chattels" includes such things as cars, ships, paintings and animals, in other words, personal belongings. Freehold and leasehold land is excluded from the definition because land is real property, not personal property.

"Things in action" is a term governing such items as shares in a company and negotiable instruments (i.e. cheques etc.) and these are specifically excluded from the definition of goods.

"Emblements" and "industrial growing crops" are those crops which do not grow naturally but have to be cultivated, e.g. potatoes.

Finally, "things attached to or forming part of the land" includes those things which grow naturally on the land, and fixtures, which are objects generally fixed to the land otherwise than merely by their own weight so that they are treated as being part of the land itself.

One part of the definition of a contract for the sale of goods which sometimes causes confusion is the phrase "property in goods". The word "property" here simply means "ownership", and it is this that is transferred from seller to buyer.

The defininition specifically states that the consideration in a contract for the sale of goods must be money. Thus, where two people strike a bargain and merely exchange one set of goods for another, this is not a contract for the sale of goods but a barter transaction. But if the consideration is money and goods, e.g. exchanging old goods plus money for new goods, the agreement will come within the ambit of the Sale of Goods Act 1979.

Distinction between sale of goods and provision of services

It is very important to distinguish between a contract for the sale of goods and a contract for the provision of services since the latter is not subject to the 1979 Act.

In order to ascertain what sort of contract is being entered into the main purpose of the contract must be examined. If the purpose is to transfer ownership of goods from the seller to the buyer, the contract is for the sale of goods. If, on the other hand, the main purpose is not to transfer ownership but is, for example, something like the provision of labour, then the contract is for the provision of services. It is the substance of the agreement that is important so that a contract for the provision of services will not become a contract for the sale of goods merely because the ownership of some goods pass under the contract, but incidentally to it.

ROBINSON v GRAVES (1935)

A contract to paint a portrait was **held** to be a contract for skill and not a contract for the sale of goods even though the ownership of the canvass and frame (i.e. goods) was transferred under the contract. This transfer of ownership was quite incidental to the main purpose of the contract.

Terms in the contract of sale

The distinction between terms and representations has alrady been discussed, as has the distinction between conditions and warranties. To recap, a condition is a term which is fundamental to the contract. A warranty is a less important term which is ancillary to the main purpose of the contract. Whether a term is a condition or a warranty is a matter for the court to decide.

The importance of this distinction lies in the remedies available for breach of a condition and warranty. S.11(3) provides that where there has been a breach of condition the injured party may repudiate the contract and sue for damages. Where there has been a breach of warranty, however, the only remedy is an action for damages. It should be noted that the injured party is not obliged to repudiate if a condition is broken, but may simply bring an action for damages.

Implied Terms

All contracts for the sale of goods are subject to specific implied terms as laid down by the 1979 Act and with the development of consumer protection law, these terms may only be excluded under certain circumstances. This is particularly advantageous to the consumer who now enjoys a favourable position when buying goods in that his statutory rights exist despite any attempt by the seller to exclude or restrict them.

Sections 12-15 provide the implied terms applicable to all contracts for the sale of goods.

S.12 – Implied terms as to title

The following terms are implied:

1) An implied condition on the part of the seller that in case of a sale he has the right to sell the goods, and in the case of an agreement to sell he will have the right at the time when property is to pass.
2) An implied warranty that the goods are free, and will remain free until property is to pass, from any charge or encumbrance not disclosed or known to the buyer before the contract was made.

3) An implied warranty that the buyer will enjoy quiet possesson of the goods except in so far as it may be disturbed by anyone entitled to the benefit of a charge or encumbrance disclosed to or known by the buyer.
4) Where it appears from the contract or may be inferred from the circumstances that the seller intends to transfer only such title as he or third party may have, the following warranties are implied:
   (*a*) that all charges and encumbrances known to the seller have been disclosed to the buyer before the contract is made, and
   (*b*) that the buyer will obtain quiet possession apart from anyone claiming under a charge or encumbrance disclosed to the buyer before the contract is made.

The main object of S.12 is to ensure that a seller has the right to sell the goods and will consequently transfer a good title to the buyer who will enjoy the goods without interference from undisclosed sources.

"Quiet possession" refers to the buyer's right not to have the goods taken away from him (e.g. by the true owner if the seller did not have the right to sell). "Charges" and "encumbrances" in the context of sale of goods means the rights of third parties over the goods e.g. a mortgagee's charge or a lien.

S.13-Implied terms as to description (i.e. any words used to identify the goods)

The following terms are implied:

1) Where there is a contract for the sale of goods by description, an implied condition that the goods will correspond with that description.

   In VARLEY v WHIPP (1900), a person selling a secondhand reaping machine described as new the previous year was **held** to be in breach of S.13 (of the Sale of Goods Act 1893 which is substantially the same as S.13 of the 1979 Act) when the machine was found by the buyer to be much older.

   Again, in BEALE v TAYLOR (1967), the seller of a car advertised it as a 1961 Herald convertible. The buyer later found that only the rear half of the car was a 1961 model, the front half being part of an earlier model. The court **held** that the seller was in breach of the condition implied by S.13.

2) If the sale is by sample as well as by description the goods must correspond with both the sample and the description.

   S.13(3) provides that a sale of goods by description includes sales where the goods are selected by the buyer, e.g. goods selected in a supermarket. In these circumstances, the goods must correspond with any description given on packaging, wrappers, labels, etc.

Sellers often take precautions against S.13 (which is strictly applied by the courts) by using such words as "more or less" or "approximately". However, a wide variation from even an approximate description will be in breach of the implied condition, e.g. where a box of matches described as having an average of 48 matches is found to contain only 35.

S.14 - Implied terms as to merchantable quality and fitness for purpose

The general rule is CAVEAT EMPTOR (let the buyer beware). Subject to the statutory provisions, there is no implied term as to the quality or fitness for any particular purpose of goods supplied under a contract of sale.

However, to this general rule there are two exceptions:

1) S.14(2) provides that, "Where the seller sells goods IN THE COURSE OF A BUSINESS, there is an implied condition that the goods supplied under the contract are of merchantable quality *except*
   (*a*) as regards defects specifically drawn to buyer's attention before the contract is made, or
   (*b*) if the buyer examines the goods before the contract is made, as regards defects which that examination ought to reveal."

   It is important to note that this provision applies to sellers selling "in the course of a business" and "business" includes "a profession and the activities of any government department . . . or local or public authority." Private sales are therefore excluded from the scope of the Act and the buyer must rely on ordinary contractual remedies if a private contract of sale is broken.

   "**Merchantable quality**" is defined by S.14(6) as "fit for the purpose or purposes for which goods of that kind are commonly bought as it is reasonable to expect having regard to any description applied to them, the price (if relevant) and all other relevant circumstances." Obviously, therefore, a businessman selling off goods which have been traded in for new goods may not be subject to such a strict interpretation of the definition as if he was selling new goods.

   Not only must the goods be merchantable at the time the contract is made, but they must remain merchantable for a reasonable time afterwards. Further, where perishable goods are sold and sent by carrier they must remain merchantable throughout a normal journey and a reasonable time thereafter.

   BEER v WALKER (1877)

   The sellers of rabbits sent some by train from London to Brighton. The rabbits were merchantable when put on the train but on arrival were putrid and useless. As the journey had been a normal one, the sellers were **held** liable for the deterioration.

2) S.14(3) provides that where the seller sells goods in the course of a business there is an implied condition that the goods are reasonably fit for any purpose made known to the seller by the buyer except where the circumstances show that the buyer does not rely, or that it is unreasonable for him to rely, on the skill or judgment of the seller.

The same condition is implied by S.61 where goods are supplied on credit and the buyer tells the credit-broker of the purpose for which he wants the goods. A credit-broker is a person who carries on the business of introducing persons who want credit to organisations willing to supply credit facilities.

The condition implied by S.14(3) is illustrated by GODLEY v PERRY (1960)

A young boy bought a toy catapult which broke when he used it causing him to lose an eye. The boy's action against the seller was successful since the catapult was not fit for the purpose for which it was bought.

If the goods are bought for a special purpose, that purpose must be made known to the seller if he is to be subject to S.14(3).

GRIFFITHS v PETER CONWAY LTD. (1939)

A woman bought a tweed coat without disclosing to the seller that she had a very sensitive skin. The woman contracted dermatitis from the coat and sued for damages for breach of the condition implied by S.14(3). Her action failed because she had not disclosed the particular purpose for which she wanted the coat, namely, wearing by a buyer with a very sensitive skin.

It is no defence to an action for breach of this implied condition that no ordinary skill and care by the seller could have detected the defect. Consequently in FROST v AYLESBURY DAIRY CO. LTD. (1905), where typhoid germs were found in milk resulting in the death of a woman who drank it, the defendants were held liable for breach of the implied condition even though the presence of the germs could only have been discovered by a careful and prolonged investigation.

S.15 – Implied terms in sales by sample

A contract of sale is a contract of sale by sample where there is an express or implied term to that effect in the contract. In a contract of sale by sample the following conditions are implied:

(*a*) that the bulk will correspond with the sample in quality;

(*b*) that the buyer will have a reasonable opportunity of comparing the bulk with the sample;

(*c*) that the goods will be free from any defect rendering them unmerchantable which would not be apparent on reasonable examination of the sample.

Two further points should be noted here. Firstly, exhibiting a sample during the course of negotiations does not always mean that the sale is by sample if there is no contractual term to that effect. Secondly, if the goods do not correspond with the sample in quality, condition (a) above will be broken even if by a simple process e.g. the application of heat (as in E. & S. Ruben v Faire Bros. (1949)) the goods can be made to correspond.

Exclusion of the Implied Terms

We have already seen that the parties to a contract for the sale of goods are free to vary or exclude the provisions of the Act except in so far as the Unfair Contract Terms Act 1977 is contravened (S.55). It is, therefore, necessary to examine the provisions of the U.C.T.A. in relation to contracts for the sale of goods.

S.6(1) U.C.T.A. provides that S.12 of the 1979 Act (title) cannot under any circumstances be excluded or restricted by any contract term. Whether or not sections 13-15 may be excluded or restricted depends upon the type of sale in question. i.e. whether it is a "consumer sale" or a "non-consumer sale". The importance of the distinction lies in the fact that S.6(2) U.C.T.A. provides "As against a person dealing as consumer, liability for breach of the obligation arising from section 13,14 or 15 of the 1979 Act . . . cannot be excluded or restricted by any contract term."

S.12 U.C.T.A. provides that a party to a contract 'deals as consumer' in relation to another party if:

(*a*) he neither makes the contract in the course of a business nor holds himself out as doing so; and

(*b*) the other party does make the contract in the course of a business; and

(*c*) the goods passing under the contract are of a type ordinarily supplied for private use or consumption.

The onus of proving that a sale is not a consumer sale is on the seller. The U.C.T.A. provides that in auction sales and sales by competitive tender the buyer is not to be regarded as a consumer.

To illustrate the distinction between the types of sale, note the following examples:

(i) Bert buys an electric fan heater from a department store for use in his home – a consumer sale.

(ii) Fred, a market gardener, buys an electric fan heater from a department store to help maintain a constant temperature in one of his greenhouses – a non-consumer sale.

In non-consumer sales, a contract term purporting to exclude or restrict any of sections 13-15 is only valid "in so far as it satisfies the requirement of reasonableness" (S.6(3) U.C.T.A.). This requirement means that the excluding term must be fair and reasonable in the circumstances. The U.C.T.A. lists five matters which may be relevant in deciding whether an excluding term is reasonable. These are:

(*a*) the strength of the bargaining positions of the parties relative to each other, taking into account alternative means by which the customer's requirements could have been met;

(*b*) whether the customer received an inducement to agree to the term or in accepting it had an opportunity of entering into a similar contract with other persons but without having to accept a similar term;

(*c*) whether the customer knew or ought reasonably to have known of the existence and extent of the term (having regard, among other things, to any custom of the trade and any previous course of dealing between the parties);

(*d*) where the term excludes or restricts any relevant liability if some condition is not complied with, whether it was reasonable at the time of the contract to expect that compliance with that condition would be practicable;

(*e*) whether the goods were manufactured, processed, or adapted to the special order of the customer.

Sale of goods where the seller is not the owner

Where the seller of goods is also the true owner of them he can obviously pass a good title to the buyer. Problems may arise, however, where the seller is not the true owner but, for example, obtained possession of the goods illegally. The general rule is NEMO DAT QUOD NON HABET, which applied to the sale of goods means where goods are sold by a person who is not the owner, the buyer obtains no better title than the seller has. S.21 enacts this rule but provides that it will not apply where –

(*a*) the seller had the authority or consent of the owner, or

(*b*) the owner is estopped from denying the seller's authority to sell.

The first of these exceptions is straight forward. The second applies in situations where the owner has behaved in such a way that the seller appeared to a third party to be the true owner. This will happen where the owner commits a fraud himself or acquiesces in the fraud of the seller.

EASTERN DISTRIBUTORS v GOLDRING (1957)

The owner of a van signed hire-purchase documents showing a dealer to be the owner, and the documents were presented to a finance company to obtain finance. The finance company bought the van from the dealer but the true owner then claimed possession on the grounds that the dealer had no authority to sell it. It was **held** that the owner was estopped from denying the dealer's authority to sell and the finance company had, therefore, acquired a good title to the van.

The 1979 Act lays down a further series of special exceptions to the nemo dat rule, all of which are designed to protect the buyer.

1) Sales by persons acting under common law or statutory powers
e.g. the right of a mortgagee (the lender) to sell the mortgaged property when the mortgagor (the borrower) defaults on repayment of the mortgage debt; the right of an innkeeper to sell the property of guests who do not pay their bill.

2) Sales ordered by the court
e.g. where the court orders goods to be sold so that the proceeds of sale can be used to settle a judgment debt.

3) Sales in market overt
"Market overt" is the term used to describe any open, public and legally constituted market in England or a shop in the City of London. S.22 states that where goods are sold in market overt the buyer acquires a good title to them provided he buys them in good faith and without notice of any defect in the title of the seller. It is essential that the goods are on display to the public and sold according to the usual custom of the market.

Sales in shops in the City of London are sales in market overt provided the sale is by the shopkeeper and not to him and provided it takes place during business hours in the public part of the shop and not in a private room.

An illustration of the effect of a sale in market overt is:

BISHOPSGATE MOTOR FINANCE CORPORATION v TRANSPORT BRAKES LTD. (1949)

A took a car which was subject to a hire-purchase agreement to Maidstone market where he instructed auctioneers to sell it. The car did not reach its reserve price but A later sold it in the area of the market to C who bought in good faith and with no knowledge of the hire-purchase agreement. It was **held** that as a private sale was according to the custom of the market, C obtained a good title under S.22.

4) Sales under a voidable title
If a buyer buys goods under a voidable contract, his title is also voidable and may be rendered void if the true owner acts in time. A voidable contract is a binding contract, but one of the parties has an option to set it aside.

S.23 provides that where the seller of goods has a voidable title to them which has not been avoided at the time of the sale, the buyer acquires a good title to the goods provided he buys them in good faith and without notice of the seller's defect of title.

It is important to note that S.23 only applies to voidable contracts and not to void contracts.

The principle in S.23 is illustrated by:

CAR & UNIVERSAL FINANCE CO. LTD. v CALDWELL (1964)

A rogue bought a car and fraudulently induced the seller to accept a cheque which was subsequently dishonoured. The seller immediately informed the police and the AA of the fraud – an act which avoided the contract. After the seller had taken this action, the rogue sold the car to an innocent third party who acquired no title since at the time he bought the car the rogue himself had no title to it.

Note (i) This case would presumably have been decided differently if the seller's action in informing the police and the AA had been done *after* the sale by the rogue to the third party.

(ii) Even if the seller had not avoided the contract in time, the third party would not have acquired a good title if he took the car with notice of the fraudulent act.

5) Sales by a Mercantile Agent

A mercantile agent is a person who in the ordinary course of his business buys, sells, or otherwise deals in goods on behalf of others. S.2 Factors Act 1889 provides that an innocent party who buys goods in good faith from such an agent acquires a good title to them even though at the time of the sale the agent's authority had been terminated. It is essential, however, that the agent was in possession of the goods or title documents to them with the consent of the owner, even if that consent was obtained by a trick or fraud.

FOLKES v KING (1923)

A handed over possession of his car to B, a mercantile agent, with instructions to sell it, but not for less than £575. The agent sold it for much less than £575 to a third party, C, who bought it in good faith. It was **held** that C acquired a good title to the car.

But note:

STADIUM FINANCE LTD. v ROBBINS (1962)

The plaintiff gave his car to a mercantile agent to see what offers he could get for it. The plaintiff retained the ignition key and accidentally left the registration book in the glove compartment of the car. The agent obtained an ignition key and broke into the glove compartment to retrieve the registration book. He then sold the car to a third party. It was **held** that the third party did not acquire a good title to the car. Although the agent was in possession of the car with the owner's consent, he was not in possession of the registration book with such consent and so did not have authority to sell the car.

6) Sale by a seller in possession
S.24 provides that where a person having sold goods retains them or the documents of title to them and then delivers or transfers them to a third party, the third party will obtain a good title to the goods provided he buys in good faith and without notice of the previous sale. The same applies if a mercantile agent disposes of the goods on behalf of the seller.

The effect of the second sale is as if it had been expressly authorised by the owner of the goods. Of course, the original buyer is not left without a remedy as he may sue the seller for breach of contract (see later).

The following example illustrates the application of S.24:
A sells goods to B but A retains possession of them (even though property has passed to B). A then sells and delivers the same goods to C. C obtains a good title to the goods provided he takes in good faith and without notice of A's sale to B. B can sue A for breach of contract.

7) Sale by a buyer in possession of the goods
S.25 provides that the delivery or transfer of goods by a buyer to whom property has not passed will have the same effect as if the sale had been by a mercantile agent in possession of the goods or title documents to them with the owner's consent. Thus, even if the buyer does not have a good title to the goods, he can pass a good title to a third party who buys from him provided the third party acts in good faith and without notice of any rights of the original seller.

S.25 only applies to contracts of sale where the property in the goods has not passed to the buyer. If property has passed there is no problem and, therefore, no need to rely on the section. So, for example, S.25 will apply where it is agreed that property shall not pass until the buyer has paid the price in full, or until his cheque has been cleared. If the condition is not fulfilled, the seller may sue the buyer for breach of contract.

E.g. X sells goods to Y, the contract providing that property shall not pass until Y's cheque is cleared. Before the cheque is cleared, Y sells the goods to Z who buys in good faith. Z acquires a good title to the goods. If Y's cheque is dishonoured, X may sue him for breach of contract.

8) Sales of motor vehicles subject to hire-purchase agreements
When goods are bought on hire-purchase, the property in the goods does not pass to the hirer until the final instalment has been

paid. Any sale by the hirer/debtor will not, therefore, pass a good title to the buyer because the property is still owned by the creditor (usually a Finance Company). However, the Hire Purchase Act 1964 Part III provides an exception in the case of motor vehicles. If someone buying a motor vehicle on hire-purchase sells it to a private purchaser before he has paid all the instalments, the purchaser will obtain a good title provided he buys in good faith and without notice of the hire-purchase agreement.

Further, if the vehicle is sold to a dealer in the motor trade before all the instalments have been paid, the dealer will not get a good title, but the first private purchaser of the vehicle from the dealer will obtain a good title provided he buys in good faith. Of course, in either case, the true owner has a remedy against the person buying on hire-purchase or the trader, or both, as the case may be.

Remedies for breach of a contract for the sale of goods

A. Remedies of the Seller

The seller has two sets of remedies, personal remedies against the buyer and remedies which may be exercised against the goods. Of those mentioned below, (1) and (2) are personal remedies, the remainder are exercisable against the goods.

(1) Action for the Price
S.49 provides that where the property in the goods has passed to the buyer and he wrongfully neglects or refuses to pay for them, the seller may maintain an action against him for the price.

However, if the parties have agreed a date on which payment is to be made and payment is not made on that date, the seller may bring an action for the price even though the goods have not been delivered or the property has not passed.

(2) An action for damages for non-acceptance
S.50 provides that where the buyer wrongfully neglects or refuses to accept and pay for the goods, the seller may bring an action for damages for non-acceptance.

The amount of damages depends upon whether or not there is an available market for the goods. If there is, the measure of damages is usually the difference between the contract price and the market price at the time the goods are rejected. If there is not an available market, the proper measure of damages is the loss of profit by the seller on the sale.

The usual rules of mitigation apply to these actions by the seller.

(3) Seller's lien
A lien is a creditor's right to retain goods belonging to a debtor until a debt has been paid. In relation to contracts for the sale of goods, the lien attaches to the goods to be sold. It should be noted that the lien relates only to the price and the goods cannot be retained pending payment of any other debt. The lien is lost when the seller is paid, when he arranges for the goods to be transferred to the buyer, when the buyer lawfully obtains possession of the goods, or when the seller waives the lien.

(4) Stoppage in transit
S.44 provides that when the buyer of goods becomes insolvent the unpaid seller has the right to resume possession of goods as long as they are in course of transit and may retain them until payment has been made. This enables the seller to recover the goods instead of having to become a creditor of the insolvent buyer with the possibility of receiving only a proportion of the contract price.

"Insolvency" in relation to the sale of goods arises where a person has ceased to pay his debts in the ordinary course of business or cannot pay them as they become due.

Goods are deemed to be "in the course of transit" from the time they are delivered to a carrier or other person for the purpose of transmission to the buyer until the buyer or his agent takes delivery of them from the carrier.

(5) The right to resell the goods
Generally, the seller has no right to resell the goods but S.48 enables him to do this:

(*a*) where the goods are perishable;
(*b*) where the unpaid seller gives notice to the buyer of his intention to resell and the buyer does not make payment within a reasonable time;
(*c*) where the seller expressly reserves the right of resale in case the buyer defaults.

B. Remedies of the Buyer

(1) The right to reject the goods.
e.g. for breach of condition.
(2) Action for damages.
e.g. for breach of condition or warranty.
(3) Action for damages for non-delivery.

S.51 provides that when the seller wrongfully neglects or refuses to deliver the goods, the buyer can maintain an action against him for damages for non-delivery. The measure of damages is the estimated loss directly and naturally resulting, in the ordinary course of events, from the seller's breach of contract. This is basically an enactment of the rule in Hadley v Baxendale.

WILLIAMS BROS. v ED. T. AGIUS LTD. (1914)

A agreed to sell coal to W at 16s. 3d. per ton. W then agreed to sell the coal to X at 19s. per ton. A did not deliver the coal. W was **held** entitled to recover damages assessed at the difference between the contract price of 16s 3d. and the market price on the day when A should have delivered which was 23s 6d. The sub-sale was therefore ignored by the court (as is generally the case).

(4) Action for specific performance.

In relation to the sale of goods, the court will only order specific performance of a contract for specific or ascertained goods and then only if the goods are unique or of some special value to the buyer. Further, specific performance will not be ordered if damages are an appropriate remedy.

Exercises (no answers given at back of book)

7.1. (*a*) Where are the terms of the contract to be found?
(*b*) Explain the 'patrol evidence' rule.
(*c*) What are the advantages of a standard form contract?
(*d*) Why is it necessary to distinguish between terms and representations?
(*e*) What is the difference between conditions and warranties? Why do we need to distinguish between the two?
(*f*) Which contracts need to be evidenced in writing and why?

7.2X. Rigsby agreed to rent his seaside villa to Dora for two weeks during the summer. The written contract specifically stated that the villa was 100 yards from the beach and had recently been redecorated.

Dora arrived for her holidays with her ten children only to discover that the villa was two miles away from the beach and had not been redecorated for five years. She immediately returned home and refused to pay Rigsby.

Advise Rigsby.

7.3. (*a*) Make a list of exclusion clauses which are frequently to be found in everyday life.
(*b*) Explain why, before 1977, exclusion clauses were not subject to a test of reasonableness.
(*c*) Read Thornton v Shoe Lane Parking 1971 and list the reasons why the exclusion clauses were not enforceable.
(*d*) Assess the extent to which the Unfair Contract Terms Act has affected the validity of exclusion clauses.
(*e*) Apply the new test of reasonableness to the exclusion clause in Photo Productions Ltd. v Securicor Ltd. 1980.

7.4X. John took a pair of trousers to a dry cleaners. He was given a numbered ticket which had to be produced in order for the cleaned garment to be returned. This he put into his pocket without examining it.

On the ticket was printed the following: "The Company and its servants accept no responsibility for any damage caused to customer's garments, whether by negligence or otherwise".

John returned to collect his trousers and found that they were badly torn. When he complained, the assistant referred him to the clause on the ticket.

Advise John.

7.5X. Stan travelled regularly between Manchester and Nottingham by coach, each time purchasing his ticket at the booking office. A notice inside each coach states: "The Company accepts not liability for injury to passengers or damage to their belongings."

On one journey the driver travels far too fast around a corner and Stan falls off his seat. He injures his head, and his expensive camera, which was on his lap, is smashed.

Advise Stan whether he can successfully obtain damages from the coach company.

7.6X. Gaffer, the owner of a business, signed an agreement with Abacus Ltd. for the installation of a computer. The contract contained a clause excluding the liability of Abacus Ltd. for unforeseeable acts of its employees.

Lonely, an employee of Abacus Ltd., deliberately tampered with the wiring of the computer during its installation. This casued a short-circuit when the power was switched on and the premises were completely destroyed by fire.

Advise Gaffer whether he can recover compensation from Abacus Ltd.

7.7. (*a*) Distinguish between contracts which must be *created* in writing, and contracts which must be *evidenced* in writing.

(*b*) State the functions of the parties involved in a contract of guarantee.

(*c*) Discuss the relationship between the application of S.40 of the Law of Property Act 1925 and 'gazumping'.

(*d*) Explain how the equitable doctrine of 'part performance' mitigates the harshness of the application of S.40.

7.8. (*a*) Define a contract for the sale of goods.

(*b*) In contracts for the sale of goods, what do you understand by "goods"?

(*c*) Distinguish between a contract for the sale of goods and a contract for the provision of services. What is the importance of the distinction?

7.9. Briefly outline the nature of the terms implied in contracts for the Sale of Goods.

(*a*) What is meant by the buyer's right to quiet possession?

(*b*) What is the meaning of 'caveat emptor'?

(*c*) Distinguish between a consumer sale and a non-consumer sale.

7.10X. Ross buys an electric heater from Sparky's Electric Shop. A sign on the counter says "Sparky accepts no liability for the poor quality of any goods sold in this shop." Ross uses the heater to heat his greenhouses at night to protect his tomatoes from the cold weather. After 3 days the heater burns out.
Advise Ross.

7.11. Explain the legal-position where goods perish before the parties agree to a contract of sale and where goods perish after the contract has been made.

7.12. (*a*) What is meant by "market overt"?
(*b*) What is a mercantile agent?

7.13. (*a*) Explain the duties of buyer and seller regarding performance of the contract of sale.
(*b*) What is meant by delivery.
(*c*) What is meant by a contract for the sale of goods stating that the delivery date is "of the essence".
(*d*) Briefly explain the rules relating to acceptance.

7.14X. Ben agrees to sell a consignment of fresh vegetables to David. Explain the legal position in the following situations:
(i) Ben delivers fresh vegetables mixed with tinned vegetables.
(ii) The consignment is agreed to be delivered in 10 instalments to be paid for separately. The 5th consignment is rotten and David refuses to accept any more instalments.

7.15. (*a*) Distinguish between the sellers' remedies against the buyer and his remedies against the goods.
(*b*) Explain the nature of the seller's lien.
(*c*) Explain the meaning of stoppage in transit.

7.16. Briefly describe in your own words
(*a*) a conditional sale agreement
(*b*) a contract of hire
(*c*) a credit sale agreement.

7.17. (*a*) Explain the meaning of "collateral contracts".
(*b*) Explain the nature of third part proceedings.
(*c*) In your own words, explain the principle in Donoghue v Stevenson.

8

Legal Points Regarding Purchasing Documentation

Learning Objectives

At the end of this chapter you should be able to:

8A **List the important legal points of purchasing documents.**

The documentation necessary was illustrated in chapters 2 & 3. The reasons for each documents are worth repeating:

Documentation

The following can be regarded as the major stages in a transaction between buyer and seller. This is not common to all businesses as some prefer to adopt their own system.

(*a*) *Enquiry*
This is a request by a retailer to a manufacturer or supplier for a copy of their price list or catalogue.

(*b*) *Price List of Catalogue*
This will be sent by the supplier. It contains a full description of the goods, prices, conditions of sale, terms, discounts, mode of carriage, minimum orders, special offers, returns procedure and any other information relevent to the buyer's needs.

A catalogue will also provide photographs of the goods to be supplied. As they are expensive to produce, a manufacturer normally has only two editions printed each year. In addition to photographs the catalogue will contain information as to sizes and ranges of goods available. It will be sent out together with a price list which is cheaper to prepare and can be up-dated at very little extra cost.

(*c*) *Order*
After deciding how and what to order the appropriate form is completed. Included on the order form should be details such as price, description, catalogue or price list number, quantity, where to send goods to, and any other special delivery instructions. It often occurs that the address for delivery differs from the address on the order. Attention must be drawn to this.

The actual writing of an order is unnecessary in quite a few cases as suppliers send representatives. They make regular visits, take the order, and try to ensure that special instructions are carried out. In some buying organisations Head Office permission is required prior to purchase. A Purchase Requisition Note then has to be made out prior to ordering. This informs the buying office or Head Office that goods are required. In many cases goods cannot be bought, by a manager, without the approval of senior management.

One obvious reason for this is the negotiation of special discounts for large bulk orders which are made by Head Office for delivery to branches. These are often known as allocations.

(*d*) *Acknowledgement*

This is sent by the supplier to the buyer acknowledging receipt of order.

(*e*) *Advice Note*

This informs the buyer that the goods have been despatched and gives details of the method of transport.

(*f*) *Delivery Note*

This accompanies the goods and enables the buyer to check them off. It is often a carbon copy of the invoice. Some organisations at this stage require an internal document, known as a Goods Received Note, to be completed. It contains the name and address of the supplier, date, number of cases or articles received, shortages, any damage and the condition of the goods.

(*g*) *Invoice*

The invoice is sent after delivery. This is the document which stipulates the price of goods bought and the total amount spent. It contains details of purchases, quantities, unit price, total price, discounts, terms for prompt payment and VAT. Invoices should be checked thoroughly to ensure correct prices have been charged, and accurate calculations have been made.

(*h*) *Credit Note*

A credit note, which is usually printed in red, will be send to the buyer for any of the following reasons: –

(i) goods have been overcharged e.g. incorrect price on invoice or incorrect additions and calculations creating an overcharge.

(ii) goods have been returned e.g. damaged, inferior goods sent as substitutes; items included in delivery but not ordered; returns for bottles, empties, cases, or gift vouchers.

(iii) cancellation of the invoice.

The value of a credit note reduces the amount owing by the buyer in the accounts of the seller.

(*j*) *Debit Note*

This is the opposite of the credit note and is sent to the buyer for any of the following reasons: –

(i) more goods were sent than had been invoiced and they have been retained by the buyer.

(ii) goods have been undercharged, e.g. wrong price quoted on invoice or incorrect addition creating an undercharge.

(iii) goods supplied were of higher quality (and therefore of higher price) than those stipulated on the invoice and have been retained by the buyer.

(iv) any omissions from the invoice e.g. items delivered but not included.

The value of a debit note increases the amount owing by the buyer in the accounts of the seller.

(*k*) *Statement*

This is sent out at the end of a trading period, usually at monthly intervals. It gives details of: –

(i) amounts purchased in that period;

(ii) any adjustments e.g. credit or debit notes;

(iii) any discounts received;

(iv) balance from previous statement (if any);

(v) payments received from the buyer during the month (if any)

The final most important figure is the amount which the buyer owes the seller who is now asking to be paid. In practice most buyers wait for the statement before paying and do not pay each individual invoice as it arrives.

(*l*) *Settlement*

The amount on the statement is paid either by cheque, Giro, postal order, money order or cash.

(*m*) *Receipt*

This is issued by the seller acknowleding payment of the amount owing. It shows the details of amount paid, how paid, date, and it is signed by an official of the company e.g. cashier. If payment is made by cheque, then no receipt is necessary. In many cases firms still continue to issue receipts as an additional check against fraud.

The documentation may be used as written evidence in any legal dispute. If an order is made verbally it should be confirmed in writing.

The design of the order form is particularly important and should include the following when applicable: –

1. The period of the contract.
2. Reference to the purchase specification if it exists.
3. Removal of rejected food or other items by the supplier.

4. Chargeable containers to be credited on return.
5. Indemnity against damage.
6. The place of delivery.
7. Invoices to be supplied within a specified time of delivery.
8. Terms of payment.
9. Notice to terminate the contract or order before completion by either part.

Exercises (no answers given at back of this book)

8.1. 1. List the major documents used in a business transaction of buying and selling.
2. Give reasons why a credit note is issued.
3. Give reasons why a debit note is issued.

8.2. Using the following details, complete an invoice: –
1 white shade @ £2.00, 1 wall clock @ £9.00, 2 wall brackets @ £1.50 each, 5 one way switches @ £2.75 each, add VAT at the rate of 15%. Use imaginary names and addresses for the supplier and the customer.

9

The Law of Agency

Learning Objectives

At the end of this chapter you should be able to:

9A Describe the law of agency as it affects purchasing.

A caterer buying either goods or services may deal with an agent who represents the seller (the principal). It is important for the buyer to understand the law of agency as it affects purchasing.

The principal authorises the agent to act for him in contract negotiations. In contracts where the principal supplies a caterer he must be an adult but the agent can be an infant. An agent can be appointed:

1. Informally – this can be done orally or by the conduct of the parties or by implication.
2. Formally – this means in writing.

If the agent had no authority the principal may still confirm the contract at a later date. This is called ratification.

The Agent's Duties

He must only act according to his authority, exercise proper skill and care, and render account if required. He must not become a competitive principal against the interests of his employer or make secret profits. He can only delegate with the consent of the principal.

The Principal's Duties

He must reward the agent properly and indemnify him for all lawful acts connected with his authority.

Types of Agent

1. Brokers – they sell but do not possess the goods of the principal.
2. Factors – they sell the principal's goods in their possession. They can also receive payment and they have a lien on the goods against payment by the principal of proper commission.

Contracts for catering supplies made with an agent

The above legal points should make it clear that the buyer of a catering organisation should take care when dealing with an agent. If there is any doubt, the principal should be contacted for clarification. It is important to know when an agency agreement terminates.

Termination of Agency

The agreement can be ended in any of the following ways.

1. The principal can revoke it at any time unless:
   (*a*) the agent has carried out his part of the contract.
   (*b*) the agency is expressed as ''irrevocable''.

If the agent continuous to act after revocation then he will be liable for the contract, if it is formed.

2. The purpose of the agency has come to an end.
3. The time of the agency, if specified, has ended.
4. The lunacy or death of the principal or the agent.
5. The bankruptcy of the principal.
6. The agent renounces the agreement.
7. By mutual agreement.

Exercises (no answers given at back of the book)

9.1. Give a definition of an agent.

9.2. State the ways in which an agent/principal relationship may be created.

9.3. Give the main rules relating to ratification by a principal of an act of his agent.

9.4. 'An agent must not become a principal as against his employer'. What does this mean?

9.5. Examine the case whether or not an agent is permitted to act in a manner to benefit himself personally when performing his principal's duties.

9.6. What is meant by the fact that an agent's acts will bind his principal provided that they are within the limits of an agent's usual authority.

9.7. What obligations does a principal have in a principal/agent relationship?

9.8. List the ways by which an agency relationship can be terminated.

10

The Legal Aspect of Storage

Learning Objectives

At the end of this chapter you should be able to:

10A **Know the statutory requirements relevant to storage of food, liquor, cleaning materials and equipment.**

The importance of hygiene and safety in the stores was discussed in chapter 3.

At level 2 it is necessary to know the statutory requirements in more detail. The following legislation will now be considered:

Food Hygiene Regulations 1970

They are designed to protect public health by securing the maintenance of sanitary and hygienic conditions on premises where food is handled. They are enforced by the local authorities.

1. Interpretation

(*a*) *Food* means food or drink intended for sale for human consumption, except milk, water, live animals or birds and drugs.

(*b*) *Food Premises* means premises on which a "food business" is carried on.

(*c*) *Food Business* means any trade or business for the purpose of which any person engages in the handling of food, *except* agricultural activity, docks, slaughterhouses, market stalls and delivery vehicles to which other regulations apply and ships where food is handled for consumption by the crew or permanent residents.

2. General Requirements

(*a*) **Sanitary Premises (Regulation 6)**

No food business shall be carried on at any insanitary premises or any premises where that food is exposed to the risk of contamination.

(*b*) **Clean Equipment (Regulation 7)**

Equipment with which food comes into contact must be kept clean and in good repair, and, except in the case of non-returnable containers, must be so constructed as to be easily cleaned, non-absorbent, and to limit the risk of contamination. Reasonable steps must be taken to keep all food containers free from contamination.

(*c*) **Domestic Premises (Regulation 8)**

A person carrying on a food business shall not give out any food or permit any food to be given out for preparation or packing by another person at any domestic premises other than those of the person carrying on the business.

3. Requirements as to the Handling of Food

(*a*) **Protection of Food (Regulation 9)**

A person handling food must take all reasonably necessary steps to protect the food from the risk of contamination. In particular he must not place it so as to risk contamination, keep unfit food near it, place it lower than 18″ from the ground in an open space unless adequately protected, or keep unscreened animal feed in a food room. He must take reasonable steps to keep open food covered.

(*b*) **Personal Cleanliness (Regulations 10/11)**

A person handling food must keep as clean as reasonably possible all parts of his body and clothing likely to come into contact with the food, keep covered with a waterproof dressing cuts or abrasions on the exposed part of his body, and refrain from spitting or the use of tobacco.

With exceptions, a person handling open food, other than raw vegetables, intoxicating liquor or soft drinks, must wear sufficient clean and washable clothing.

(*c*) **Carriage and Wrapping of Food (Regulation 12)**

Food must not be carried in a container together with any article from which there is a risk of contamination or with any live animal or poultry unless reasonable precautions are taken to prevent contact.

All wrappings or containers must be clean and free from the risk of contamination and no printed material other than that designed exclusively for that purpose shall be allowed to come into contact with food other than uncooked vegetables.

(*d*) **Infections (Regulation 13)**

A person handling food who becomes aware that he is suffering from, or is the carrier of, certain infections such as typhoid, dysentry or other infection likely to cause food poisoning must see that the Medical Officer of Health is immediately informed.

4. Requirements Relating to Food Premises (Regulations 14 – 17)

(*a*) **Soil Drainage Systems**

No fresh air intake into such system may be situated in a food room, and every inlet into such system must be trapped.

(*b*) **Water Cisterns**

No water cistern supplying a food room shall supply a sanitary convenience unless an anti-contamination system exists.

(*c*) **Sanitary Conveniences**

Sanitary conveniences in food premises must be kept clean, in working order, properly lighted and ventilated and so placed that offensive odours cannot penetrate a food room, and a prominent notice must be displayed in a suitable position requesting users to wash their hands after use.

No room containing a sanitary convenience may be used as a food room, nor connect directly with a room used for handling open food.

(*d*) **Water Supply**

A sufficient supply of clean and wholesome water must be provided in all food premises.

(*e*) **Wash-hand basins**

Suitable, sufficient and clean wash-hand basins in good repair must be supplied together with an adequate supply of hot and cold water, soap, nail brushes and clean towels.

(*f*) **First Aid**

Sufficient and accessible first aid materials must be kept available.

(*g*) **Accommodation for clothing**

Where open food is handled suitable accommodation for clothes and shoes not worn during working hours must be supplied.

(*h*) **Food washing facilities**

Suitable, sufficient and clean sinks or other washing facilities in good repair supplied with hot and cold water, soap and clean cloths must be available for washing food and equipment where open food is handled.

(*i*) **Lighting**

Every food room must be sufficiently lighted.

(*j*) **Ventilation**

Suitable and sufficient ventilation must be maintained in every food room where the humidity or temperature is not controlled.

(*k*) **Sleeping Place**

No food room shall be used as a sleeping place, nor shall a food room used for handling open food communicate directly with a sleeping place.

(*l*) **Cleanliness and Repair**

All parts of the structure of a food room shall be kept clean and in good repair.

(*m*) **Refuse**

No refuse or filth shall be allowed to accumulate in a food room.

(*n*) **Temperature of Food**

Meat, fish, imitation gravy and food containing eggs, or milk (with a number of exceptions including bread, cakes, chocolate etc.) must be brought without delay to, and kept at, a temperature above 145 degrees Fahrenheit or below 50 degrees Fahrenheit, unless: –

(i) exposed for immediate sale, or

(ii) brought to the premises within four hours before the opening of the business and exposed for sale upon the opening of the business, or

(iii) kept available for replenishment of food exposed for sale (being a reasonably necessary quantity).

5. *Administration and Enforcement*

(*a*) **Offences**

(i) A person engaged in handling food shall be guilty of an offence if he fails to comply with the regulations where appropriate.

(ii) A person carrying on a food business shall be guilty of an offence if any of the regulations (other than 10 and 13) as respects that food business are contravened or he fails to take reasonable steps to secure compliance with regulations 10 and 13 by a person under his employ or control.

(iii) A person having control of management of persons engaged in the handling of food, but not himself carrying on a food business, shall be guilty of an offence if he fails to take all reasonable steps to secure compliance by such persons with the regulations.

(*b*) **Penalties**

These are the same as under the Food and Drugs Act, 1955.

The Health and Safety at Work Act 1974

The Act gives a framework which provides a new system of regulations and codes of practice. The old Acts like the Factories Act 1961 will apply until their provisions are replaced. The policy making body is the Health and Safety Commission. The inspectors of the Health and Safety Executive enforce the Act but some powers are retained by local authorities.

Section 1

This sets out the main objectives:

(*a*) to secure the health, safety and welfare of persons at work.

(*b*) to protect persons other than persons at work against health and safety risks caused by work activities.

(*c*) to control the storing and use of dangerous substances.

(*d*) to control the emission of noxious and offensive substances.

An organization in the hotel and catering industry has to comply with general duties specified in section 2 of the Act, if it is classed as an employer. Similar duties are placed on employees under section 7, the self employed under section 3 and occupiers of work places under section 4.

Section 2

The following duties are owned by the employer:

(*a*) to provide and maintain equipment and systems which are safe and are without risk to health.

(*b*) to ensure the safe handling, storage use and transport of articles and substances.

(*c*) to provide the required information, training, instruction and supervision.

(*d*) to maintain the work place and access so that it is safe and without risk to health.

(*e*) to provide a safe working environment.

The employer must prepare and revise when necessary a written statement of the general policy for health and safety and give notice of it to the employees. Failure to abide by the safety policy rules can result in a fine.

Since 1978 recognized trade unions have been allowed to appoint safety representatives from the employees. The safety representatives are to be consulted on safety matters, allowed to inspect premises and plant and investigate complaints from employees regarding health safety and welfare. The representatives need time and training to carry out their function and the regulations allow time off with pay.

Section 6

This places duties on manufacturers and suppliers to hotel and caterers:

(*a*) to ensure supplies are safer and without risk to health.

(*b*) to provide information for the safe use of supplies.

Section 7

This places duties on the employee:

(*a*) to take reasonable care of his own and others health and safety while at work.

(*b*) to co-operate with the employer to enable him to fulfil his duties.

An offending employee can be fined.

Section 20

This sets out the powers of inspectors. They can:

(*a*) enter premises.

(*b*) make investigations and examinations as appropriate.

(*c*) issue either an Improvement or a Prohibition Notice.

(*d*) prosecute as a last resort. This may mean a fine or even up to two years imprisonment.

The Factories Act 1961

This is the best example of the old law now being enforced by the new authority. Section 175 gives a general definition of a factory. These must be premises in which manual workers are employed for making, altering or adapting articles for sale. A factory is also likely to have an office which will be covered by the Offices Shops and Railway Premises Act 1963. Catering premises are likely to be subject to both the Factories Act (the store area) and the Offices Shops and Railway Premises Act (the stores office). The occupier which usually means the employer will be responsible for health, safety and welfare.

Exercises (no answers given at back of the book)

10.1. (*a*) Define in your own words the term 'hygiene'.

(*b*) Give three symptoms of possible food poisoning.

(*c*) What are likely to be the effects of poor hygiene on customers, on sales, and on the image of the business?

(*d*) What powers does the environmental health inspector have?

(*e*) Name the legislation which relates to hygiene.

10.2. (*a*) Give three examples of how you personally can minimise the risk of passing on any infection.

(*b*) For what reasons may premises and/or equipment be regarded as unhygienic?

(*c*) What is meant by the term "sell by" date and why is it used?

(*d*) What special facilities may be necessary for the handling and storage of food?

(*e*) What benefits can a business achieve from careful attention to hygiene?

10.3. (*a*) Define negligent behaviour and give one example of such behaviour.

(*b*) State four provisions of the Offices, Shops and Railway Premises Act 1963 which relate to safety.

(*c*) State in your own words what "reasonably practicable" means.

(*d*) What duties have been imposed on employers by the Health and Safety at Work Act 1974?

(*e*) What penalties may be imposed on those who break this law?

11

Stocktaking and Stores Accounting

Learning Objectives

At the end of this chapter you should be able to:

11A **Understand and carry out stocktaking and stores accounting procedures.**

Yield Testing

This was mentioned briefly in chapter 5 (Page 46). Yield testing can be illustrated by looking at an experiment to see if the use of aluminium foil reduces the loss in weight after cooking both chicken and topside of beef. The results are shown in exhibit 11.1.

Exhibit 11.1

	Kg before cooking	*Kg after cooking*	*% loss*	*% loss/saving using foil*
Chicken				
Conventional	1.4	1.021	27%	
Using Foil	1.4	1.191	15%	12% saving
Topside of beef				
Conventional	2.75	2.183	21%	
Using Foil	2.75	1.93	30%	9% loss

The yield is the usable part of a food item which is available to be served after preparation.

A standard yield occurs when a standard method of preparation and portioning is applied to a food item purchased to a known standard.

Yield testing is essential for those catering organisations who wish to operate a system of standard recipes, portion control and standard costing.

Methods of Pricing Stores Issues

The pricing of stores issued was shown in chapter 3.

However, as you will no doubt be aware from your own experience, the cost of items do not remain fixed over a period of time. Therefore in a period of one year a stores item may well have several prices, especially food and beverage prices. The cost office must decide which price to use, and they will usually adopt one of three acceptable methods of pricing stores issues.

In the examples which follow, the same basic information is used to illustrate the three methods.

Received	
19-1	*Number and cost per item*
January	10 at £15 each = £150
March	10 at £17 each = £170
August	20 at £20 each = £400
Issued	*Number issued*
19-1	
April	8
December	24

1. First In, First Out Method (abbreviated as F.I.F.O.)

With this method the first goods received are deemed to be issued first, goods from earlier receipts are treated as being issued before any of the goods from later receipts.

In this case the cost of the goods issued is stated to be £120 + £440 = £560.

	Received	Issue Price	Stock after each transaction
January	10 at £15 each		10 at £15 each = £150
March	10 at £17 each		10 at £15 each = £150 10 at £17 each = £170 = £320
April		8 at £15 each = £120	2 at £15 each = £30 10 at £17 each = £170 = £200
August	20 at £20 each		2 at £15 each = £30 10 at £17 each = £170 20 at £20 each = £400 = £600
December		2 at £15 each = £30 10 at £17 each = £170 12 at £20 each = £240 = £440.	8 at £20 each = £160

2. Last In, First Out Method (abbreviated as L.I.F.O.)

This method treats each issue of goods as being made from the last lot of goods received previous to the date of issue. If that lot of goods is not enough then the balance of the issue is treated as being made from the next previous lot still unissued, and so on.

	Received	Issue Price	Stock after each transaction
January	10 at £15 each		10 at £15 each = £150
March	10 at £17 each		10 at £15 each = £150 10 at £17 each = £170 = £320
April		8 at £17 each = £136	10 at £15 each = £150 2 at £17 each = £34 = £184
August	20 at £20 each		10 at £15 each = £150 2 at £17 each = £34 20 at £20 each = £400 = £584
December		20 at £20 each = £400 2 at £17 each = £34 2 at £15 each = £30 = £464	8 at £15 each = £120

In this case the cost of the goods issued is stated to be £136 + £464 = £600.

3. Average Cost Method

Each time there is a receipt of goods the average cost of the goods held in stock is recalculated. Any issues then made are at that price until another receipt of goods when the price is recalculated for further issues, and so on.

	Received	Issued	Average Cost per unit of stock held £	Number of units in stock	Total value of stock £
January	10 at £15 each		15	10	150
March	10 at £17 each		16	20	320
April		8 at £16 each = £128	16	12	192
August	20 at £20 each		18.5	32	592
December		24 at £18.5 each = £444	18.5	8	148

In this case the cost of the goods issued is stated to be £128 + £444 = £572.

Periodic Inventory Valuation Methods

So far we have looked at materials or goods being issed and the records being kept on a perpetual basis, meaning by this that each issue or sale was compared with the receipts strictly on a chronological basis and the price of issue calculated accordingly. The record was, therefore, being maintained perpetually throughout the year. For accounting purposes, however, especially in financial accounting, the calculation of the cost of the goods issued or sold may not be determined until the end of the accounting year. When this is done the exact date of issue or sale during the year is ignored – it is just looked at from the point of view of the total issued or sold. Using the average cost method the issue price is the average cost for the whole year rather than the different averages at different points in time. The LIFO method assumes that the last goods to come in during the year are the first to be issued, instead of the last to be received before the issue was made. The FIFO method will, however, give the same answer no matter whether the perpetual or the periodic method is used.

As an illustration of the way that the two methods can give different answers is shown in Exhibit 11.2

Exhibit 11.2

The following details are relevant to the receipt and issue of goods. There was no opening stock of goods.

Exhibit 11.2

		Receipts	*Issues*	
19-1	January	9 at £20 each	May	5 items
	July	6 at £30 each	November	4 items

Perpetual Inventory – Average Cost

	Received	Issued	Average Cost per unit of stock held	Number of units in stock	Total value of stock
					£
January	9 at £20		20	9	180
May		£5 at £20	20	4	80
July	6 at £30		26	10	260
November		4 at £26	26	6	156

Periodic Inventory – Average Cost

Received	9 at £20	=	180
	6 at £30	=	180
	15		£360

Fifteen items cost a total of £360, therefore the average cost at which issues will be priced is $\frac{£360}{15}$ = £24 each. As 9 items have been issued the total price that they will be charged out as cost of goods sold or materials used is 9×£24 = £216. Compare this with the issue price of 5×£20 plus 4×£26 = £204 using the perpetual inventory method. The closing stocks are 6×£24 = £144 under the periodic inventory method and £156 under the perpetual inventory method.

Similarly the LIFO method of pricing issues will give different answers, in fact 5×£20 plus 4×£30 = £220 with the perpetual method and 6×£30 plus 3×£20 = £240 with the period method. The FIFO method will give the same answer under both methods, that of 9×£20 = £180 for the cost of the issues.

Firms operating standard costing will use standard recipes and standard prices.

Exercises

11.1(*a*) Briefly explain LIFO, FIFO and Average Cost methods of pricing non-perishable stores issues.

(*b*) The following receipts and issues are made of a particular wine: –

	Receipts		*Issue*
	Quantity	*Price/Bottle*	*Quantity*
January	50	£1.25	42
February	30	£1.35	24
March	30	£1.40	22

Prepare a statement showing the pricing of the issues and stock in hand using the FIFO method of pricing stores issues.

11.2. Describe two methods of pricing the issues of wine stocks. Illustrate your answer with the following data:

Wine 47 Half-Bottles

1 9 - 4		*Purchases at Cost*			*Issues (Sales)*
Jan	1	36@70p each	Jan	20	29
Feb	5	48@80p each	Feb	19	50
Mar	17	42@90p each	Mar	30	40

Compute closing stock at each month end.

11.3X. An industrial firm buys frozen meat pies for use in its vending machines in packs of 100 and retails them (each pie) at 20p. The following are the purchases and sales for the quarter ended March 19-7.

	Purchases	*Sales*	*Losses*
January	10 packs at £10 per pack	900	50
February	15 packs at £12 per pack	1300	100
March	10 packs at £14 per pack	800	50

(*a*) Compute the closing stocks of pies at each month end using
  (i) FIFO method.
  (ii) LIFO method.

(*b*) Prepare a quarterly trading account using the stocks computed in (*a*). Which method of pricing stores issues returns the highest profit?

11.4(*a*) From the following figures calculate the closing stock-in-trade that would be shown using (i) F.I.F.O., (ii) L.I.F.O., (iii) A.V.C.O. methods on a perpetual inventory basis.

	Bought		*Sold*
January	24 at £10 each	June	30 at £16 each
April	16 at £12.50 each	November	34 at £18 each
October	30 at £13 each		

(*b*) Draw up Trading Accounts using each of the three methods.

11.5X. P. Paul has been in business for three years, deals in only one product, and has used the F.I.F.O. method of valuing stock-in-trade on a perpetual inventory basis. The figures of receipts and sales are as follows:

		Receipts		*Sales*
Year 1	January	28 at £10 each	March	11 at £16 each
	April	12 at £10 each	August	15 at £16 each
	November	14 at £11 each	December	10 for £16.5 each
Year 2	February	9 at £12 each	April	17 for £17 each
	June	10 at £13 each	July	8 for £17 each
	August	8 at £12 each	December	30 for £19 each
	November	20 at £13 each		
Year 3	January	15 at £15 each	February	15 for £19 each
	April	10 at £16 each	November	32 for £22 each
	June	10 at £17 each		
	October	20 at £19 each		

You are required to calculate the valuation of the closing stock-in-trade for each of the three years. Also construct Trading Accounts for the three years.

11.6X. What would the stock-in-trade valuations have been at the end of each of the three years in 11.5X if the L.I.F.O. method had been used. Also draw up the Trading Accounts.

12

Costing Concepts

Learning Objectives

At the end of this chapter you should be able to:

12A **Understand the various types of cost and how they relate to catering operations.**

12B **Prepare an Operating Statement.**

A catering organisation operating a costing system is likely to operate a system of absorption costing but the concept of marginal costing may be useful in some organisations e.g. seasonal establishments.

Absorption Costing

Costs are divided into:

1. *Direct Costs* i.e. costs which can be identified with or allocated to a catering activity (e.g. kitchen production) or an operated department or a cost centre.
2. *Indirect Costs* i.e. costs which are difficult to allocate to an activity or department or cost centre.

Apart from where a standard system is in use, there will be quite wide differences about which costs are classified as direct costs and those which are indirect costs. Some organisations attempt to identify as direct costs not only direct materials, but also labour and overhead expenses. On the other hand some restrict direct costs to materials and labour only, whilst others restrict it even further to direct materials only.

The indirect costs may be charged to an activity by a predetermined indirect overhead rate e.g. a percentage based on sales or direct costs. Costs are often used to determine selling prices which should be sufficient to absorb all costs and leave a satisfactory net profit. This of course would not apply to subsidised catering prices, which are common in industrial canteens and staff restaurants, as here it would be the value of the service to the firm which would be most important, rather than basing everything on net profit.

Suppose that in the last period the sales and costs for catering had been:

	% of Sales		as % of Food Direct Costs		£	
Sales		100		250		100,000
Less Direct Food Costs	40		100		40,000	
,, Indirect Costs	50	90	125	225	50,000	90,000
Net Profit		10		25		10,000

In the column for % of Sales it can be seen that a Margin[1] of 60% covered Indirect Costs 50%, leaving 10% for Net Profit. If this was the aim of the following period and there were to be no changes in the organisation, then the same margin could be used. Similarly the mark-up used was 150% to cover 125% Indirect Costs leaving net profit of 25% (equalling 10% of Sales).

Food and beverage operations in the profit making organisation may work as follows using an à la carte operation:

1. Identify the cost of a menu item by using dish costing and portion control – say £1 for a fish course.
2. Use a 60% Margin to obtain the exclusive sales price of £2.50. This price is expected to absorb all other costs and give a 10% net profit margin per unit.
3. The unit cost statement would be: –

	£	*% margin*
Direct Food Cost	1.00	40
Indirect Costs	1.25	50
Net Profit	0.25	10
	2.50	100

If the statement is expressed in mark-up terms it would be:

	£	*% mark-up*
Direct Food Costs	1.00	100
Indirect Costs	1.25	125
Net Profit	0.25	25
	2.50	250

This last statement illustrates the use of a predetermined rate. If 150% mark-up was required to cover indirect costs and net profit, then this same percentage rate would be added on to all direct food costs for the whole of the period.

Footnote:

1. The terms Margin and Mark-up were explained in Chapter 4.

Marginal Costing

The concept divides costs into:

1. *Fixed costs* i.e. costs which do not vary with activity or sales or output.
2. *Variable costs* i.e. costs which do vary with a change in activity. The problem is that variable costs may or may not vary exactly in proportion to a change in sales activity.

Some costs are part fixed and part variable, for example telephone expenses are part rental (fixed) and a charge per call (variable). This variable part is unlikely to be in direct proportion to an increase or decrease in sales, even though it is obviously connected.

The above difficulties result in many accountants abandoning the idea of a marginal costing system. However the concept is gaining ground and is used in the industry for both break-even analysis and seasonal decisions regarding opening or closing during the 'off' season. This can be simply illustrated in Exhibit 12.1.

Exhibit 12.1

J. Jones, who owned a holiday resort guest house opened in the off season last year. He analysed his profit and loss account for the year between the on-season and the off-season as follows:

Profit and Loss Account

	Whole year		*On-season*		*Off-season*	
	£	£	£	£	£	£
Sales		100,000		90,000		10,000
Less: Food Costs	20,000		18,000		2,000	
Other Costs	65,000	85,000	56,000	74,000	9,000	11,000
Net Profit (Loss)		15,000		16,000		(1,000)

The owner may decide to shut down during the off-season, as he appears to be losing £1,000, which would be saved by shutting down. However, although the food costs are variable, some of the other costs will be variable whilst others will be fixed and will have to be paid whether the guest house is open or shut. Such items as rent, rates, fire insurance are payable whether the guest house is open or not.

If the guest house had been shut down during the off-season the Profit and Loss Account for the whole year might be:

Profit and Loss Account (whole year)

	£	£
Sales		90,000
Less: Food Costs	18,000	
Other Costs	62,000	80,000
Net Profit		10,000

This shows that net profit for the year would be reduced by £5,000 if the guest house had been shut down. The reason for this is that of the £9,000 other costs during the off-season, £6,000 would have had to be paid whether the guest house was open or not.

Such a wrong decision to shut down could be avoided if the Profit and Loss Accounts had been drafted using marginal costing principles. This uses the basic concept of marginal costing, as compared with absorption costing which can be illustrated:

	Absorption Costing		*Marginal Costing*
	SALES		SALES
less	FOOD COSTS	*less*	VARIABLE COSTS
and	OTHER COSTS	=	CONTRIBUTION
=	NET PROFIT	*less*	FIXED COSTS
		=	NET PROFIT

Using marginal costing, any project which has a positive contribution (i.e. Sales are greater than Variable Costs), will be of benefit to the organisation. Such a contribution will help to pay fixed costs, and will therefore help to increase net profit (or reduce net loss).

If, therefore, the original Profits and Loss Account had been drafted in marginal costing terms it would have been as follows:

Profit and Loss Account

	Whole year		*On-season*		*Off-season*	
	£	£	£	£	£	£
Sales		100,000		90,000		10,000
Less Variable Costs						
Food Costs	20,000		18,000		2,000	
Other Costs	32,000	52,000	29,000	47,000	3,000	5,000
Contribution		48,000		43,000		5,000
Less Fixed Costs		33,000				
Net Profit		15,000				

As the off-season showed a contribution of £5,000 then it was obviously worthwhile keeping the guest house open.

Marginal Costing + Break-even Analysis

Marginal costing is the basis of break even calculations.

Definition of Break-even

It may be defined as the level of catering activity or sales where the organisation makes no profit or loss.

Two calculations are useful.

1. Break-even point = $\dfrac{\text{Fixed Costs per period}}{\text{Contribution per unit of output or sales.}}$
2. Sales − Fixed Costs − Variable Cost = 0

Break-even can be expressed in terms of sales £ or volume e.g. number of covers, sleeper nights etc.

The following example shows the above calculations:

A restaurant has average spending power of £5 per cover and variable costs of £2 per cover. In a given period the fixed costs are £3,000, calculate the break-even point in sales and number of covers.

Calculation 1

$$\frac{\text{Fixed Costs}}{\text{Contribution per unit}} = \frac{£3000}{£5 - £2} = \frac{£3000}{£3}$$

= 1000 Covers or £5000 Sales

This can be checked:

	£
Sales	5000
Variable costs 1000 × 2	2000
Contribution	3000
Fixed Costs	3000
Profit	Nil

Calculation 2

	Sales − F.C.	−	VC	=	0
	Sales − 3000	−	40% of sales	=	0
therefore	60% of Sales	=	£3000		
″	Sales	=	$\frac{3000}{0.6 \text{ or } 60\%}$	=	£5,000

Break-even charts or graphs

There are several methods of drawing break-even charts.

Exhibit 12.2 and 12.3 show two methods using the above date and assuming a capacity of 2000 covers. It should be observed that both methods produce the same sales and total cost lines and of course, the same break-even point.

Exhibit 12.2

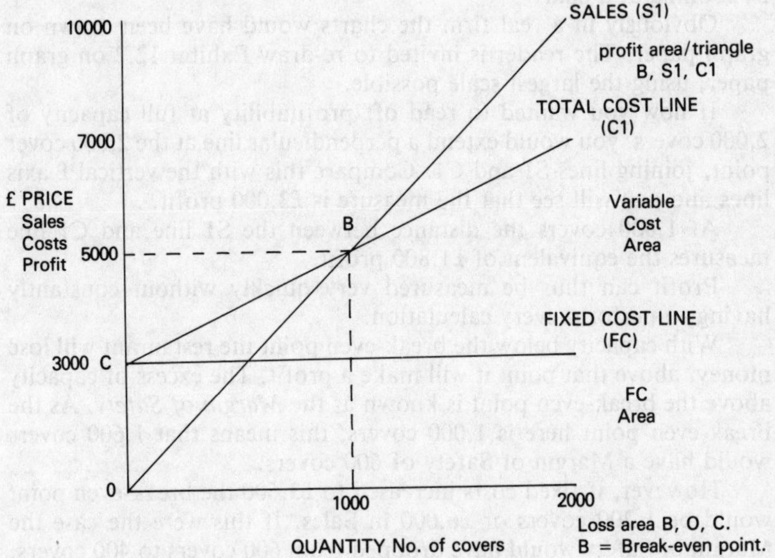

Exhibit 12.3

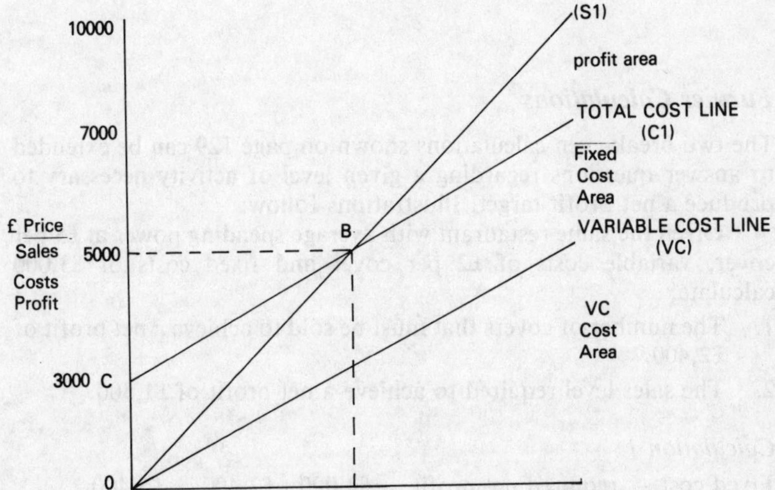

Charts can be more useful to management than calculations, as it is normally easier to see the profit/loss at different numbers of covers by looking at a chart.

Obviously in a real firm the charts would have been drawn on graph paper. The reader is invited to re-draw Exhibit 12.2 on graph paper, using the largest scale possible.

If now you wanted to read off profitability at full capacity of 2,000 covers, you would extend a perpendicular line at the 2,000 cover point, joining lines S1 and C1. Compare this with the vertical £ axis lines and you will see that the measure is £3,000 profit.

At 1,600 covers the distance between the S1 line and C1 line measures the equivalent of £1,800 profit.

Profit can thus be measured very quickly without constantly having to perform every calculation.

With capacity below the break-even point the restaurant will lose money, above that point it will make a profit. The excess of capacity above the break-even point is known as the *Margin of Safety*. As the break-even point here is 1,000 covers, this means that 1,600 covers would have a Margin of Safety of 600 covers.

However, if fixed costs increased to £3,600 the break-even point would be 1,200 covers or £6,000 in Sales. If this were the case the Margin of Safety would have dropped from 600 covers to 400 covers.

Further Calculations

The two break-even calculations shown on page 129 can be extended to answer questions regarding a given level of activity necessary to produce a net profit target. Illustrations follow:

Given the same restaurant with average spending power at £5 per cover, variable costs of £2 per cover and fixed costs of £3,000 calculate:

1. The number of covers that must be sold to achieve a net profit of £2,400.
2. The sales level required to achieve a net profit of £1,500.

Calculation 1

$$\frac{\text{Fixed cost + required net profit}}{\text{Contribution per unit}} = \frac{£3{,}000 + £2{,}400}{£5 - £2} = \frac{£5{,}400}{£3}$$

$$= 1{,}800 \text{ covers}$$

This can be checked as follows:

	£
Sales would be 1,800 × £5	9,000
less Variable costs 1,800 × £2	3,600
Therefore contribution would be	5,400
less Fixed costs	3,000
Therefore net profit would be	2,400

Calculation 2

$$\frac{\text{Fixed cost + required net profit}}{\text{Contribution per unit}} = \frac{£3{,}000 + £1{,}500}{£5 - £2} = \frac{£4{,}500}{£3}$$

$$= 1{,}500 \text{ covers}$$

$$= 1{,}500 \times 5 = £7{,}500 \text{ Sales}$$

This can also be checked as follows:

	£
Sales would be	7,500
less Variable costs at 40%	3,000
Therefore Contribution would be	4,500
less Fixed Costs	3,000
Therefore net profit would be	1,500

Looking at the charts you drew on graph paper for Exhibit 12.1 you should be able to tackle the problems just shown as Calculation 1 and 2 by visual inspection.

Exercises

12.1. A cafe produces a three course meal menu at an average food cost per meal of £1.20. From past records the food cost averages 50% of selling price and labour and overheads 40% of selling price which allows 10% for net profit.

(*a*) Calculate the selling price (ex. VAT).
(*b*) Calculate the labour and overhead costs.
(*c*) Calculate the net profit.
(*d*) Express labour and overheads as a percentage of food cost.
(*e*) Draw up a Unit Cost Statement in £.

12.2. If the cafe in 12.1 sold 1,000 meals in a given period and the labour and overheads during the period were actually £1,000. Draw up P & L Statement for the period.

12.3. If the £1,000 labour and overheads in 12.2 was ½ variable in direct proportion to sales calculate:

(*a*) The contribution per unit.

(*b*) Draw up a Contribution Statement for the period.

(*c*) Calculate the price necessary to produce a net profit for the period of £500, if all other factors are constant.

12.4. A restaurant has a monthly capacity of 2,500 covers and an average selling price of £4 per cover. The Gross Profit % or margin is 60% and the fixed expenses are £3,000 per month.

(*a*) Prepare a break even chart on the graph paper provided and read off
  i) The break even point in covers and £'s.
  ii) The margin of safety in covers and £'s.

(*b*) Calculate the break even point if the fixed expenses rise by 20%.

12.5X. The OPEL Restaurant has available the following Profit & Loss Statement for year ended 31st December 19-5.

Sales		£20,000
Food cost		9,000
Gross Profit		£11,000
Salaries		4,000
Wages (variable)		5,000
Fixed expenses		2,000
Variable expenses		1,000
	LOSS	£1,000

The Restaurant operates 50 weeks per year and Food Stocks are sufficient to cover 2 weeks on average.

Calculate:

(*a*) Sales (turnover) required to break-even on present performance:

(*b*) The Average Food Stock.

The newly appointed Manager believes he can reduce Food Cost to 40% of Sales and turnover can be increased by 50%. (Assume variable expenses will be in same proportion to sales as in 19-5).

Evaluate and comment on his proposals.

12.6. (a) Define the terms and give examples of DIRECT AND INDIRECT COSTS.

(*b*) The Ella Salmon is a small Spanish Restaurant with indirect costs amounting to £351 per week and it is required to allocate these costs to the restaurant and bar in proportion to their respective floor areas. The areas involved are as follows:

Entrance and toilets	150 square feet
Bar and Cellar	250 square feet
Restaurant/Kitchen	500 square feet

Calculate the amount to be allocated to each source of income.

12.7X(*a*) Define the terms and give examples of FIXED AND VARIABLE COSTS.

(*b*) It is proposed to open a new restaurant at a capital cost of £20,000. Market and financial appraisal by the owners have produced the following figures:

Rent	£2,500 per annum
Rates	£850 per annum
Manager's Salary	£6,000 per annum
Insurance	£250 per annum
Depreciation	£900 per annum
Food/drink cost	40% of sales income
Casual labour	8% of sales income

It is hoped to attract customers with an average spend of £2 per cover, but the owner has no idea of how many covers he will need to serve before he breaks even or before he makes sufficient profit to justify the capital invested.

You are required to:

i) Complete the table on the graph paper taking three sample levels of annual output at 8,000; 12,000 and 16,000 customers.

ii) Draw up and label the break even chart to illustrate the position.

iii) Read off the break even point and margin of safety.

iv) If the owner requires a 15% return on capital, find what level of output he should operate at in order to make the required net profit. What is this in terms of 'covers per day' if he plans to open for 350 days per year?

13

Sales Mix and its Effect on Profitability

Learning Objectives

At the end of this chapter you should be able to:
13A Appreciate the effect of sales mix on profitability.

The results of a restaurant for a month may be displayed in an operating statement based on either absorption or marginal costing principles.

ABSORPTION COSTING OPERATING STATEMENT

		£	%
Sales		5,000	100
Cost of Food & Beverage		2,000	40
Gross Profit		3,000	60
Labour Costs	1,300		26
Overheads	600	1,900	12
Net Profit		1,100	22

MARGINAL COSTING OPERATING STATEMENT

	£	%
Sales	5,000	100
Variable Costs	2,000	40
Contribution	3,000	60
Fixed Costs	1,900	38
Net Profit	1,100	22

In the above examples Food and Beverage is assumed to be variable and labour and overheads are assumed to be fixed.

Sales Mix – If the above sales were split Food £3,000, Beverages £1,700, Cigarettes £300, the sales mix would be:

$$\text{Food } \frac{3000}{5000} \times \frac{100}{1} = 60\%$$

$$\text{Beverages } \frac{1700}{5000} \times \frac{100}{1} = 34\% \qquad \text{Cigarettes } \frac{300}{5000} \times \frac{100}{1} = 6\%$$

If sales mix items have different gross profit % then this will have an effect on the overall gross profit. If sales of an item with a high gross profit % increases in volume then this will increase the overall gross profit much more than an increase in a sale of an item with a low gross profit percentage.

Suppose in the above example the gross profit percentages were food 65%, beverages 50%, cigarettes 10% the gross profit would be:

		Sales Mix	GP %	Sales Mix	Gross Profit
	£	%		% × GP%	£
Food	3000	60	65	0.390	1950
Beverages	1700	34	50	0.170	850
Cigarettes	300	6	10	0.006	30
		100			
GP weighted by Sales Mix				0.566	2830

GP in £ would be 2830 (.566 × 5000)

Let us compare an increase in sales of 10% on food with a 10% increase in cigarettes.

10% increase in Food

	Sales GP%		£	
Food	3,300 × 0.65	=	2,145	
Beverages	1,700 × 0.50	=	850	
Cigarettes	300 × 0.10	=	30	
Overall Gross Profit			3,025	an increase of £195

10% increase in Cigarettes

	Sales GP%		£	
Food	3,000 × 0.65	=	1,950	
Beverages	1,700 × 0.50	=	850	
Cigarettes	330 × 0.10	=	33	
Overall Gross Profit			2,833	an increase of £3

In exactly the same way, a change in Gross Profit % on a high selling item affects overall GP much more than in a low selling item.

Let us compare a drop of 5% in Gross Profit % on food with a 5% drop on beverages.

5% drop in Food Gross Profit %

	Sales GP%		£	
Food	3,000 × 0.60	=	1,800	
Beverages	1,700 × 0.50	=	850	
Cigarettes	300 × 0.10	=	30	
			2,680	decrease of £150

5% Drop in Beverages GP

	Sales GP%		£	
Food	3,000 × 0.65	=	1,950	
Beverages	1,700 × 0.45	=	765	
Cigarettes	300 × 0.10	=	30	
			2,745	decrease of £85

Exercises

13.1. You are responsible for setting food and beverage selling prices in a large hotel organisation:

Set restaurant prices inclusive of 15% VAT (no service charge) for each course from the following budgeted information:

Course	*Sales Mix %*	*Gross Profit % (Margin)*
A	10	50
B	40	60
C	20	65
D	30	70

The expected number of covers in the budget period is 10,000. The fixed expense for the period is £33,000 and the target net profit for the restaurant is £30,000.

13.2. The Queen's Restaurant reports the following statistics for Monday 31st January: –

Number of Sales	*Item*	*Average Item Price £*	*Expected Gross Profit %*
50	Table d'Hote Meals	4.95	65
40	A la Carte Starters	0.95	70
57	A la Carte Main Course	5.25	62
25	A la Carte Sweets	0.45	52
47	A la Carte Coffee	0.40	70

N.B. Ignore V.A.T. etc.

Utilising the above information: –

i) Calculate the overall Gross Profit %.
ii) Calculate the average spend per person.
iii) Calculate the sales mix.

13.3. Ambrune Restaurants are opening a new restaurant.

The owners estimate the average: –

i) weekly demand to be 1,000 covers.
ii) weekly overheads (all fixed) to be £4,000.
iii) food costs and sales mix percentages to be: –

	Food Cost %	*Sales Mix %*
Main dishes	40	55
Starters/Sweets	36	25
Wine	30	20

The owners required the restaurant to achieve a weekly profit of £725.

Using the information above, you are required to establish prices for the individual courses of the meal.

N.B. Ignore V.A.T.

13.4X. The York Restaurant reports the following statistics: –

	Year 1	Year 2
Sales (£)	150,000	170,000
Customers	40,000	42,500
Gross Profit %		
Food	60	65
Drink	50	50
Tobacco	10	11
Sales Mix %		
Food	60	50
Drink	30	40
Tobacco	10	10

From the above information: –

(*a*) Calculate the average spend per customer, for each year.

(*b*) Calculate the overall Gross Profit and Gross Profit percentage for each year.

(*c*) Comment on the effect of the change in gross profit.

13.5X. The Charter Restaurant are reviewing their prices. The owners estimate the average:

i) Weekly demand to be 2,000 covers.

ii) Weekly net profit to be £1,000.

iii) Weekly overheads to be £5,000.

iv) Food Costs and Sales Mix percentages to be: –

	Sales Mix %	*Food Cost %*
Starters	20	35
Main Dishes	60	40
Sweets	20	45

Using the above information, you are required to establish prices for the individual courses of the meal.

Ignore VAT.

13.6. A Restaurant Owner is proposing to redesign his premises to accommodate a small cocktail bar. He has conducted a small market survey and believes that whilst initially his old customers will spend approximately the same per head, it would now be split up 25% bar and 75% food. Eventually however, he expects to attract a higher average spending power customer and enjoy greater weekly turnover up to £2,000 per week.

Before alterations commence the weekly turnover is £1,000 per week (food only) and his gross profit is 60% overall.

After alterations he plans to price the bar to give a 35% G.P (i.e. low in order to attract customers) and maintain the same margin on the food as previously.

You are required to:

(*a*) Advise the owner what the new G.P. (£) will be assuming weekly turnover is the same as before alterations.

(*b*) Project what the G.P. (£) is going to be if turnover climbs to £1,700 per week with the same bar: food ratio of 25%:75%.

(*c*) Explain to the owner what effect an alteration in the sales mix from 25%:75% (bar/food) to 30%:70% (bar/food) would have on the G.P. at the £1,700 level of turnover.

(*d*) Calculate the G.P. (£) that would be produced given the conditions detailed in (c.) above EXCEPT assume that the GP% on the bar is raised to 45% and the food G.P.% is dropped to 50%.

13.7X. (*a*) Describe two possible ways in which inclusive tariffs may be broken down for departmental accounting purposes.

(*b*) The Swin Dale Hotel charges £230 per week (inclusive of all meals and VAT). It provides table d'hote menus for non-residents at £3.22 (inc. VAT) for lunch, and £5.75 (inc. VAT) for dinner. The cost of providing breakfast is calculated at 55 pence and the gross profit target on all meals is 45%.

Calculate:

(i) How the income per guest per week would be apportioned between meals, accommodation and VAT.

(ii) The nightly charge for bed and breakfast inclusive of VAT.

13.8X. The capital cost of the Kosmo King (a small speciality restaurant with jazz pianist) was £50,000, and the owner requires an annual net profit of 16% of this figure. The restaurant turns over 350 covers per week for 52 weeks of the year.

Labour costs (including the pianist) and other fixed costs total £500 per week. The following menu structure together with sales mix percentages has applied in the past:

	Food Cost %	*Sales Mix %*
Starters	40	30
Main courses	55	60
Sweets	45	10

You are required to calculate:

(i) the annual net profit required
(ii) the overall gross profit to be achieved
(iii) an inclusive price for the whole meal
(iv) a price for the individual courses if required.

14

Costing and Pricing Related to Food and Beverage Sales

Learning Objectives

At the end of this chapter you should be able to:

14A **Make costing calculations relating to units of sale of food and beverages.**

Beverages

Bar Prices

Bar prices may be determined by market factors. In the case of public houses, owned by breweries employing their own unit managers, the prices will be set by the brewery.

However, licensed restaurants, hotels and free houses may set prices based on *Cost* and *Margin* (Gross profit as % of Sales). See chapter 4.

This can be illustrated:

A brand of bottled beer costs £0.18 per bottle.

The pricing policy is 55% MARGIN. Set the bar price inclusive of VAT at 15%.

MARGIN OF 55% GIVES COST OF 45%. Therefore in this case 45% is £0.18 per bottle, therefore Ex. SELLING PRICE = £0.18 $\times \frac{100}{45}$ = £0.40

therefore PRICE INCLUDING VAT = £0.40 × 1.15 = £0.46

Non alcoholic Beverages (i.e. teas and coffees) may also be priced based on cost and a given margin. The margin is usually higher than for alcoholic beverages:

A cup of coffee costs 5p to produce and is sold for 25p excluding VAT. i.e. 25p = 100% therefore gross profit = 20p and the GP% = $\frac{20}{25} \times 100 = 80\%$.

Meat, Poultry and Fish Costing

The above foods can be purchased pre-portioned but the practice of boning and trimming before cooking and carving is still common.

If portion control is in operation the weight of a portion will be known. It would be wrong to cost this portion weight at the cost price per kg. of meat etc. purchased. Obviously the loss due to preparation should be taken into account. This can be illustrated by an example:

40 kg of beef are purchased @ £5 per kg. After preparation 250 portions are obtained at 100g per portion.

The cost of the meat served is:

Total Cost 40 kg × 5 = £200

therefore portion cost $\frac{£200}{250} = £0.80$

The meat served can also be given at cost per kg. served.

i.e. 250 portions × 100g each = 25 kg.

25kg of meat served cost £200

therefore 1kg. of meat served cost $\frac{200}{25} = £8$ per kg.

The above calculations can be expressed as a formula:

$$\text{cooked meat price per kg} = \frac{\text{raw meat price per kg} \times \text{raw meat weight}}{\text{cooked meat weight}}$$

$$\text{,,} \quad = \frac{£5 \times 40\text{kg.}}{25\text{kg.}} = \underline{\underline{£8}}$$

$$\text{cooked meat price per portion} = \frac{\text{raw meat price per kg} \times \text{raw meat weight}}{\text{number of portions}}$$

$$\text{,,} \quad = \frac{£5 \times 40}{250} = \underline{\underline{£0.80}}$$

25kg of prepared meat from raw meat of 40kg may be expressed as a percentage. i.e. $\frac{25}{40} \times 100 = 62.5\%$

again in formula: $\text{cooked price per kg} = \frac{\text{raw meat price per kg} \times 100}{\text{cooked meat \% of raw meat}}$

$$\text{,,} \quad = \frac{5 \times 100}{62.5} = \underline{\underline{£8}}$$

Exercises

14.1. The latest consignment of wine 17 on a restaurant's wine list was invoiced:

invoiced:	10 cases	£270
	less 20% trade discount	54
		£216
	add 15% VAT	32.40
		£248.40

There are 12 bottles in a case. Price 1 bottle for the wine list inclusive of VAT given a pricing policy of 70% margin.

14.2. An hotel purchases 5 cases (dozens) of 26 oz. Whisky at a total price of £403.65 inclusive VAT at the Standard rate. Assuming that there are 32 measures to the bottle, and the required Gross Profit percentage is 60%, calculate: –

(*a*) Unit cost per bottle
(*b*) Cost per measure
(*c*) Selling price per measure ex. VAT
(*d*) Selling price per measure inc. VAT at the Standard Rate, rounded up to the nearest penny

N.B. Workings correct to three decimal places.

14.3. A joint weighing 9.2 kg is purchased at £3.10 per kg, and when boned, produces 1.7 kg of bones valued at 10p per kg. Determine: –

(*a*) the cost per kilo of useable meat
(*b*) the cost per kilo of served meat if cooking loss is 40%.

14.4X. A bar operates with measures of one third and one sixth of a gill for the appropriate drinks and serves wine in glasses which hold a portion size of 4½ fluid ounces. Required GP% = 55%. Calculate the selling price – rounded off to nearest p – (including VAT at 15%) for the following drinks given the information below:

Drink	*Bottle size*	*Bottle cost (exc. VAT)*
Gin	26⅔ fl oz	£6.38
Creme de menthe	24 fl oz	£5.60
Tio Pepe	75 fl oz	£3.10
Muscadet	70 cl	£3.45
Martini	150 cl	£3.95

14.5X(*a*) Complete the following conversions:

1 litre	=...........pints	=...........fluid ounces	
1 kilo	=...........lb		
1 pint	=...........litre	=...........fluid ounces	
1 lb	=...........kilo	=...........grams	
1 gill	=...........fluid oz	=...........litre	
1/6 gill	=...........fluid oz	=...........litre	

(*b*) Use the above to calculate: –

How many 1/6 gill measures there are in bottles of the following sizes: 26⅔ fluid oz, 40 fluid oz, 75 cl, 70 cl, 100 cl.

14.6X. If a bar manager wishes to achieve a gross profit of 51% on every sale, calculate his selling price for the following drinks (add VAT at 15%): Whisky 19 pence per measure, Sherry 15 pence per measure, Bottled Beer 22 pence per measure. These cost prices do not include VAT.

15

Costing and Pricing Methods used in Various Catering Establishments

Learning Objectives

At the end of this chapter you should be able to:

15A **Understand the factors which influence function costing and the pricing methods used in various catering establishments**

Banqueting

Many hotels and restaurants offer a banqueting or special functions service. This service will include wedding receptions, dinner parties and maybe conferences, in addition to banqueting.

This service may be considered important enough to appoint a banqueting manager, who will be responsible for marketing, pricing, costing and control and possibly production and service.

The following is one example of the work involved:

A wedding reception has been ordered for 100 guests. Precise details of food per guest has been given and costed at £4 per head. The labour and overheads will cost £230 for the function.

The functions manager then prices the function per guest both exclusive and inclusive of VAT. The policy of the hotel is 10% net profit on banqueting sales.

Sales = Food Cost + Labour and Overheads + net profit.
S = £400 + £230 + 10% of S.

by using normal arithmetical techniques and deducting 10% of S from both sides of the equation.
therefore 90% of S = £630
therefore S = £700 or £7 per head (excluding VAT).

Price per guest inclusive of VAT = £7 × 1.15 = £8.05.

Some hotels offer a choice of set menu for wedding receptions e.g.

Menu A £3 per head at cost
B £4 per head at cost
C £5 per head at cost

Labour and overheads are £2 per cover or guest.

Each reception should make a profit of £1 per guest. Set selling prices including VAT for each menu.

	Food Cost	+	Labour & Overheads	+	Net Profit	= S* × 1.15	=	inclusive selling price
A	£3	+	£2	+	£1	= 6 × 1.15	=	£6.90
B	£4	+	£2	+	£1	= 7 × 1.15	=	£8.05
C	£5	+	£2	+	£1	= 8 × 1.15	=	£9.20

*S = Sales exclusiuve of V.A.T.

These prices are often part of an attractive advertising brochure.

Some special functions require extras, for example music in the form of a band or disco.

The extra cost is simply added in the above formula to determine the selling price.

This can be illustrated:

A Rugby Club is to hold its annual dinner dance. There will be 250 guests, the food and beverage costs will be £4 per head. The charge for the disco is £100 plus flowers for the dignatories wives £50. Labour and Overheads are costed at £600. The hotelier requires a net profit of £250.

Sales = Food and Beverage Cost + Extras + Labour/Overheads + Net Profit

S = 250 × £4 = 1000 + 150 + 600 + 250 = £2000

Price per guest $\frac{2000}{250}$ = £8 Ex. VAT.

Inc. VAT. £8 × 1.15 = £9.20

Industrial Catering

Most industrial firms offer canteen and or staff restaurant facilities to their employees. Some employers are prepared to subsidise the meals i.e. the selling price is less than the cost.

The employer must decide on a reasonable price structure or the employees will not use the canteen facility. Providing a canteen may be an important objective of the management and one which they are prepared to subsidise. The amount or rate of this contribution must be decided.

The following is an example of determining a subsidised pricing policy:

A canteen caters for an average of 100 lunches per day, for 300 days per year.

The food cost will average 80p per meal and the labour and overheads for the canteen are budgeted at £13,000 p.a. The firm will subsidise these costs by £1,000 p.a.

Calculate the selling price excluding VAT and also including VAT and calculate the pricing policy as a percentage of food cost (Mark up not margin).

Calculations

	£	£
No. of meals per annum 30,000		
Food costs per annum 30,000 × 80p =		24,000
Other costs	13,000	
less subsidy	1,000	12,000
Total sales must be		36,000

Selling price excluding VAT = $\frac{£36{,}000}{30{,}000}$ = £1.20

Selling price including VAT = £1.20 × 1.15 = £1.38.

Mark up = $\frac{\text{Selling price £1.20} - \text{Food cost 80p}}{\text{Food cost 80p}} = \frac{40}{80} \times \frac{100}{1} = 50\%$

This can be summarised in a profit and loss statement:

	£
Sales, excluding VAT	36,000
Food cost	24,000
Gross Profit	12,000
Labour and overheads	13,000
Loss subsidised by employer	1,000

Price Sensitivity

Using cost as the basis for setting selling prices may cause problems if the prospective customer is sensitive to price increases. The sales manager must judge the market for a particular activity, and if the market is competitive it may be better to set a price for the 'representative customer'. A restaurant may find that a competitive price for a table d'hote menu is £4.60 per person including VAT.

From past records he may require a 55% margin to cover labour, overheads and net profit.

He will wish to calculate the food cost available to give his food and beverage operations staff a guide to the preparation of a suitable menu.

The first step is to extract the VAT from the representative customer or average spend.

£4.60 × $\frac{100}{115}$ = £4.00 net of VAT

55% margin or Gross Profit will leave 45% for food cost; therefore food and beverage cost per cover will be 0.45 × £4.00 = £1.80.

High and Low Margin Returns

The above restaurant will be a low margin return restaurant because the average for restaurant operation is 60%. Another restaurant may require a high margin return, e.g. 65%, because the labour and overheads are more expensive.

A comparison of a high margin and a low margin return restaurant can now be given for the same period.

POPULAR RESTAURANT	£	%	*LUXURY RESTAURANT*	£	%
Sales 25,000 × £4	100,000	100	10,000 × £10	100,000	100
Food Cost 25,000 × £1.80	45,000		10,000 × £3.50	35,000	
Gross Profit	55,000	55		65,000	65
Labour Cost	24,000	24		30,000	30
Overheads	21,000	21		25,000	25
Net Profit	10,000	10		10,000	10

The low return popular restaurant has a representative customer price of £4 and requires a high volume of sales to achieve £10,000 net profit.

The high return luxury restaurant achieves the same net profit by serving many fewer customers. The better service and the higher food cost per head justify the average spend of £10.

Apportionment of Hotel Costs

The main sales department is ''ROOMS'. Licensed hotels usually operate a 'RESTAURANT' and a 'BAR' department in addition to rooms.

The cost of sales in the restaurant and bar will be direct materials, i.e. food and beverages. Some other materials may be allocated to departments, but materials which cannot be easily allocated will be treated as indirect materials and assumed to be part of overheads if all overheads are considered to be indirect.

In chapter 4 labour costs were introduced and hotels should be able to allocate most labour costs 'direct' to one of the three departments. Again some labour costs cannot be easily allocated, e.g. the salary of a typist, and will be treated as indirect.

Indirect labour and overheads (including some indirect materials) can be apportioned ιo the sales departments. There are several methods.

Methods of Apportionment

1. Based on Sales

In a given period hotel sales are £40,000 rooms, £50,000 restaurant and £10,000 bar. Indirect labour is £10,000 and overheads £15,000.

These will be apportioned:

	Indirect Labour		*Overheads*	
		£		£
Rooms	£10,000 × 40% =	4,000	£15,000 × 40% =	6,000
Restaurant	£10,000 × 50% =	5,000	£15,000 × 50% =	7,500
Bar	£10,000 × 10% =	1,000	£15,000 × 10% =	1,500

The main criticism of using sales as the base is that it does not take into account the different rates of Gross Profit in the 'sales mix'. The average Gross Profit % are rooms 100%, restaurant 60%, bar – a mixture of wines, beers, spirits, tobacco all with different Gross Profit rates. If sales is used as a base some department managers will claim, with justification, that their departments are charged with an unfair share of the indirect costs of the organisation.

Another objection is that sales vary from one period to another and yet many costs do not vary with sales change.

2. Based on time spent

This will require 'time recording' which is not a feature in many hotels. If time-sheets are kept the indirect costs of labour are in effect converted to 'direct' labour costs. Any unallocated labour will have to be apportioned in some way.

3. Metering

This applies to gas, electricity, and water charges. If subsidiary meters are supplied to each department then what is normally described as an indirect cost will become direct.

4. Based on Floor area

The costs which apply to the hotel as a whole, which are difficult to allocate to a department, may be suitably apportioned to a department in proportion to the floor area the department occupies. The areas should be available on the architect's plan of the hotel. The following is an example:

The hotel plan shows that all bedrooms are on the upper floors and there is a restaurant, bar and usual facilities on the ground floor:

		Area in square metres
GROUND FLOOR	Restaurant	1,800
	Kitchens	1,200
	Bar	1,000
	Other facilities	2,000
UPPER FLOORS		6,000

Apportion indirect wages of £500 and indirect overheads of £1,000 to the departments – Rooms, Restaurant and Bar.

The department areas are 6,000m, 3,000m, 1,000m or 60%, 30%, 10%.

Apportionment Calculations

	Rooms	*Rest.*	*Bar*	*Total*
	60%	30%	10%	100%
Indirect Wages	£300	£150	£50	£500
,, Overheads	£600	£300	£100	£1,000

It will be noticed that the area of 'other facilities' has been ignored. Obviously the hotel does not make a specific charge for 'other facilities', therefore it is ignored in apportioning overheads.

Exercises

15.1. You are preparing your banqueting prices for the coming season. You estimate the Food Cost for Menu H. for fifty covers to be £89.60. Your Staff and Overhead Charges for such a banquet are estimated at £146.05. Determine: –

(*a*) the charge per cover to attain a Net Profit of 15% (Ignore VAT)
(*b*) the estimated net profit from a banquet of fifty covers using this menu.

15.2. (*a*) Contrast the traditional methods of calculating menu and banquet prices.
(*b*) Calculate the banquet price (exclusive of VAT) from the following: Numbers of guests 100, Food cost per guest £2, Wages £150, Overheads £100, Net profit 10% on Sales.

15.3X. Quote an inclusive price for a banquet for 100 people requiring a food and beverage cost of £5 per head. The labour and overheads expenses are standard at £4 per head for special functions and the expected net profit is 25% of sales exclusive of VAT.

15.4. An industrial firm has 400 employees, 70% on average will use the canteen for 250 days per annum.

The average food cost of a meal will be £0.80. The following costs will be allocated to the canteen: labour £23,000 p.a., overheads £12,000 p.a.

The management have decided to charge £0.75 ex. VAT for canteen meals. Calculate the subsidy.

15.5X. An industrial canteen sells an average of 100 meals per day and opens 250 days per annum.

The average food cost is budgeted at £0.20 per meal and the labour and overheads to be allocated to the canteen service will be £3,000 per annum. The pricing policy is to break-even.

Calculate the price to be charged both ex. VAT and VAT inclusive (15%).

15.6. The Pine Hotel has a total guest occupancy of 630 sleeper/nights per week. Average occupany is 60% and floor areas are as follows:

		Square feet
1st Floor (Bedrooms & corridors)		4,200
2nd Floor (Bedrooms & corridors)		4,200
3rd Floor (Bedrooms & corridors)		4,200
Ground Floor:	Kitchen and restaurant	2,700
	Bar	400
	Lounge	900
	Corridors	200
Direct wages per annum:		£
	Kitchen and restaurant	156,000
	House*	148,000
	Bar	32,000
Direct expenses per annum:		
	Kitchen and restaurant	102,000
	House*	123,000
	Bar	26,000

Overheads amount to £172,000 per annum. The net profit required on accommodation is 20% on sales.

You are required to calculate, to the nearest £, the average charge per week for accommodation, and also the tariff per sleeper/night.

**These are all allocated to Rooms Department.*

15.7. A temperance hotel operates two departments and analyses the wages between the two. The manager's salary and the overheads are apportioned to the departments according to sales. Prepare a profit and loss statement for the month of June from the following:

Sales – rooms £6,000 restaurant £4,000. Direct labour – rooms £700 restaurant £600. Food cost £40%. Managers salary £800 per month, overheads £1,500 per month.

15.8X. The George Hotel's sales for a given period were £220,000 split rooms £76,000, restaurant £122,000, bar £22,000.

Apportion indirect wages of £11,000 and overheads of £17,600 to the operated departments according to the sales mix.

15.9. Allocate the indirect expenses £16,950 of The Grand Hotel to the sales departments based on the following floor areas – bedrooms 8,200 m^2 restaurant and kitchen 2,100, bar 1,000, lounge 600, service areas 3,000.

15.10X. The floor areas in a licensed hotel are in the following proportions:

Department 1, rooms 30%, Department 2 restaurant 40%, Department 3 bar 20% Services areas 10%.

Allocate the managers salary £9,900 per annum to the 3 operated departments.

15.11X. The following costs are estimated for a banquet of 100 covers:

Wages £155.20; Butcher £19.50; Greengrocer £74.60; Dairy £8.30; Fishmonger £54.60; Stores £80.20; Overheads £110.30.

You are required to:

(*a*) Calculate what charge per cover should be made in order to achieve a net profit of 15%.
(*b*) What rate of gross profit will be made?
(*c*) Express the
i) wages and,
ii) overheads as a percentage of sales.

15.12X. A table d'hote menu has been costed at an average price per customer (based on expected dish popularity) at £1.21 per customer. The restaurant of a local hotel is selling a similar product for £2.80 inclusive of VAT. In order to be competitive what gross percentage would you suggest should be employed to set a 'reasonable' selling price.

15.13X. A function has been prepared for 50 people. It is estimated that the food would cost the hotel £1.95 per person and that the other costs would be Casual waitresses £23.60, and overheads £25.00. The normal profit target of the establishment is 13% (net profit). What price would you charge the party per person inclusive of VAT at 15%.

15.14 (*a*) Explain what you understand by the concept of 'range of price discretion' with reference to the high fixed cost and low fixed cost sections of the hotel and catering industry.

(*b*) The fixed costs of the Samantha restaurant were £5,296 per annum, and the variable cost per cover was £1.96. When the total covers for the year amounted to 4,341, what selling price per cover should have been charged:

(i) in order to make a net profit of 22% on sales
(ii) in order to break even on the operation
(iii) if the restaurant was happy (for certain customers) to make only a small 'contribution' towards fixed costs and net profit of 14 pence per cover.

16

Value Added Tax

Learning Objectives

At the end of this chapter you should be able to:

16A Know what is meant by Value Added Tax, the current rate and the general areas to which it applies.

This tax (VAT) was introduced in the UK on 1st April 1973. At the time of writing this book, Hotel and Catering organisations with a turnover (net sales p.a.) of £18,700 must register. This threshold (starting point) was £5,000 in 1973 and the current trend is to increase the threshold annually in line with inflation. The reader must therefore check what is the amount of the current threshold.

The registered catering firm must charge the current rate of VAT (15%[1] at the time of writing this book) on the sales of catering services i.e. food beverages and accommodation. Some sales will be either:

1. Zero rated – supplies technically taxable but currently the tax rate is NIL.
2. Exempt – supplies which are not intended to be taxed.

Full details of Zero rate and exempt supplies are given in HM Customs & Excise Notice No. 701.

Catering (notice 709)

VAT is chargeable at standard rate (15%) on the supply of food and drink for consumption on the premises in which it is supplied or for immediate consumption near the place of supply. This means sales by restaurants, cafes, hotels, boarding houses, pubs, snack bars, canteens, street stalls, railway kiosks, supplies on trains and other transport.

Cold 'Take away' food, for example sandwiches and cakes is 'zero rated'. Hot 'take-away' food is standard rated e.g. fish and chips, chinese 'take-aways'.

1. Note: This rate may vary from time to time. In the first ten years of VAT there had been three different basic rates, 8%, 10%, and 15% at the time this book was writtern.

Hotels include motels, inns, guest houses, residential clubs. VAT is chargeable at standard rate for accommodation, meals, drinks and 'service charges'.

The following hotel items are not chargeable.

1. Accommodation where the stay is in excess of 4 weeks.
2. Visitors' paid out.
3. Newspapers sold to guests.

Duties of the Registered Firm

1. Charge the appropriate rate on sales
2. Issue tax invoices if requested
3. Record all sales (Outputs) and expenditure (Inputs). Food as an 'Input' is zero rated
4. File VAT returns with Customs and Excise
5. Keep a VAT account.

Sales Invoices

Sales are called outputs for VAT.

Exhibit 16.1 is a typical invoice issued by a Restaurant or Hotel for a wedding reception.

Exhibit 16.1

VAT Registration No. 1234 5678	The Sea View Hotel, The Promenade, Dolphin Bay. 1st September, 19-5
To: D. Prendergast, 45 Charles Street, Colwyn Bay.	
Wedding Reception	
70 guests @ £8	560.00
VAT @ 15%	84.00
	£644.00

Where a cash discount is offered for speedy payment, VAT is calculated on an amount represented by the value of the invoice, less such a discount. In exhibit 16.1 if a cash discount of £20 had been offered then the VAT would have been £81 i.e. 15% of £560 − £20 = £540. Even if the cash discount is lost because of late payment, the VAT will not change.

Cash Sales

Sales for cash are usual in restaurants and bars and often the sale is recorded in a cash register without the issue of an invoice.

At the end of a period (say a month) these cash sales will have been recorded including VAT. Suppose they were £2,300.

It will be necessary to extract the VAT as follows (we are using a rate of 15% VAT in this example).

Cash sales without VAT + VAT = Cash Sales with VAT.
100% + 15% = 115%
£2,000 + £300 = £2,300

$$\text{VAT} = \frac{15}{115} \times 2{,}300 = £300$$

Note: You will often know only the gross amount of an item, this figure will in fact be made up of the net amount plus VAT. To find the amount of VAT which has been added to the net amount, a formula capable of being used with any rate of VAT can be used. It is:

$$\frac{\text{\% Rate of VAT}}{100 + \text{\% Rate of VAT}} \times \text{Gross Amount} = \text{VAT in £}$$

In the case just seen the VAT was worked out as

$$\frac{15}{100 + 15} \times £2{,}300 = \frac{15}{115} \times £2{,}300 = £300$$

This means that the net amount can be calculated: Gross Amount £2,300 − VAT £300 = £2,000.

Let us try this with other figures. Suppose that the gross amount of sales was £1,650 and the rate of VAT was 10%. Find the amount of VAT and the net amount before VAT was added.

Using the formula: –

$$\frac{10}{100 + 10} \times £1{,}650 = \frac{10}{110} \times £1{,}650 = £150.$$

Therefore the net amount was £1,500, which with VAT £150 added, becomes £1,650 gross.

Value Added Tax and Purchases

In the kind of firm with which we are concerned in this chapter, we will be able to claim refunds for VAT paid on items bought. These items bought are known as inputs for VAT.

For each period, if VAT on outputs (sales) is greater than VAT on inputs (items bought), then the firm will have to pay the difference between these amounts to the Customs and Excise.

If VAT on inputs (items bought) is greater than VAT on outputs (sales), then the firm will collect the difference from the Customs and Excise.

Exhibit 16.2 shows a purchases invoice.

Food supplies bought by the hotel, restaurant etc are not subject to VAT. The same would apply to any private individual buying food from any sort of retail food store, e.g. from butchers, grocers, greengrocers, supermarkets etc.

Exhibit 16.2

E. Lyal Ltd
College Avenue
St Albans
Hertfordshire

INVOICE No. K453/A

Date: 1/3/19-2
Your order No. BB/667

To: W. Frank & Co
Hayburn Road
Stockport

Terms: Strictly net 30 days
VAT Reg. No. 2422 1896

	£
50 bottles of Wine No. 7 × £3 each	150
30 bottles of Wine No. 8 × £4 each	120
	270
Less Trade discount at 33⅓%	90
	180
Add VAT 15%	27
	207

Exercises

16.1. Define
- (*a*) V.A.T.
- (*b*) Current percentage rates of V.A.T.
- (*c*) Dish Costing
- (*d*) Service Charge
- (*e*) Normal percentage rates of service charge
- (*f*) Cash Discount
- (*g*) Trade Discount.

16.2. (*a*) An hotel account of £35.21 is subject to V.A.T. at the standard rate of 15% and 10% Service Charge. Calculate the total amount due.

(*b*) A restaurant bill of £29.01 is inclusive of 12½% Service Charge and V.A.T. at the Standard rate of 15%. Calculate: –

(i) the amount of V.A.T.
(ii) the amount of Service Charge
(iii) the amount exclusive of V.A.T. and Service Charge

(*c*) Calculate the selling price of a Dish costing 62p where the required Gross Profit is 60%.

(*d*) The selling price of a Dish including V.A.T. at the Standard Rate of 15% is £3.95. Calculate the Gross Profit percentage if the cost price is £1.48.

16.3X. Find out what is the current THRESHOLD for registration as a registered firm.

16.4X. Define

(*a*) Inputs
(*b*) Outputs
(*c*) Input Tax
(*d*) Output Tax.

16.5. Name one advantage and one disadvantage of a firm below current VAT threshold not registering.

17

The Accounting Equation

Learning Objectives

At the end of this chapter you should be able to:

17A Record financial transactions in a balance sheet.

17B Calculate the capital from assets and liabilities.

The whole of accounting and book-keeping is based upon a very simple idea. This is called the accounting equation, which sounds complicated, but in fact it is very straightforward indeed.

It can be expressed by saying that if a firm is to come into existence, and start trading, then it needs resources. Let us assume that in the first place it is the owner of the business who has supplied all of the resources. This can be shown as:

Resources in the business = Resources supplied by the owner

In book-keeping and accounting terms are used to describe things, as in any other kinds of activity. The amount, expressed in money, of the resources supplied by the owner is called 'Capital'. The actual resources that are then in the business are called 'Assets'. This means that the accounting equation above, when the owner has supplied all of the resources, can be shown as:

Assets = Capital

Usually, however, someone other than the owner has supplied some of the assets. The amount owing to this person for these assets is given the name 'liabilities'. The equation has now changed to:

Assets = Capital + Liabilities

You can see that the two sides of the equation will have the same totals. This is because you are dealing with the same thing from two different points of view. It is:

Resources: What they are = Resources: Who supplies them
(Assets) (Capital + Liabilities)

It is a fact that the totals of each side will always equal one another, and that this will always be true no matter how many transactions are entered into. The actual assets, capital and liabilities may change, but the equality of assets with that of the total of capital and liabilities will always hold true.

Assets consist of property of all kinds, such as buildings, machinery, stocks of goods and motor vehicles, also benefits such as debts owing by customers and the amount of money in the bank account.

In catering 'Stocks of Goods' means stocks of items of food and beverages for resale.

Liabilities consist of money owing for goods supplied to the firm, and for expenses, also for loans made to the firm.

Capital is often called the owner's equity or net worth.

Later we will consider rather more precise definitions as to what we mean by the terms 'book-keeping' and 'accounting'. At this point all we need to know is that 'book-keeping' is concerned with the work of entering information into accounting records, and afterwards maintaining such records properly. 'Accounting', at this point in the book, can be said to be concerned with the various uses of such records.

The Balance Sheet and the Effects of Business Transactions

The accounting equation is expressed in a statement called the Balance Sheet. It is not the first book-keeping record to be made, but it is a convenient place to start to consider accounting.

The Introduction of Capital

On 1 May 19-7 B. Blake started in business and deposited £5,000 into a bank account opened specially for the business. The balance sheet would appear:

B. Blake
Balance Sheet as at 1 May 19-7

Assets	£		£
Cash at bank	5,000	Capital	5,000
	5,000		5,000

The Purchase of an Asset by Cheque

On 3 May 19-7 Blake buys a building for £3,000. The effect of this transaction is that the cash at bank is decreased and a new asset, buildings, appears.

B. Blake

Balance Sheet as at 3 May 19-7

Assets	£		£
Buildings	3,000	Capital	5,000
Cash at bank	2,000		
	5,000		5,000

The Purchase of an Asset and the Incurring of a Liability

On 6 May 19-7 Blake buys some goods for £500 from D. Smith, and agrees to pay for them some time within the next two weeks. The effect of this is that a new asset, stock of goods, is acquired, and a liability for the goods is created. A person to whom money is owed for goods is known in accounting language as a creditor.

B. Blake

Balance Sheet as at 6 May 19-7

Assets	£	*Capital and Liabilities*	£
Buildings	3,000	Capital	5,000
Stock of goods	500	Creditor	500
Cash at bank	2,000		
	5,500		5,500

Sale of an Asset on Credit

On 10 May 19-7 goods which had cost £100 were sold to J. Brown for the same amount, the money to be paid later. The effect is a reduction in the stock of goods and the creation of a new asset. A person who owes the firm money is known in accounting language as a debtor.

The balance sheet now appears as:

B. Blake
Balance Sheet as at 10 May 19-7

Assets	£	*Capital and Liabilities*	£
Buildings	3,000	Capital	5,000
Stock of goods	400	Creditor	500
Debtor	100		
Cash at bank	2,000		
	5,500		5,500

Sale of an Asset for Immediate Payment

On 13 May 19-7 goods which had cost £50 were sold to D. Daley for the same amount, Daley paying for them immediately by cheque. Here one asset, stock of goods, is reduced, while another asset, bank, is increased. The balance sheet now appears:

B. Blake
Balance Sheet as at 13 May 19-7

Assets	£	*Capital and Liabilities*	£
Buildings	3,000	Capital	5,000
Stock of goods	350	Creditor	500
Debtor	100		
Cash at bank	2,050		
	5,500		5,500

The Payment of a Liability

On 15 May 19-7 Blake pays a cheque for £200 to D. Smith in part payment of the amount owing. The asset of bank is therefore reduced, and the liability of the creditor is also reduced. The balance sheet now appears:

B. Blake
Balance Sheet as at 15 May 19-7

Assets	£	*Capital and Liabilities*	£
Buildings	3,000	Capital	5,000
Stock of goods	350	Creditor	300
Debtor	100		
Cash at bank	1,850		
	5,300		5,300

Collection of an Asset

J. Brown, who owed Blake £100, makes a part payment of £75 by cheque on 31 May 19-7. The effect is to reduce one asset, debtor, and to increase another asset, bank. This results in a balance sheet as follows:

B. Blake
Balance Sheet as at 31 May 19-7

Assets	£	*Capital and Liabilities*	£
Buildings	3,000	Capital	5,000
Stock of goods	350	Creditor	300
Debtor	25		
Cash at bank	1,925		
	5,300		5,300

It can be seen that every transaction has affected two items. Sometimes it has changed two assets by reducing one and increasing the other. Other times it has reacted differently. A summary of the effect of transactions upon assets, liabilities and capital is shown below.

Example of Transaction		
1. Buy goods on credit.	Increase Asset (Stock of Goods)	Increase Liability (Creditors)
2. Buy goods by cheque.	Increase Asset (Stock of Goods)	Decrease Asset (Bank)
3. Pay creditor by cheque.	Decrease Asset (Bank)	Decrease Liability (Creditors)
4. Owner pays more capital into the bank.	Increase Asset (Bánk)	Increase Capital
5. Owner takes money out of the business bank for his own use.	Decrease Asset (Bank)	Decrease Capital
6. Owner pays creditor from private money outside the firm.	Decrease Liability (Creditors)	Increase Capital

Each transaction has therefore maintained the equality of the total of assets with that of capital and liabilities. This can be shown:

Number of transaction as above	*Asset*	*Liabilities and Capital*	*Effect on balance sheet totals*
1	+	+	Each side added to equally.
2	+		A plus and a minus both on the assets side
	−		cancelling out each other.
3	−	−	Each side has equal deductions.
4	+	+	Each side has equal additions.
5	−	−	Each side has equal deductions.
6		−	A plus and a minus both on the liabilities
		+	side cancelling out each other.

Note:

(i) Anyone who has studied book-keeping or accounting previously may well question the validity of having assets on the left-hand side of the balance sheet and capital and liabilities on the right-hand side, as previously they used to be opposite to that. However, the Companies Act 1981 lays it down that in two-sided balance sheets assets must be shown on the left-hand side of the balance sheet and capital and liabilities on the right-hand side. In the interests of standardisation, and to avoid confusion, the balance sheets for sole traders and partnerships will also be drawn up in the same way.

In fact the new method does make book-keeping and accounting much easier to learn than previously. It is however a point to bear in mind when looking at other textbooks which have not been updated.

Exercises

17.1. You are to complete the gaps in the following table:

	Assets	*Liabilities*	*Capital*
	£	£	£
(*a*)	12,500	1,800	?
(*b*)	28,000	4,900	?
(*c*)	16,800	?	12,500
(*d*)	19,600	?	16,450
(*e*)	?	6,300	19,200
(*f*)	?	11,650	39,750

17.2X. You are to complete the gaps in the following table:

	Assets	*Liabilities*	*Capital*
	£	£	£
(*a*)	55,000	16,900	?
(*b*)	?	17,200	34,400
(*c*)	36,100	?	28,500
(*d*)	119,500	15,400	?
(*e*)	88,000	?	62,000
(*f*)	?	49,000	110,000

17.3. Distinguish from the following list the items that are liabilities from those that are assets:

(i) Office machinery
(ii) Loan from C. Shirley
(iii) Fixtures and fittings
(iv) Motor vehicles
(v) We owe for goods
(vi) Bank balance.

17.4X. Classify the following items into liabilities and assets:

Motor vehicles
Premises
Creditors for goods
Stock of goods
Debtors
Owing to bank
Cash in hand
Loan from D. Jones
Machinery.

17.5. State which of the following are shown under the wrong classification for J. White's business:

Assets	*Liabilities*
Loan from C. Smith	Stock of goods
Cash in hand	Debtors
Machinery	Money owing to bank
Creditors	
Premises	
Motor vehicles.	

17.6X. Which of the following are shown under the wrong headings:

Assets	*Liabilities*
Cash at bank	Loan from J. Graham
Fixtures	Machinery
Creditors	Motor vehicles
Building	
Stock of goods	
Debtors	
Capital	

17.7. A. Smart sets up a new business. Before he actually sells anything he has bought Motor Vehicles £2,000. Premises £5,000, Stock of goods £1,000. He did not pay in full for his stock of goods and still owes £400 in respect of them. He had borrowed £3,000 from D. Bevan. After the events just described, and before trading starts, he has £100 cash in hand and £700 cash at bank. You are required to calculate the amount of his capital.

17.8X. T. Charles starts a business. Before he actually starts to sell anything he has bought, Fixtures £2,000, Motor Vehicles £5,000 and a stock of goods £3,500. Although he has paid in full for the fixtures and the motor vehicle, he still owes £1,400 for some of the goods. J. Preston had lent him £3,000. Charles, after the above, has £2,800 in the business bank account and £100 cash in hand. You are required to calculate his capital.

17.9. Draw up A. Foster's balance sheet from the following as at 31 December 19-4:

	£
Capital	23,750
Debtors	4,950
Motor vehicles	5,700
Creditors	2,450
Fixtures	5,500
Stock of goods	8,800
Cash at bank	1,250

17.10X. Draw up Kelly's balance sheet as at 30 June 19-2 from the following items:

	£
Capital	13,000
Kitchen Equipment	9,000
Creditors	900
Stock of goods	1,550
Debtors	275
Cash at bank	5,075
Loan from C. Smith	2,000

17.11. Complete the columns to show the effects of the following transactions:

	Effect upon		
	Assets	*Liabilities*	*Capital*
(*a*) We pay a creditor £70 in cash			
(*b*) Bought fixtures £200 paying by cheque			
(*c*) Bought goods on credit £275			
(*d*) The proprietor introduces another £500 cash into the firm			
(*e*) J. Walker lends the firm £200 in cash			
(*f*) A debtor pays us £50 by cheque			
(*g*) We return goods costing £60 to a supplier whose bill we had not paid			
(*h*) Bought additional premises paying £5,000 by cheque.			

17.12X. Complete the columns to show the effects of the following transactions:

	Effect upon Assets	Liabilities	Capital
(*a*) Bought motor van on credit £500			
(*b*) Repaid by cash a loan owed to P. Smith £1,000			
(*c*) Bought goods for £150 paying by cheque			
(*d*) The owner puts a further £5,000 cash into the business			
(*e*) A debtor returns to us £80 goods. We agree to make an allowance for them.			
(*f*) Bought goods on credit £220			
(*g*) The owner takes out £100 cash for his personal use			
(*h*) We pay a creditor £190 by cheque.			

17.13. C. Sangster has the following items in his balance sheet as on 30 April 19-4:

Capital £18,900; Loan from T. Sasso £2,000; Creditors £1,600; Fixtures £3,500; Motor Vehicle £4,200; Stock of Goods £4,950; Debtors £3,280; Cash at Bank £6,450; Cash in Hand £120.

During the first week of May 19-4 Sangster:

(i) Bought extra stock of goods £770 on credit.
(ii) One of the debtors paid us £280 in cash.
(iii) Bought extra fixtures by cheque £1,000.

You are to draw up a balance sheet as on 7 May 19-4 after the above transactions have been completed.

17.14X. C. Samuels has the following balance sheet as at 31 March 19-5:

Balance Sheet as at 31 March 19-5

Capital and Liabilities	£	*Assets*	£
Capital	14,400	Buildings	6,000
Loan from L. Stennett	2,000	Motor vehicle	4,000
Creditors	1,600	Stock of Goods	2,000
		Debtors	2,800
		Cash at bank	3,200
	18,000		18,000

The following transactions occur:

2 April Paid a cheque of £500 to a creditor.
8 April A debtor paid C. Samuels £300 by cheque.
10 April L. Stennett is repaid £1,000 by cheque.

Draw up a Balance Sheet on 10 April 19-5 after the transactions have been completed.

18

The Double Entry System of Book-keeping

Learning Objectives

At the end of this chapter you should be able to:

18A **Record financial transactions in the ledger.**

18B **Prepare a trial balance as at a given date.**

We have seen that each transaction affects two items. If we want to show the effect of every transaction when we are doing our book-keeping, we will have to show the effect of a transaction on each of the two items. For each transaction this means that a book-keeping entry will have to be made to show an increase or decrease of that item, and another entry to show the increase or decrease of the other item. From this you will probably be able to see that the term 'Double Entry System' of book-keeping is very appropriate, as each entry is made twice (double entry).

In Chapter 17 we drew up a new balance sheet after each transaction. You could do this easily if you had only a few transactions per day, but if there were hundreds of transactions each day it would become impossible for you to draw up hundreds of different balance sheets. You simply would not have enough time.

The double entry system has an account (meaning details of transactions in that item) for every asset, every liability and for capital. Thus there will be a Premises Account (for transactions in premises), a Motor Vans Accounts (for transactions in Motor Vans), and so on for every asset, liability and for capital.

Each account should be shown on a separate page. The double entry system divides each page into two halves. The left-hand side of each page is called the debit side, while the right-hand side is called the credit side. The title of each account is written across the top of the account at the centre.

You must not think that the words 'debit' and 'credit' in book-keeping mean the same as the words 'debit' or 'credit' in normal language usage. If you do, you will become very confused.

This is a page of an accounts book:

Title of account written here	
Left-hand side of the page. This is the 'debit' side.	Right-hand side of the page. This is the 'credit' side.

If you have to make an entry of £10 on the debit side of the account, the instructions could say 'debit the account with £10' or 'the account needs debiting with £10'.

In Chapter 17 transactions were to increase or decrease assets, liabilities or capital. Double entry rules for accounts are:

Accounts	*To record*	*Entry in the account*
Assets	an increase	Debit
	a decrease	Credit
Liabilities	an increase	Credit
	a decrease	Debit
Capital	an increase	Credit
	a decrease	Debit

Let us look once again at the accounting equation:

	Assets	=	*Liabilities*	*and*	*Capital*
To increase each item	Debit		Credit		Credit
To decrease each item	Credit		Debit		Debit

The double-entry rules for liabilities and capital are the same, but they are exactly the opposite as those for assets. This is because assets are on the opposite side of the equation and therefore follow opposite rules.
Looking at the accounts the rules will appear as:

Any asset account	
Increases	*Decreases*
+	−

Any liability account	
Decreases	*Increases*
−	+

Capital account	
Decreases	*Increases*
−	+

We haven't enough space in this book to put each account on a separate page, so we will have to list the accounts under each other. In a real firm at least one full page would be taken for each account.

The entry of a few transactions can now be attempted:

1. The proprietor starts the firm with £1,000 in cash on 1 August 19-6.

Effect	*Action*
(*a*) Increases the asset of cash in the firm	Debit the cash account
(*b*) Increases the capital	Credit the capital account

These are entered:

Cash

19-6	£			
Aug 1	1,000			

Capital

			19-6	£
			Aug 1	1,000

The date of the transaction has already been entered. Now there remains the description which is to be entered alongside the amount. The double entry to the item in the cash account is completed by an entry in the capital account, therefore the word 'Capital' will appear in the cash account. Similarly, the double entry to the item in the capital account is completed by an entry in the cash account, therefore the word 'Cash' will appear in the capital account.

It always used to be the custom to prefix the description on the debit side of the books with the word 'To', and to prefix the description on the credit side of the books with the word 'By'. These have now fallen into disuse in modern firms, and as they serve no useful purpose they will not be used in this book.

The finally completed accounts are therefore:

Cash

19-6	£			
Aug 1 Capital	1,000			

Capital

			19-6	£
			Aug 1 Cash	1,000

2. A motor van is bought for £275 cash on 2 August 19-6.

Effect	*Action*
(*a*) Decreases the asset of cash	Credit the cash account
(*b*) Increases the asset of motor van	Debit the motor van account

Cash

		19-6	£
		Aug 2 Motor van	275

Motor Van

19-6	£		
Aug 2 Cash	275		

3. Fixtures bought on credit from Catering Fitters £115 on 3 August 19-6.

Effect	*Action*
(*a*) Increase in the asset of fixtures	Debit fixtures account
(*b*) Increase in the liability of the firm to Catering Fitters	Credit Catering Fitters account

Fixtures

19-6	£		
Aug 3 Catering Fitters	115		

Catering Fitters

		19-6	£
		Aug 3 Fixtures	115

4. Paid the amount owing in cash to Catering Fitters on 17 August 19-6.

Effect	*Action*
(*a*) Decrease in the asset of cash	Credit the cash account
(*b*) Decrease in the liability of the firm to Catering Fitters	Debit Catering Fitters account

Cash

		19-6	£
		Aug 17 Catering Fitters	115

Catering Fitters

19-6	£		
Aug 17 Cash	115		

Transactions to date

Taking the transactions numbered 1 to 4 above, the records will now appear:

Cash

19-6	£	19-6	£
Aug 1 Capital	1,000	Aug 2 Motor van	275
		,, 17 Catering Fitters	115

Capital

		19-6	£
		Aug 1 Cash	1,000

Motor Van

19-6	£		
Aug 2 Cash	275		

Catering Fitters

19-6	£	19-6	£
Aug 17 Cash	115	Aug 3 Fixtures	115

Fixtures

19-6	£		
Aug 3 Catering Fitters	115		

A Further Worked Example

Now you have actually made some entries in accounts you are to go carefully through the following example. Make certain you can understand every entry.

		Transactions	*Effect*	*Action*
19-4				
May	1	Started a catering business putting £1,000 into a business bank account.	Increases asset of bank. Increases capital of proprietor.	Debit bank account. Credit capital account.
,,	3	Bought machinery on credit from Unique Machines £275.	Increases asset of machinery. Increases liability to Unique Machines.	Debit machinery account. Credit Unique Machines account.
,,	4	Withdrew £200 cash from the bank and placed it in the cash till.	Decreases asset of bank. Increases asset of cash.	Credit bank account. Debit cash account.
,,	7	Bought motor van paying in cash £180.	Decreases asset of cash. Increases asset of motor van.	Credit cash account. Debit motor van account.
,,	10	Sold some of machinery for £15 on credit to B. Barnes.	Decreases asset of machinery. Increases asset of money owing from B. Barnes.	Credit machinery account. Debit B. Barnes account.
,,	21	Returned some of machinery value £27 to Unique Machines.	Decreases asset of machinery. Decreases liability to Unique Machines.	Credit machinery account. Debit Unique Machines.
,,	28	B. Barnes pays the firm the amount owing, £15, by cheque.	Increases asset of bank. Decreases asset of money owing by B. Barnes.	Debit bank account. Credit B. Barnes account.
,,	30	Bought another motor van paying by cheque £420.	Decreases asset of bank. Increases asset of motor vans.	Credit bank account. Debit motor van account.
,,	31	Paid the amount of £248 to Unique Machines by cheque.	Decreases asset of bank. Decreases liability to Unique Machines.	Credit bank account. Debit Unique Machines.

In account form this is shown:

Bank

	£		£
May 1 Capital	1,000	May 4 Cash	200
,, 28 B. Barnes	15	,, 30 Motor van	420
		,, Unique Machines	248

Cash

	£		£
May 4 Bank	200	May 7 Motor van	180

Capital

			£
		May 1 Bank	1,000

Machinery

	£		£
May 3 Unique Machines	275	May 10 B. Barnes	15
		,, 21 Unique Machines	27

Motor Van

	£		
May 7 Cash	180		
,, 30 Bank	420		

Unique Machines

	£		£
May 21 Machinery	27	May 3 Machinery	275
,, 31 Bank	248		

B. Barnes

	£		£
May 10 Machinery	15	May 28 Bank	15

YOU SHOULD NOW ATTEMPT EXERCISES 18.1 TO 18.6X BEFORE READING FURTHER. SEE END OF CHAPTER.

The Asset of Stock

The stock of goods in a business is constantly changing because some is bought, some is sold, some is returned to the suppliers and some is returned by the firm's customers.

To keep a check on the movements of stock, an account is opened for each type of dealing in goods. Thus we will have the following accounts:

Purchases Account	For the purchase of goods
Sales Account	For the sale of goods
Returns Inwards Account	For goods returned to the firm by its customers
Returns Outwards Account	For goods returned by the firm to its suppliers

As stock is an asset, and these four accounts are all connected with this asset, the double entry rules are those used for assets.

We can now look at some entries:

Purchase of Stock on Credit (Food and Beverages)

1 August. Goods costing £165 are bought on credit from D. Henry.

First, the twofold effect of the transactions must be considered in order that the book-keeping entries can be worked out.

1. The asset of stock is increased. An increase in an asset needs a debit entry in an account. Here the account concerned is a stock account showing the particular movement of stock, in this case it is the 'Purchases' movement so that the account concerned must be the purchases account.
2. An increase in a liability. This is the liability of the firm to D. Henry in respect of the goods bought which have not yet been paid for. An increase in a liability needs a credit entry, so that to enter this aspect of the transaction a credit entry is made in D. Henry's account.

Purchases

	£		
Aug 1 D Henry	165		

D. Henry

			£
		Aug 1 Purchases	165

Purchases of Stock for Cash

2 August. Goods costing £22 are bought, cash being paid for them immediately.

1. The asset of stock is increased, so that a debit entry will be needed. The movement of stock is that of a purchase, so that it is the purchases account which needs debiting.
2. The asset of cash is decreased. To reduce an asset a credit entry is called for, and the asset is that of cash so that the cash account needs crediting.

Cash

			£
		Aug 2 Purchases	22

Purchases

	£		
Aug 2 Cash	22		

Sales of Stock on Credit (Food and Beverages Sales)

3 August. Sold goods on credit for £250 to J. Lee.

1. The asset of stock is decreased. For this a credit entry to reduce an asset is needed. The movement of stock is that of a 'Sale' so the account credited is the sales account.
2. An asset account is increased. This is the account showing that J. Lee is a debtor for the goods. The increase in the asset of debtors requires a debit and the debtor is J. Lee, so that the account concerned is that of J. Lee.

Sales

			£
		Aug 3 J. Lee	250

J. Lee

	£		
Aug 3 Sales	250		

Sales of Stock for Cash

4 August. Goods are sold for £55, cash being received immediately upon sale.

1. The asset of cash is increased. This needs a debit in the cash account to show this.
2. The asset of stock is reduced. The reduction of an asset requires a credit and the movement of stock is represented by 'Sales'. Thus the entry needed is a credit in the sales account.

Sales

			£
		Aug 4 Cash	55

Cash

	£		
Aug 4 Sales	55		

Cash sales in restaurants are usual, but credit sales arrangements are quite common as well.

Returns Inwards

5 August. Goods which had been previously sold to F. Lowe for £29 are now returned by him.

1. The asset of stock is increased by the goods returned. Thus a debit representing an increase of an asset is needed, and this time the movement of stock is that of 'Returns Inwards'. The entry therefore required is a debit in the returns inwards account.
2. A decrease in an asset. The debt of F. Lowe to the firm is now reduced, and to record this a credit is needed in F. Lowe's account.

Returns Inwards

	£		
Aug 5 F. Lowe	29		

F. Lowe

			£
		Aug 5 Returns Inwards	29

An alternative name for a Returns Inwards Account would be a Sales Returns Account.

In hotels and restaurants Returns Inwards are usually referred to as 'ALLOWANCES TO GUESTS'.

Returns Outwards

6 August. Goods previously bought for £96 are returned by the firm to K. Ho.

1. The asset of stock is decreased by the goods sent out. Thus a credit representing a reduction in an asset is needed, and the movement of stock is that of 'Returns Outwards' so that the entry will be a credit in the returns outwards account.
2. The liability of the firm to K. Ho is decreased by the value of the goods returned to him. The decrease in a liability needs a debit, this time in K. Ho's account.

Returns Outwards

			£
		Aug 6 K. Ho	96

K. Ho

	£		
Aug 6 Returns outwards	96		

An alternative name for a Returns Outwards Account would be a Purchases Returns Account.

A Worked Example

May 1 Bought goods on credit £68 from D. Small
,, 2 Bought goods on credit £77 from A. Lyon & Son
,, 5 Sold goods on credit to D. Hughes for £60
,, 6 Sold goods on credit to M. Spencer for £45
,, 10 Returned goods £15 to D. Small
,, 12 Goods bought for cash £100
,, 19 M. Spencer returned £16 goods to us
,, 21 Goods sold for cash £150
,, 22 Paid cash to D. Small £53
,, 30 D. Hughes paid the amount owing by him £60 in cash
,, 31 Bought goods on credit £64 from A. Lyon & Son.

Purchases

19-5	£		
May 1 D. Small	68		
,, 2 A. Lyon & Son	77		
,, 12 Cash	100		
,, 31 A. Lyon & Son	64		

Sales

		19-5	£
		May 5 D. Hughes	60
		,, 6 M. Spencer	45
		,, 21 Cash	150

Returns Outwards

		19-5	£
		May 10 D. Small	15

Returns Inwards

19-5	£		
May 19 M. Spencer	16		

D. Small

19-5	£	19-5	£
May 10 Returns outwards	15	May 1 Purchases	68
,, 22 Cash	53		

A. Lyon & Son

		19-5	£
		May 2 Purchases	77
		,, 31 Purchases	64

D. Hughes

19-5	£	19-5	£
May 5 Sales	60	May 30 Cash	60

M. Spencer

19-5	£	19-5	£
May 6 Sales	45	May 19 Returns inwards	16

Cash

19-5	£	19-5	£
May 21 Sales	150	May 12 Purchases	100
,, 30 D. Hughes	60	,, 22 D. Small	53

Special Meaning of 'Sales' and 'Purchases'

It must be emphasized that 'Sales' and 'Purchases' have a special meaning in accounting when compared to ordinary language usage.

'Purchases' in accounting means the purchase of those goods which the firm buys with the prime intention of selling.

In catering *only* goods classed as food and beverages will be included in 'Purchases'.

Similarly, 'Sales' means the sale of those goods in which the firm normally deals and were bought with the prime intention of resale. The word 'Sales' must never be given to the disposal of items other than food and beverages.

Failure to keep to these meanings would result in the different forms of stock account containing something other than goods sold or for resale. Obviously in the case of hotels, charges for accommodation will be classed as sales.

Comparison of Cash and Credit Transactions for Purchases and Sales

The difference between the records needed for cash and credit transactions can now be seen.

The complete set of entries for purchases of goods where they are paid for immediately needs entries:

1. Credit the cash account.
2. Debit the purchases account.

On the other hand the complete set of entries for the purchase ot goods on credit can be broken down into two stages. First, the purchase of the goods and second, the payment for them.

The first part is:

1. Debit the purchases account.
2. Credit the supplier's account.

While the second part is:

1. Credit the cash account.
2. Debit the supplier's account.

The difference can now be seen in that with the cash purchase no record is kept of the supplier's account. This is because cash passes immediately and therefore there is no need to keep a check of indebtedness to a supplier. On the other hand, in the credit purchase the records should reveal the identity of the supplier to whom the firm is indebted until payment is made.

A study of cash sales and credit sales will reveal a similar difference.

Cash Sales	*Credit Sales*
Complete entry:	First part:
Debit cash account	Debit customer's account
Credit sales account	Credit sales account
	Second part:
	Debit cash account
	Credit customer's account

YOU SHOULD NOW ATTEMPT EXERCISES 18.6 TO 18.9X BEFORE READING FURTHER. SEE END OF CHAPTER.

The Double Entry System for Expenses. The Effect of Profit or Loss on Capital

On 1 January the assets and liabilities of a firm are:

Assets: Fixtures £10,000, Stock £7,000,
Cash at Bank £3,000.

Liabilities: Creditors £2,000

The Capital is found by the formula

Assets − Liabilities = Capital.

In this case capital works out at £10,000 + £7,000 + £3,000 − £2,000 = £18,000.

During January the whole of the £7,000 stock is sold for £11,000 cash. On the 31 January the assets and liabilities have become:

Assets: Fixtures £10,000, Stock Nil, Cash at Bank £14,000.

Creditors: Creditors £2,000

The capital can be calculated:

Assets £10,000 + £14,000 − liabilities £2,000 = £22,000

It can be seen that capital has increased from £18,000 to £22,000 = £4,000 increase because the £7,000 stock was sold for £11,000, a profit of £4,000. Profit therefore increases capital.

Old Capital + Profit = New Capital
£18,000 + £4,000 = £22,000

On the other hand a loss would reduce the capital so that it would become:

Old Capital − Loss = New Capital

Profit or Loss and Sales

Profit will be made when goods are sold at more than cost price, whilst the opposite will mean a loss.

Profit or Loss and Expenses

While the firm is selling its goods there will be expenses other than the cost of the goods being sold. Every firm has other expenses such as rent, salaries, wages, telephone expenses, motor expenses and so on. Every extra £1 of expenses will mean £1 less profit.

It would be possible simply to have one account with the title 'Expenses Account'. However, rather than just know that the overall total of expenses was £50,000 it would be more useful if we knew exactly how much of that figure was for Rent, how much for Motor Expenses and so on. An expense account is therefore opened for each type of expense.

Debit or Credit

We have to decide whether expense accounts are to be debited or credited with the costs involved. Assets involve expenditure by the firm and are shown as debit entries. Expenses also involve expenditure by the firm and therefore should also be debit entries.

You could look at it another way. An expense will reduce profit which will reduce capital. Reductions in capital needs debits, and therefore the expense accounts should be debit entries.

Effect of Transactions

A few illustrations will demonstrate the double entry required.

1. The rent of £20 is paid in cash.

Here the twofold effect is:

(*a*) The asset of cash is decreased. This means crediting the cash account to show the decrease of the asset.

(*b*) The total of the expenses of rent is increased. As expense entries are shown as debits, and the expense is rent, so the action required is the debiting of the rent account.

Summary: Credit the cash account with £20.
Debit the rent account with £20.

2. Motor expenses are paid by cheque £55.

The twofold effect is:

(*a*) The asset of money in the bank is decreased. This means crediting the bank account to show the decrease of the asset.

(*b*) The total of the motor expenses paid is increased. To increase an expenses account needs a debit, so the action required is to debit the motor expenses account.

Summary: Credit the bank account with £55
Debit the motor expenses account with £55.

3. £60 cash is paid for telephone bills.
(*a*) The asset of cash is decreased. This needs a credit in the cash account to decrease the asset.
(*b*) The total of telephone expenses is increased. Expenses are shown by a debit entry, therefore to increase the expense account in question the action required is to debit the telephone expenses account.
Summary: Credit the cash account with £60.
Debit telephone expenses account with £60.

It is now possible to study the effects of some more transactions showing the results in the form of a table:

		Increase	*Action*	*Decrease*	*Action*
19-6					
June 1	Paid for postage stamps by cash £5	Expense of postages	Debit postages account	Asset of cash	Credit cash account
,, 2	Paid for advertising by cheque £29	Expense of advertising	Debit advertis-ing account	Asset of bank	Credit bank account
,, 3	Paid wages by cash £90	Expense of wages	Debit wages account	Asset of cash	Credit cash account
,, 4	Paid insurance by cheque £42	Expense of insurance	Debit insurance account	Asset of bank	Credit bank account

The above four examples can now be shown in account form:

Cash

		19-6	£
		June 1 Postages	5
		,, 3 Wages	90

Bank

		19-6	£
		June 2 Advertising	29
		,, 4 Insurance	42

Advertising

19-6	£		
June 2 Bank	29		

Insurance

19-6	£		
June 4 Bank	42		

Postages

19-6	£		
June 1 Cash	5		

Wages

19-6	£		
June 3 Cash	90		

It is clear that from time to time the proprietor will want to take cash out of the business for his private use. In fact he will sometimes take goods. This will be dealt with later. However, whether the withdrawals are cash or goods they are known as 'Drawings'. Drawings in fact decrease the claim of the proprietor against the resources of the business, in other words they reduce the amount of capital. According to the way in which the accounting formula is represented by debits and credits the decrease of capital needs a debit entry in the capital account. However, the capital account is a very important account, and to save it from getting full up with all the minor details a 'Drawings Account' is opened and the debits are entered there.

An example will demonstrate the twofold effect of cash withdrawals from the business.

Example: 25 August 19-6. Proprietor takes £50 cash out of the business for his own use.

Effect	*Action*
1. Capital is decreased by £50	Debit the drawings account £50
2. Cash is decreased by £50	Credit the cash account £50

Cash

		19-6	£
		Aug 25 Drawings	50

Drawings

19-6	£		
Aug 25 Cash	50		

YOU SHOULD NOW ATTEMPT EXERCISES 18.10 AND 18.11X BEFORE READING FURTHER. SEE END OF CHAPTER.

Balancing off Accounts

What you have been reading about so far is the recording of transactions in the books by means of debit and credit entries. Every so often we will have to look at each account to see what is revealed by the entries.

Probably the most obvious reason for this is to find out how much our customers owe us in respect of meals we have sold to them on credit. In most firms the custom is that this should be done at the end of each month. Let us look at the account of one of our customers, D. Knight, at the end of a month.

D. Knight

19-6	£	19-6	£
Aug 1 Sales	158	Aug 28 Cash	158
,, 15 ,,	206		
,, 30 ,,	118		

You can see that Knight still owed £206 + £118 = £324 at the end of 31 August 19-6. Our firm will thus start its business for the next month on 1 September 19-6 with that amount owing to it. To show that our firm is carrying these outstanding items from one period to the next one, the 'balance' on each account is found. The 'balance' is the accounting term meaning the arithmetical difference between the two sides of an account.

To balance off an account:

(i) First add up the side of the account having the greatest total.
(ii) Second, insert the difference (the balance) on the other side of the account so as to make the totals of each side equal. When doing this, ensure that the two totals are written on a level with each other.
(iii) The balance has now been entered in the period which has finished, it now has to be entered on the other side of the books to ensure that double-entry of the item is carried out. This is done by making the second entry on the next line under the totals. Let us see Knight's account now 'balanced' off:

D. Knight

19-6	£	19-6	£
Aug 1 Sales	158	Aug 28 Cash	158
,, 15 ,,	206	,, 31 Balance carried down	324
,, 30 ,,	118		
	482		482
Sept 1 Balance brought down	324		

We can now look at another account prior to balancing:

H. Henry

19-6		£	19-6		£
Aug 5 Sales		300	Aug 25 Returns Inwards		50
,, 25 Sales		540	,, 29 Bank		250

This time, and we will always do this in future, for it will save us from unnecessary writing, we will abbreviate 'carried down' to 'c/d' and 'brought down' to 'b/d'.

H. Henry

19-6		£	19-6		£
Aug 5 Sales		300	Aug 24 Returns Inwards		50
,, 28 Sales		540	,, 29 Bank		250
			,, 31 Balance	c/d	540
		840			840
Sept 1 Balance	b/d	540			

Notes:

1. The date given to Balance c/d is the last day of the period which is finishing, and Balance b/d is given the opening date of the next period.
2. As the total of the debit side originally exceeded the total of the credit side, the balance is said to be a debit balance. This being a personal account (for a person), the person concerned is said to be debtor – the accounting term for anyone who owes money to the firm. The use of the term debtor for a person whose account has a debit balance can again thus be seen.

If accounts contain only one entry it is unnecessary to enter the total. A double line ruled under the entry will mean that the entry is its own total. For example:

B. Walters

19-6		£	19-6		£
Aug 18 Sales		51	Aug 31 Balance	c/d	51
Sept 1 Balance	b/d	51			

If an account contains only one entry on each side which are equal to one another, totals are again unnecessary. For example:

D. Hylton

19-6		£	19-6		£
Aug 6 Sales		214	Aug 12 Bank		214

Credit Balances

Exactly the same principles will apply when the balances are carried down to the credit side. We can look at two accounts of our suppliers which are to be balanced off.

E. Williams

19-6		£	19-6		£
Aug 21 Sales		100	Aug 2 Purchases		248
			,, 18 ,,		116

K. Patterson

19-6		£	19-6		£
Aug 14 Returns Outwards		20	Aug 8 Purchases		620
,, 28 Bank		600	,, 15 Purchases		200

When balanced these will appear as:

E. Williams

19-6		£	19-6		£
Aug 21 Bank		100	Aug 2 Purchases		248
,, 31 Balance	c/d	264	,, 18 ,,		116
		364			364
			Sept 1 Balance	b/d	264

K. Patterson

19-6		£	19-6		£
Aug 14 Returns Outwards		20	Aug 8 Purchases		620
,, 28 Bank		600	,, 15 Purchases		200
,, 31 Balance	c/d	200			
		820			820
			Sept 1 Balance	b/d	200

Computers and Book-keeping Machinery

Throughout the main part of this book the type of account used shows the left-hand side of the account as the debit side, and the right-hand side is shown as the credit side. However, when most computers or book-keeping equipment is used the style of the ledger account is different. It appears as three columns of figures, being one column for debit entries, another column for credit entries, and the last column for the balance. If you have a current account at a bank your bank statements will normally be shown using this method.

The accounts used in this chapter will now be redrafted to show the ledger accounts drawn up in this way.

D. Knight

	Debit	**Credit**	**Balance (and whether debit or credit)**
19-6	£	£	£
Aug 1 Sales	158		158 Dr
,, 15 ,,	206		364 Dr
,, 28 Cash		158	206 Dr
,, 31 Sales	118		324 Dr

H. Henry

	Debit	*Credit*	*Balance*
19-6	£	£	£
Aug 5 Sales	300		300 Dr
,, 24 Returns		50	250 Dr
,, 28 Sales	540		790 Dr
,, 29 Bank		250	540 Dr

B. Walters

	Debit	*Credit*	*Balance*
19-6	£	£	£
Aug 18 Sales	51		51 Dr

D. Hylton

	Debit	*Credit*	*Balance*
19-6	£	£	£
Aug 6 Sales	214		214 Dr
,, 12 Bank		214	0

E. Williams

		Debit	Credit	Balance
19-6		£	£	£
Aug	2 Purchases		248	248 Cr
,,	18 Purchases		116	364 Cr
,,	21 Bank	100		264 Cr

K. Patterson

		Debit	Credit	Balance
19-6		£	£	£
Aug	8 Purchases		620	620 Cr
,,	14 Returns	20		600 Cr
,,	15 Purchases		200	800 Cr
,,	28 Bank	600		200 Cr

It will be noticed that the balance is calculated afresh after every entry. This can be done quite simply when using book-keeping machinery or a computer because it is the machine which automatically calculates the new balance. However, when manual methods are in use it is often too laborious to have to calculate a new balance after each entry, and it also means that the greater the number of calculations the greater the possible number of errors. For these reasons it is usual for students to use two-sided accounts. However, it is important to note that there is no difference in principle, the final balances are the same using either method.

The Trial Balance

You have already seen that the method of book-keeping in use is that of the double entry method. This means:

1. For each debit entry there is a corresponding credit entry.
2. For every credit entry there is a corresponding debit entry.

All the items recorded in all the accounts on the debit side should equal in *total* all the items recorded on the credit side of the books. To see if the two totals are equal, or in accounting terminology to see if the two sides of the books 'balance', a Trial Balance may be drawn up periodically.

A form of a trial balance could be drawn up by listing all the accounts and adding together all the debit entries, at the same time adding together all the credit entries. Using the worked exercise on pages 174 and 175 such a trial balance would appear as follows, bearing in mind that it would not be drawn up until after all the entries had been made, and will therefore be dated as on 31 May 19-6.

Trial Balance as on 31 May 19–6

	Dr	Cr
	£	£
Purchases	309	
Sales		255
Returns outwards		15
Returns inwards	16	
D. Small	68	68
A. Lyon & Son		141
D. Hughes	60	60
M. Spencer	45	16
Cash	210	153
	708	708

However, this is not the normal method of drawing up a trial balance, but it is the easiest to understand in the first instance. Usually, a trial balance is a list of balances only, arranged as to whether they are debit balances or credit balances. If the above trial balance had been drawn up using the conventional balances method it would have appeared as follows:

Trial Balance as on 31 May 19–6

	Dr	Cr
	£	£
Purchases	309	
Sales		255
Returns outwards		15
Returns inwards	16	
A. Lyon and Son		141
M. Spencer	29	
Cash	57	
	411	411

Here the two sides also 'balance'. The sums of £68 in D. Small's account, £60 in D. Hughes' account, £16 in M. Spencer's account and £153 in the cash account have however been cancelled out from each side of these accounts by virtue of taking only the balances instead of totals. As equal amounts have been cancelled from each side, £297 in all, the new totals should still equal one another, as in fact they do at £411.

This latter form of trial balance is the easiest to extract when there are more than a few transactions during the period, also the balances are either used later when the profits are being calculated, or else appear in a balance sheet, so that it is not just for ascertaining whether or not errors have been made that trial balances are extracted.

You should now be able to attempt the remainder of the exercises at the end of this chapter.

Exercises

18.1. Complete the following table:

	Account to be debited	Account to be debited
(*a*) Bought office machinery on credit from D. Isaacs Ltd.		
(*b*) The proprietor paid a creditor, C. Jones, from his private monies outside the firm		
(*c*) A debtor, N. Fox, paid us in cash.		
(*d*) Repaid part of loan from P. Exeter by cheque		
(*e*) Returned some of office machinery to D. Isaacs Ltd.		
(*f*) A debtor, N. Lyn, paid us by cheque.		
(*g*) Bought motor van by cash.		

18.2X. Complete the following table showing which accounts are to be debited and which to be credited:

	Account to be debited	Account to be credited
(*a*) Bought motor lorry for cash		
(*b*) Paid creditor, T. Lue, by cheque		
(*c*) Repaid P. Lopez's loan by cash		
(*d*) Sold motor lorry for cash		
(*e*) Bought office machinery on credit from Ultra Ltd		
(*f*) A debtor, A. Hill, pays us by cash		
(*g*) A debtor, J. Cross, pays us by cheque		
(*h*) Proprietor puts a further amount into the business by cheque		
(*i*) A loan of £200 in cash is received from L. Lowe		
(*j*) Paid a creditor, D. Lord, by cash.		

18.3. You are required to open the asset and liability and capital accounts and record the following transactions for June 19-4 in the records of C. Williams.

19-4

June 1 Started business with £2,000 in cash.
,, 2 Paid £1,800 of the opening cash into a bank account for the business
,, 5 Bought office furniture on credit from Betta-Built Ltd. for £120
,, 8 Bought a motor van paying by cheque £950
,, 12 Bought kitchen machinery from Evans & Sons on credit £560
,, 18 Returned faulty office furniture costing £62 to Betta-Built Ltd
,, 25 Sold some of the kitchen machinery for £75 cash
,, 26 Paid amount owing to Betta-Built Ltd £58 by cheque
,, 28 Took £100 out of the bank and put it in the cash till
,, 30 J. Smith lent us £500 – giving us the money by cheque.

18.4. Write up the various accounts needed in the books of S. Russell to record the following transactions:

19-4

April 1 Opened business with £10,000 in the bank
,, 3 Bought office equipment £700 on credit from J. Smith Ltd
,, 6 Bought motor van paying by cheque £3,000
,, 8 Borrowed £1,000 from H. Thompson – he gave us the money by cheque
,, 11 Russell put further capital into the firm in the form of cash £500
,, 12 Paid £350 of the cash in hand into the bank account
,, 15 Returned some of the office equipment costing £200 – it was faulty – to J. Smith Ltd.
,, 17 Bought more office equipment, paying by cash £50
,, 19 Sold the motor van, as it had proved unsuitable, to R. Jones for £3,000. R. Jones will settle for this by three payments later this month
,, 21 Received a loan in cash from J. Hawkins £400
,, 22 R. Jones paid us a cheque for £1,000
,, 23 Bought a suitable motor van £3,600 on credit from Phillips Garages
,, 26 R. Jones paid us a cheque for £1,800
,, 28 Paid £2,000 by cheque to Phillips Garages Ltd
,, 30 R. Jones paid us cash £200.

18.5X. Write up the asset, capital and liability accounts in the books of C. Williams to record the following transactions:

19-5

June 1 Started business with £5,000 in the bank
,, 2 Bought motor van paying cheque £1,200
,, 5 Bought office fixtures £400 on credit from Young Ltd.
,, 8 Bought motor van on credit from Super Motors £800
,, 12 Took £100 out of the bank and put it into the cash till
,, 15 Bought office fixtures paying by cash £60
,, 19 Paid Super Motors a cheque for £800
,, 21 A loan of £1,000 cash is received from J. Jarvis
,, 25 Paid £800 of the cash in hand into the bank account
,, 30 Bought more office fixtures paying by cheque £300.

18.6X. Write up the accounts to record the following transactions:

19-3

March 1 Started business with £1,000 cash
,, 2 Received a loan of £5,000 from M. Chow by cheque, a bank account being opened and the cheque paid into it
,, 3 Bought machinery for cash £60
,, 5 Bought display equipment on credit from Better-View Machines £550
,, 8 Took £300 out of the bank and put it into the cash till
,, 15 Repaid part of Chow's loan by cheque £800
,, 17 Paid amount owing to Better-View Machines £550 by cheque
,, 24 Repaid part of Chow's loan by cash £100
,, 31 Bought additional machinery, this time on credit from D. Smith for £500.

18.7. You are required to write up the following in the books:

19-4

July 1 Started business with £500 cash
,, 3 Bought goods for cash £85
,, 7 Bought goods on credit £116 from E. Morgan
,, 10 Sold goods for cash £42
,, 14 Returned goods to E. Morgan £28
,, 18 Bought goods on credit £98 from A. Moses
,, 21 Returned goods to A. Moses £19
,, 24 Sold goods to A. Knight £55 on credit
,, 25 Paid E. Morgan's account by cash £88
,, 31 A. Knight paid us his account in cash £55.

18.8. You are to enter the following in the accounts needed:

19-6

Aug 1 Started business with £1,000 cash
,, 2 Paid £900 of the opening cash into the bank
,, 4 Bought goods on credit £78 from S. Holmes
,, 5 Bought a motor van by cheque £500
,, 7 Bought goods for cash £55
,, 10 Sold goods on credit £98 to D. Moore
,, 12 Returned goods to S. Holmes £18
,, 19 Sold goods for cash £28
,, 22 Bought fixtures on credit from Kingston Equipment Co. £150
,, 24 D. Watson lent us £100 paying us the money by cheque
,, 29 We paid S. Holmes his account by cheque £60
,, 31 We paid Kingston Equipment Co by cheque £150.

18.9X. Enter up the following transactions in the records:

19-5

May 1 Started business with £2,000 in the bank
,, 2 Bought goods on credit from C. Shaw £900
,, 3 Bought goods on credit from F. Hughes £250
,, 5 Sold goods for cash £180
,, 6 We returned goods to C. Shaw £40
,, 8 Bought goods on credit from F. Hughes £190
,, 10 Sold goods on credit to G. Wood £390
,, 12 Sold goods for cash £210
,, 18 Took £300 of the cash and paid it into the bank
,, 21 Bought machinery by cheque £550
,, 22 Sold goods on credit to L. Moore £220
,, 23 G. Wood returned goods to us £140
,, 25 L. Moore returned goods to us £10
,, 28 We returned goods to F. Hughes £30
,, 29 We paid Shaw by cheque £860
,, 31 Bought machinery on credit from D. Lee £270.

18.10. You are to enter the following transactions, completing double-entry in the books for the month of May 19-7:

19-7
May 1 Started business with £2,000 in the bank
,, 2 Purchased goods £175 on credit from M. Mills
,, 3 Bought fixtures and fittings £150 paying by cheque
,, 5 Sold goods for cash £275
,, 6 Bought goods on credit £114 from S. Wong
,, 10 Paid rent by cash £15
,, 12 Bought stationery £27, paying by cash
,, 18 Goods returned to M. Mills £23
,, 21 Let off part of the premises receiving rent by cheque £5
,, 23 Sold goods on credit to U. Henry for £77
,, 24 Bought a motor van paying by cheque £300
,, 30 Paid the month's wages by cash £117
,, 31 The proprietor took cash for himself £44.

18.11X. Write up the following transactions in the records of D. DaSilva:

Feb 1 Started business with £3,000 in the bank and £500 cash
,, 2 Bought goods on credit from: T. Small £250; C. Todd £190; V. Ryan £180.
,, 3 Bought goods for cash £230
,, 4 Paid rent in cash £10
,, 5 Bought stationery paying by cheque £49
,, 6 Sold goods on credit to: C. Crooks £140; R. Rogers £100; B. Grant £240
,, 7 Paid wages in cash £80
,, 10 We returned goods to C. Todd £60
,, 11 Paid rent in cash £10
,, 13 R. Rogers returns goods to us £20
,, 15 Sold goods on credit to: J. Burns £90; J. Smart £130; N. Thorn £170
,, 16 Paid rates by cheque £130
,, 18 Paid insurance in cash £40
,, 19 Paid rent by cheque £10
,, 20 Bought motor van on credit from C. White £600
,, 21 Paid motor expenses in cash £6
,, 23 Paid wages in cash £90
,, 24 Received part of amount owing from B. Grant by cheque £200
,, 28 Received refund of rates £10 by cheque
,, 28 Paid following by cheque: T. Small £250; C. Todd £130; C. White £600.

18.12. You are to enter up the necessary amounts for the month of May from the following details, and then balance off the accounts and extract a trial balance as at 31 May 19-6:

19-6
May 1 Started firm with capital in cash of £250
,, 2 Bought goods on credit from the following persons: D. Ellis £54; C. Mendez £87; K. Gibson £25; D. Booth £76; L. Lowe £64.
,, 4 Sold goods on credit to: C. Bailey £43 B. Hughes £62; H. Spencer £176
,, 6 Paid rent by cash £12
,, 9 Bailey paid us his account by cheque £43
,, 10 H. Spencer paid us £150 by cheque
,, 12 We paid the following by cheque: K. Gibson £25; D. Ellis £54
,, 15 Paid carriage by cash £23
,, 18 Bought goods on credit from C. Mendez £43; D. Booth £110
,, 21 Sold goods on credit to B. Hughes £67
,, 31 Paid rent by cheque £18.

18.13. Enter up the books from the following details for the month of March, and extract a trial balance as at 31 March 19-4:

19-6

March 1 Started business with £800 in the bank
,, 2 Bought goods on credit from the following persons: K. Henriques £76; M. Hyatt £27; T. Braham £56
,, 5 Cash sales £87
,, 6 Paid wages in cash £14
,, 7 Sold goods on credit to: H. Elliott £35; L. Lindo £42; J. Carvalho £72
,, 9 Bought goods for cash £46
,, 10 Bought goods on credit from: M. Hyatt £57; T. Braham £98
,, 12 Paid wages in cash £14
,, 13 Sold goods on credit to: L. Lane £32; J. Carvalho £23
,, 15 Bought fixtures on credit from Betta Ltd £50
,, 17 Paid M. Hyatt by cheque £84
,, 18 We returned goods to T. Braham £20
,, 21 Paid Betta Ltd a cheque for £50
,, 24 J. Carvalho paid us his account by cheque £95
,, 27 We returned goods to K. Henriques £24
,, 30 J. King lent us £60 by cash
,, 31 Bought a motor van paying by cheque £400.

18.14X. Record the following details for the month of November 19-3 and extract a trial balance as at 30 November:

Nov 1 Started with £5,000 in the bank
,, 3 Bought goods on credit from T. Henriques £160; J. Smith £230; W. Rogers £400; P. Bonitto £310
,, 5 Cash sales £240
,, 6 Paid rent by cheque £20
,, 7 Paid rates by cheque £190
,, 11 Sold goods on credit to: L. Matthews £48; K. Alberga £32; R. Hall £1,170
,, 17 Paid wages by cash £40
,, 18 We returned goods to: T. Henriques £14; P. Bonitto £20
,, 19 Bought goods on credit from: P. Bonnitto £80; W. Rogers £270; D. Diaz £130
,, 20 Goods were returned to us: K. Alberga £2; L. Matthews £4
,, 21 Bought motor van on credit from U. Z. Motors £500
,, 23 We paid the following by cheque: T. Henriques £146; J. Smith £230; W. Rogers £300
,, 25 Bought another motor van, paying by cheque immediately £700
,, 26 Received a loan of £400 cash from A. Williams
,, 28 Received cheques from: L. Matthews £44; L. Alberga £30
,, 30 Proprietor brings a further £300 into the business, by a payment into the business bank account

19

The Preparation of Final Accounts

Learning Objectives

At the end of this chapter you should be able to:

19A Make adjustments for accrued expenditure, payments in advance and provisions.

19B Prepare a Trading and Profit and Loss Account and a Balance Sheet of a sole trader from a trial balance and adjustments.

You have seen that there can be quite a few reasons why book-keeping records may be kept. One thing is certain, and that is that one of the main reasons will be that of providing the information from which the proprietor will be able to calculate profits earned by the business, or the losses incurred by it.

The profits are calculated by drawing up a special account called a Trading and Profit and Loss Account.

One of the most important uses of the Trading and Profit and Loss Accounts is the comparison of the results achieved with those of past periods. When doing this it is extremely useful for caterers, as you will see more fully later, to calculate two sorts of profits. These are:

Gross Profit (calculated in the Trading Account)	This is the excess of sales over the cost of goods sold in the period. (i.e. cost of food and beverages used)
Net Profit (calculated in the Profit and Loss Account)	What remains after all other costs used up in the period have been deducted from the gross profit.

The trial balance of Stephens Café, Exhibit 19.1, drawn up as on 31 December 19-5 after the completion of his first year in business can now be looked at.

Exhibit 19.1

Stephens Café
Trial Balance as on 31 December 19-5

	Dr	*Cr*
	£	£
Sales		3,850
Purchases	2,900	
Rent	240	
Lighting	150	
General expenses	60	
Fixtures and fittings	500	
Debtors	680	
Creditors		910
Bank	1,510	
Cash	20	
Drawings	700	
Capital		3,000
Wages	1,000	
	7,760	7,760

We can now start to draw up the trading account using the information in Exhibit 19.1, but we will soon find that we have a problem. Sales less cost of goods sold is the definition of gross profit. The figure of sales is given as £3,850, but we are not told the cost of goods sold.

You may well possibly, as a first thought, imagine that Purchases £2,900 would be the figure for the cost of goods sold. Certainly, if all the goods bought had been sold, then purchases and cost of goods sold would mean exactly the same thing. But very few businesses immediately sell all the food and drink they buy. They will have unsold goods, called stock.

To calculate cost of goods sold we need to find the value of the stock of unsold goods. This cannot be discovered by looking at the book-keeping records. The only way that Stephens Café can do this is by a stocktaking on 31 December 19-5 after the business of that day. By stocktaking is meant that he would make a list of all the unsold food and beverages and then find out their value. The value he would normally place on them would be the cost price of the goods. Assume that this was £1,360. The cost of purchases less the cost of unsold goods would equal the cost of goods sold, ignoring losses by theft or wastage. This figure would then be deducted from the figure of sales to find the gross profit.

Stephens could perform this calculation arithmetically:

Sales – Cost of goods sold (Purchases – unsold stock)	= Gross Profit
£3,850 – (£2,900 – £1,360)	= £2,310

This however is not performing the task by using double entry accounts. In double entry the balance of the sales account is transferred to the trading account by debiting the sales account (thus closing it) and crediting the trading account. The balance of the purchases account would then be transferred by crediting the purchases account (thus closing it) and debiting the trading account. Now the accounts connected with stock movements have been closed, and accounts are being drawn up to a point in time, in this case 31 December 19-5. At this point of time Stephens has an asset, namely stock (of unsold goods), for which no account exists. This must be corrected by opening a stock account and debiting the amount of the asset to it. Now as already stated, the closing stock needs to be brought into the calculation of the gross profit, and the calculation of the gross profit is effected in the trading account. Therefore the credit for the closing stock should be in the trading account thus completing the double entry.

It is now usual for the trading and profit and loss accounts to be shown under one combined heading, the trading account being the top section and the profit and loss account being the lower section of this combined account. This account is often referred to as 'Revenue Account' or 'Profit and Loss Statement'.

Stephens Café

Trading and Profit and Loss Account for the year ended 31 December 19-5

	£		£
Purchases	2,900	Sales	3,850
Gross profit c/d	2,310	Closing stock	1,360
	5,210		5,210
		Gross profit b/d	2,310

The balance shown on the trading account is shown as gross profit rather than being described as a balance. When found the gross profit is carried down to the profit and loss section of the account.

The accounts so far used appear as follows:

Sales

19-5	£	19-5	£
Dec 31 Trading A/c	3,850	Dec 31 Balance b/d	3,850

Purchases

19-5	£	19-5	£
Dec 31 Balance b/d	2,900	Dec 31 Trading A/c	2,900

Stock

19-5	£		
Dec 31 Trading A/c	1,360		

The entry of the Closing Stock on the credit side of the trading and profit and loss account is in effect a deduction from the purchases on the debit side. In present-day accounting it is usual to find the closing stock actually shown as a deduction from the purchases on the debit side, and the figure then disclosed being described as 'cost of goods sold'. This is illustrated in Exhibit 19.2.

The costs used up in the year, in other words the expenses of the year, are transferred to the debit of the profit and loss account. It may also be thought, quite rightly so, that, as the fixtures and fittings have been used during the year with the subsequent deterioration of the asset, that something should be changed for this use. The methods for doing this are left until later.

The revised trading account with the addition of the profit and loss account is shown as Exhibit 19.2.

Exhibit 19.2

Stephens Café

Trading and Profit and Loss Account for the year ended 31 December 19-6

	£		£
Purchases	2,900	Sales	3,850
Less Closing stock	1,360		
Cost of goods sold	1,540		
Gross Profit c/d	2,310		
	3,850		3,850
Rent	240	Gross profit b/d	2,310
Lighting	150		
General expenses	60		
Wages	1,000		
Net profit	860		
	2,310		2,310

The expense accounts closed off will now appear as:

Rent

19-5	£	19-5	£
Dec 31 Balance b/d	240	Dec 31 Profit and Loss A/c	240

Lighting Expenses

19-5	£	19-5	£
Dec 31 Balance b/d	150	Dec 31 Profit and Loss A/c	150

General Expenses

19-5	£	19-5	£
Dec 31 Balance b/d	60	Dec 31 Profit and Loss A/c	60

Wages

19-5	£	19-5	£
Dec 31 Balance b/d	1,000	Dec 31 Profit and Loss A/c	1,000

Net profit increases the capital of the proprietor. The credit entry for the net profit is therefore in the capital account. Drawings reduce the capital, and accordingly at the end of each period the drawings are transferred to the debit side of the capital account. The capital account, showing these transfers, and the drawings account now closed are as follows:

Capital

19-5	£	19-5	£
Dec 31 Drawings	700	Jan 1 Cash	3,000
,, 31 Balance c/d	3,160	Dec 31 Net Profit from Profit and Loss A/c	860
	3,860		3,860
		19-6	
		Jan 1 Balance b/d	3,160

Drawings

19-5	£	19-5	£
Dec 31 Balance b/d	700	Dec 31 Capital	700

You will have noticed that not all the items in the trial balance have been used in the Trading and Profit and Loss Account. The remaining balances are assets or liabilities or capital, they are not expenses or sales. We are going to use these later when we draw up a balance sheet, for as you have seen in Chapter 17, assets, liabilities and capital are contained in balance sheets.

In Exhibit 19.3, although it is not necessary to redraft the trial balance after the trading and profit and loss accounts have been prepared, it will be useful to do so in order to establish which balances still remain in the books. The first thing to notice is that the stock account, not originally in the trial balance, is in the redrafted trial balance, as the item was not created as a balance in the books until the trading account was prepared. These balances will be used by us when we start to look at the balance sheets.

Exhibit 19.3

Stephens Café
Trial Balance as on 31 December 19-5
(after Trading and Profit and Loss Accounts completed)

	Dr	*Cr*
	£	£
Fixtures and fittings	500	
Debtors	680	
Creditors		910
Stock	1,360	
Bank	1,510	
Cash	20	
Capital		3,160
	4,070	4,070

Balance Sheets

After the trading and profit and loss accounts have been completed, a statement is drawn up in which the remaining balances in the books are arranged according to whether they are asset balances or liability or capital balances. This statement is called a balance sheet. The assets are shown on the left-hand side and the liabilities on the right-hand side.

It is very important to know that the balance sheet is not part of the double-entry system. This contrasts with the Trading and Profit and Loss Account which is part of double-entry. The use of the word 'account' indicates that it is part of double-entry.

You saw earlier in this chapter that when we took sales, purchases and the various expenses into the profit calculations we actually made an entry in each account showing that the item had been transferred to the Trading Account or the Profit and Loss Account. The balance sheet however is not part of double-entry, it is simply a list of the balances remaining after the Trading and Profit and Loss Accounts have been prepared. Therefore we do *not* transfer items from accounts to the balance sheet, and accordingly we do *not* make any entries in the various accounts when we draw up a balance sheet.

Let us now look again at Exhibit 19.3, the trial balance of Stephens Café as on 31 December 19-5 *after* the Trading and Profit and Loss Account had been prepared.

We can now draw up a balance sheet as at 31 December 19-5, Exhibit 19.4. You saw examples of balance sheets earlier. We will not worry at this point whether or not the balance sheet is set out in good style.

Exhibit 19.4

Stephens Café

Balance Sheet as at 31 December 19-5

Assets	£	*Capital and liabilities*	£
Fixtures and fittings	500	Capital	3,160
Stock	1,360	Creditors	910
Debtors	680		
Bank	1,510		
Cash	20		
	4,070		4,070

Remember, all of the balances per Exhibit 19.3 still remain in the accounts, *no* entries were made in the accounts for the purpose of drawing up the balance sheet.

Balance Sheet Layout

In balance sheets we do not want all the items shown in any order. We would really want them displayed so that desirable information could easily be seen.

For people such as bank managers, accountants and investors who look at a lot of different balance sheets, we would want to keep to a set pattern so as to enable comparison of balance sheets to be made easier. What you are about to look at is a suggested method for displaying items in balance sheets.

Let us look at the assets side first. We are going to show the assets under two headings, Fixed Assets and Current Assets.

Assets are called Fixed Assets when they are of long life, are to be used in the business and were *not* bought with the main purpose of resale. Examples are buildings, machinery, motor vehicles and fixtures and fittings.

On the other hand, assets are called Current Assets when they represent cash or are primarily for conversion into cash or have a short life. An example of a short-lived asset is that of the stock of oil held to power the boilers in a hotel, as this will be used up in the near future. Other examples of current assets are cash itself, stocks of goods, debtors and bank balances.

There is a choice of two methods of listing the assets under their respective headings. The first, being the most preferable since it helps standardize the form of sole traders' accounts with those of limited companies, is that the assets are listed starting with the most permanent asset, or to put it another way, the most difficult to turn into cash, progressing to the asset which is least permanent or easiest to turn into cash. The fixed assets will thus appear under that heading followed by the current assets under their heading. The other method, used by banks but fast falling into disuse in most other kinds of organizations, is the complete opposite. In this method it is the least permanent asset that appears first and the most permanent asset which appears last.

Using the first method an illustration may now be seen of the order in which assets are displayed:

Fixed Assets

Land and buildings
Fixtures and fittings
Machinery and Equipment
Motor vehicles

Current Assets

Stock
Debtors
Bank
Cash

The order with which most students would disagree is that stock has appeared before debtors. On first sight stock would appear to be more easily realizable than debtors. In fact, however, debtors could normally be more quickly turned into cash by factorizing them, i.e. selling the rights to the amounts owing to a finance company for an agreed amount. On the other hand, to dispose of all the stock of a business is often a long and difficult task. Another advantage is that the method follows the order in which full realization of the asset takes place. First, before any sale takes place there must be a stock of goods, which when sold on credit turns into debtors, and when payment is made by the debtors it turns into cash.

The order of the other side of the balance sheet is preferably that of starting with capital, progressing via Long-Term Liabilities such as loans not requiring repayment within the near future, and finishing with Current Liabilities, being liabilities such as debts for goods which will have to be discharged in the near future. This then would be the order in which the claims against the assets would be met. The other method of listing the liabilities is the complete opposite of this, starting with current liabilities and finishing at the bottom with capital. This method conflicts with most company accounts and is best avoided if the benefits of standardization are to be attained.

Exhibit 19.5 shows Exhibit 19.4 drawn up in better style. Also read the notes following the exhibit.

Exhibit 19.5

Stephens Café
Balance Sheet as at 31 December 19-5

Fixed Assets	£	£	*Capital*	£	£
Furniture and fittings		500	Cash introduced	3,000	
			Add Net profit for the year	860	
Current Assets					
Stock	1,360			3,860	
Debtors	680		Less Drawings	700	
Bank	1,510				3,160
Cash	20	3,570	*Current Liabilities*		
			Creditors		910
		4,070			4,070

Notes to Exhibit 19.5

1. A total for capital and for each class of assets and liabilities should be shown, e.g. the £3,570 total of current assets. For this purpose the individual figures of current assets are inset and the resultant total extended into the end column.
2. It is not necessary to write the word 'account' after each item.
3. The proprietor will obviously be most interested in his capital. To have merely shown the balance of £3,160 would invariably invite his request to show how the final balance of the capital account had been arrived at. To overcome this, accounting custom always shows the full details of the capital account. Compare this with the other items above where only the closing balance is shown.
4. Compare the date on the balance sheet with that on the trading and profit and loss account. You can see from these that the essential natures of these two statements are revealed. A trading and profit and loss account is a period statement, because it covers a specifed period of time, in this case the whole of 19-5. On the other hand a balance sheet is a position statement; it is drawn up at a particular point in time, in this case at the precise end of 19-5.

YOU SHOULD NOT ATTEMPT EXERCISES 19.1 TO 19.4X BEFORE READING FURTHER. SEE END OF CHAPTER.

Trading and Profit and Loss Accounts and Balance Sheets: Further Considerations

1. Returns Inwards and Returns Outwards

In Chapter 18 we introduced the idea of different accounts for different movements of stock. We thus had sales, purchases, returns inwards and returns outwards accounts. When we looked at the preparation of a trading account on page 195, we did not have a returns inwards account or returns outwards account in the trial balance. This was so that your first look at a trading account would not be made difficult.

However, a large number of firms will return goods to their suppliers (returns outwards), and will have to make allowances to their customers (returns inwards). When we calculate the gross profit these returns will have to come into our calculations. Let us suppose that in Exhibit 19.1, the trial balance of Stephens Café, the balances showing stock movements had instead been as follows:

Trial Balance as at 31 December 19-5

	Dr	*Cr*
	£	£
Sales		4,000
Purchases	3,120	
Returns inwards	150	
Returns outwards		220

Looking at Exhibit 19.1, you can see that originally we had used an example of Sales £3,850 and Purchases £2,900. If it had been as now shown instead, we can now look at what the Trading Account would have been for the year, and what gross profit would have been.

Comparing the two instances, they do in fact amount to the same things as far as gross profit is concerned. Sales were £3,850 in the original example. In the new example we should really deduct returns inwards to get the correct figure for goods sold to customers and *kept* by them, i.e. £4,000 – £150 = £3,850. Purchases were £2,900; in the new example we should really deduct returns outwards to get the correct figure of purchases *kept* by us. The gross profit will remain at £2,310 as per Exhibit 19.1.

The trading account will appear as in Exhibit 19.6.

Exhibit 19.6

Trading and Profit and Loss Account for the year ended 31 December 19-5

	£	£		£	£
Purchases	3,120		Sales	4,000	
Less Returns outwards	220	2,900	*Less* Returns inwards	150	3,850
Less Closing stock		1,360			
Cost of goods sold		1,540			
Gross profit c/d		2,310			
		3,850			3,850

The term used for Sales less Returns Inwards is often called 'Turnover'. In the illustration in Exhibit 19.6 it is £3,850.

2. *Carriage*

Carriage (cost of transport of goods) into a firm is called Carriage Inwards. Carriage of goods out of a firm to its customers is called Carriage Outwards. A contract caterer may have Carriage Outwards.

When you buy goods the cost of carriage inwards may either be included as part of the price, or else the firm may have to pay separately for it. Suppose you were buying exactly the same goods. One supplier might sell them to you for £100, and he would deliver the goods and not send you a bill for carriage. Another supplier might sell the goods to you for £95, but you would have to pay £5 to a haulage firm for carriage inwards, i.e. a total cost of £100.

To keep cost of buying goods being shown on the same basis, carriage inwards is always added to the purchases in the Trading Account.

Carriage outwards to customers is not part of our firm's expenses in buying goods, and is always entered in the profit and loss account.

Let us suppose that in the illustration shown in this chapter, the goods had been bought for the same total figure of £3,120, but in fact £2,920 was the figure for purchases and £200 for carriage inwards. The trial balance and trading account appear as Exhibit 19.7.

Exhibit 19.7

Trial Balance as at 31 December 19-5

	Dr	*Cr*
	£	£
Sales		4,000
Purchases	2,920	
Returns inwards	150	
Returns outwards		220
Carriage inwards	200	

Trading and Profit and Loss Account for the year ended 31 December 19-5

	£	£		£	£
Purchases	2,920		Sales	4,000	
Less Returns outwards	220	2,700	*Less* Returns inwards	150	3,850
Carriage inwards		200			
		2,900			
Less Closing stock		1,360			
Cost of goods sold		1,540			
Gross profit c/d		2,310			
		3,850			3,850
			Gross profit b/d		2,310

You can see that Exhibits 19.1, 19.6 and 19.7 have been concerned with the same overall amount of goods bought and sold by the firm, at the same overall prices. Therefore, as shown, in each case the same gross profit of £2,310 is shown.

Stephens Café Second Year

At the end of his second year of trading, on 31 December 19-6, Stephens Café extracts another trial balance.

Exhibit 19.8

Stephens Café

Trial Balance as at 31 December 19-6

	Dr	*Cr*
	£	£
Sales		6,700
Purchases	4,260	
Lighting	190	
Rent	240	
Wages	1,520	
General expenses	70	
Carriage outwards	110	
Premises	2,000	
Fixtures and fittings	750	
Debtors	1,200	
Creditors		1,900
Bank	120	
Cash	40	
Loan from J. Wedderburn		1,000
Drawings	900	
Capital		3,160
Stock (at 31 December 19-5)	1,360	
	12,760	12,760

The stock shown in the trial balance is that brought forward from the previous year on 31 December 19-5; it is therefore the opening stock of 19-6. The closing stock at 31 December 19-6 can only be found by stocktaking. Assume it amounts at cost to be £2,940.

Let us first of all calculate the cost of goods sold, showing our calculation in a normal arithmetical fashion.

	£
Stock of goods at start of year	1,360
Add purchases	4,260
Total goods available for sale	5,620
Less what remains at the end of the year:	
i.e. stock of goods at close	2,940
Therefore cost of goods that have been sold	2,680

We can look at a diagram to illustrate this, Exhibit 19.9.

Exhibit 19.9

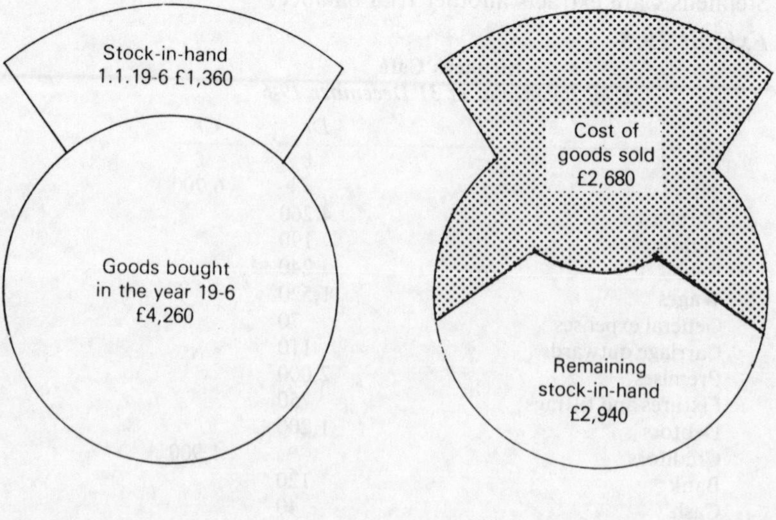

The sales were £6,700, so Sales £6,700 – Cost of Goods Sold £2,680 = Gross Profit £4,020.

Now the trading and profit and loss accounts can be drawn up using double-entry. See Exhibit 19.10.

Exhibit 19.10

Stephens Café

Trading and Profit and Loss Account for the year ended 31 December 19-6

	£		£
Opening stock	1,360	Sales	6,700
Add Purchases	4,260		
	5,620		
Less Closing stock	2,940		
Cost of goods sold	2,680		
Gross profit c/d	4,020		
	6,700		6,700
Wages	1,520	Gross profit b/d	4,020
Lighting expenses	190		
Rent	240		
General expenses	70		
Carriage outwards	110		
Net profit	1,890		
	4,020		4,020

The balances now remaining in the books, including the new balance on the stock account, are now drawn up in the form of a balance sheet. See Exhibit 19.11.

Exhibit 19.11

Stephens Café

Balance Sheet as at 31 December 19-6

Fixed Assets	£	£	*Capital*	£	£
Shop premises		2,000	Balance 1 Jan 19-6	3,160	
Fixtures and fittings		750	Add Net profit for year	1,890	
		2,750		5,050	
			Less Drawings	900	
Current Assets					4,150
Stock	2,940		*Long-term liability*		
Debtors	1,200		Loan from J. Wedderburn		1,000
Bank	120		*Current Liabilities*		
Cash	40		Creditors		1,900
		4,300			
		7,050			7,050

Stock Account

It is perhaps helpful if the stock account covering both years can now be seen:

Stock

19-5	£	19-6		£
Dec 31 Trading A/c	1,360	Jan 1	Trading A/c	1,360
19-6				
Dec 31 Trading A/c	2,940			

Final Accounts

The term 'Final Accounts' is often used to mean collectively the trading and profit and loss accounts and the balance sheet. The term can be misleading as the balance sheet is not an account.

YOU SHOULD NOW ATTEMPT EXERCISES 19.5 AND 19.6X BEFORE READING FURTHER. SEE END OF CHAPTER.

Depreciation of Fixed Assets: Calculations

On page 198 you have read that assets are called Fixed Assets when they are of long life, are to be used in the business and are *not* bought with the main purpose of resale.

However, fixed assets such as machinery, motor vans, fixtures and even buildings, do not last forever. If the amount received (if any) on disposal is deducted from the cost, the difference is called depreciation.

It is obvious that the only time that depreciation can be calculated accurately is when the fixed asset is disposed of, and the difference between the cost to its owner and the amount received on disposal is then ascertained. If a motor van was bought for £1,000 and sold five years later for £20, then the amount of depreciation is £1,000 – £20 = £980.

Depreciation is thus the part of the cost of the fixed asset consumed during its period of use by the firm. It has been a cost for services consumed in the same way as costs for such items as wages, rent, electricity, etc. Depreciation is, therefore, an expense and will need charging to the profit and loss account before calculating net profit or loss. You can see that the only real difference between the cost of depreciation for a motor vehicle and the cost of, say, petrol for the motor vehicle is that the petrol cost is used up in a day or two, whereas the cost of the motor vehicle is spread over several years. Both costs are costs of the business.

Methods of Calculating Depreciation Charges

The two main methods in use are the Straight Line Method and the Reducing Balance Method. It is generally regarded that, although other methods may be needed in certain cases, the straight line method is the one that is generally most suitable.

1. Straight Line Method

By this method, sometimes also called the Fixed Instalment Method, the number of years of use is estimated. The disposal value of the asset at the end of those years is also estimated. This figure is then divided by the number of years, to give the depreciation charge each year.

For instance if a mini bus was bought for £22,000, we thought we would keep it for 4 years and then sell it for £2,000, the depreciation to be charged would be:

$$\frac{\text{Cost (£22,000)} - \text{Disposal value (£2,000)}}{\text{Number of years of use (4)}} = \frac{\text{£20,000}}{4}$$

= £5,000 depreciation each year for 4 years

If, after 4 years, the mini bus would have had no disposal value, the charge for depreciation would have been:

$$\frac{\text{Cost (£22,000)}}{\text{Number of years use (4)}} = \frac{\text{£22,000}}{4}$$

= £5,500 depreciation each year for 4 years.

2. Reducing Balance Method

By this method a fixed percentage for depreciation is deducted from the cost in the first year. In the second or later years the same percentage is taken of the reduced balance (i.e. cost less depreciation already charged). This method is also known as the Diminishing Balance Method.

If a machine is bought for £10,000, and depreciation is to be charged at 20 per cent, the calculations for the first 3 years would be as follows:

	£
Cost	10,000
First year: Depreciation (20%)	2,000
	8,000
Second year: Depreciation (20% of £8,000)	1,600
	6,400
Third year: Depreciation (20% of £6,400)	1,280
	5,120

Using this method much larger amounts are charged in the earlier years of use as compared with the last years of use. It is often justified that repairs and upkeep in the early years will not cost as much as when the asset becomes old. It is contended that:

In the early years A higher charge for depreciation + A lower charge for repairs and upkeep	will tend to be fairly equal to	*In the later years* A lower charge for depreciation + A higher charge for repairs and upkeep

Exhibit 19.12 gives a comparison of the calculations using the two methods, if the same cost is given for the two methods.

Exhibit 19.12

A firm have just bought a billing machine for £8,000. It will be kept in use for 4 years, when it will be disposed of for an estimated amount of £500. They ask for a comparison of the amounts charged as depreciation using both methods.

For the straight line method a figure of (£8,000 − £500) ÷ 4 = £7,500 ÷ 4 = £1,875 per annum is to be used. For the reducing balance method a percentage figure of 50 per cent will be used.

	Method 1 Straight Line		*Method 2 Reducing Balance*
	£		£
Cost	8,000		8,000
Depreciation: Year 1	1,875	(50% of £8,000)	4,000
	6,125		4,000
Depreciation: Year 2	1,875	(50% of £4,000)	2,000
	4,250		2,000
Depreciation: Year 3	1,875	(50% of £2,000)	1,000
	2,375		1,000
Depreciation: Year 4	1,875	(50% of £1,000)	500
Disposal value	500		500

This illustrates the fact that using the reducing balance method has a much higher charge for depreciation in the early years, and lower charges in the later years.

Revaluation Method of Calculating Depreciation

This can be used for small items of equipment such as china, cutlery, linen and glass.

The depreciation is based on inventories (stock taking).

Exhibit 19.13

Inventory of Glass 31st December 19-2		£700
Inventory of Glass 31st December 19-3		£600
Therefore Depreciation for year 19-3	=	£100

Double Entry Records for Depreciation

Looking back quite a few years, the charge for depreciation always used to be shown in the fixed asset accounts themselves. This method is now falling into disuse but as a reasonable number of firms still use it this will be illustrated and called the 'old method'.

The method now becoming increasingly popular is where the fixed assets accounts are always kept for showing the assets at cost price. The depreciation is shown accumulating in a separate 'provision for depreciation' account.

We can now look at an illustration, using the same information but showing the records using both methods.

In a business with financial years ended 31 December a machine is bought for £2,000 on 1 January 19-5. It is to be depreciated at the rate of 20 per cent using the reducing balance method. The records for the first two years are now shown:

1. The Old Method

Here the double-entry for each year's depreciation charge is:

Debit the depreciation account
Credit the asset account

and then, this is transferred to the profit and loss account, by the following:

Debit the profit and loss account
Credit the depreciation account

Kitchen Machinery

19-5	£	19-5	£
Jan 1 Cash	2,000	Dec 31 Depreciation	400
		,, ,, Balance c/d	1,600
	2,000		2,000
19-6		19-6	
Jan 1 Balance b/d	1,600	Dec 31 Depreciation	320
		,, ,, Balance c/d	1,280
	1,600		1,600
19-7			
Jan 1 Balance b/d	1,280		

Depreciation

19-5	£	19-5	£
Dec 31 Machinery	400	Dec 31 Profit and Loss	400
19-6		19-6	
Dec 31 Machinery	320	Dec 31 Profit and Loss	320

Profit and Loss Account for the year ended 31 December

19-5 Depreciation	400
19-6 Depreciation	320

Usually shown on the balance sheet as follows:

Balance Sheet as at 31 December 19-5

	£	£
Kitchen Machinery at cost	2,000	
Less Depreciation for the year	400	
		1,600

Balance Sheet as at 31 December 19-6

Kitchen Machinery as at 1 January 19-6	1,600	
Less Depreciation for the year	320	
		1,280

2. The Modern Method

Here, no entry is made in the asset account for depreciation. Instead, the depreciation is shown accumulating in a separate account.

The double entry is:
Debit the profit and loss account
Credit the provision for depreciation account

Kitchen Machinery

19-5	£		
Jan 1 Cash	2,000		

Provision for Depreciation – Machinery

19-5	£	19-5	£
Dec 31 Balance c/d	400	Dec 31 Profit and Loss	400
19-6		19-6	
Dec 31 Balance c/d	720	Jan 1 Balance b/d	400
		Dec 31 Profit and Loss	320
	720		720
		19-7	
		Jan 1 Balance b/d	720

Profit and Loss Account for the year ended 31 December

19-5 Depreciation	400
19-6 Depreciation	320

Now the balance on the Machinery Account is shown on the balance sheet at the end of each year less the balance on the Provision for Depreciation Account.

Balance Sheet as at 31 December 19-5

	£	£
Kitchen Machinery at cost	2,000	
Less Depreciation to date	400	1,600

Balance Sheet as at 31 December 19-6

	£	£
Kitchen Machinery at cost	2,000	
Less Depreciation to date	720	1,280

The modern method is much more revealing as far as the balance sheet is concerned. By comparing the depreciation to date with the cost of the asset, a good indication as to the relative age of the asset can be obtained. In the second and later balance sheets using the old method no such indication is available. For instance, using the *old method,* a car costing £6,000 and of which £5,600 has been charged as depreciation is obviously very near the end of its useful life. A car costing £600, and of which only £200 has been charged for depreciation, is fairly new. You can tell this type of thing when you look at the balance sheet using the *modern* method, but you have no idea of the age of a fixed asset with a balance sheet using the *old* method. The modern method is therefore to be preferred as it gives you better information.

The Sale of An Asset

When we charge depreciation on a fixed asset we are having to make guesses. We cannot be absolutely certain how long we will keep the asset in use, nor can we be certain at the date of purchase how much the asset will be sold for when we dispose of it. To get our guesses absolutely correct would be quite rare. This means that when we dispose of an asset, the cash received for it is usually different from our original guess.

We can show this by looking back to the illustration already shown in this chapter. At the end of 19-6 the value of the machinery on the balance sheet is shown as £1,280. Using the old method of charging depreciation in the machinery account, we can now see the entries needed if (*a*) the machinery was sold on 2 January 19-7 for £1,400, and then (*b*) if instead it had been sold for £1,220.

(*a*) Asset sold at a profit
Book-keeping entries needed –

For cheque received:	Dr Bank
	Cr Machinery Account
For profit on sale:	Dr Machinery Account
	Cr Profit and Loss Account

Kitchen Machinery

19-7	£	19-7	£
Jan 1 Balance b/d	1,280	Jan 2 Bank	1,400
Dec 31 Profit and Loss	120		
	1,400		1,400

Bank

19-7	£		
Jan 2 Kitchen Machinery	1,400		

Profit and Loss Account for the year ended 31 December 19-7

			£
		Profit on sale of machinery	120

(*b*) Asset sold at a loss

Book-keeping entries needed –

For cheque received:	Dr Bank
	Cr Machinery Account
For loss on sale:	Dr Profit and Loss Account
	Cr Machinery Account

Kitchen Machinery

19-7	£	19-7	£
Jan 1 Balance b/d	1,280	Jan 2 Bank	1,220
		Dec 31 Profit and Loss	60
	1,280		1,280

Bank

19-7	£		
Jan 2 Kitchen Machinery	1,220		

Profit and Loss Account for the year ended 31 December 19-7

	£		
Loss on sale of machinery	60		

For the purposes of this book if the reader can understant the book-keeping entries needed using the old method then that is sufficient. For the sake of those students who will need to know how to enter the items using the modern method, the description is now given.

(i) Transfer the cost price of the asset sold to an Assets Disposal Account (in this case a Machinery Disposals Account).	Dr Machinery Disposals Account Cr Machinery Account
(ii) Transfer the depreciation already charged to the Assets Disposal Account.	Dr Provision for Depreciation – Machinery Cr Machinery Disposals Account
(iii) For remittance received on disposal.	Dr Cash Book Cr Machinery Disposals Account
(iv) Transfer balance (difference) on Machinery Disposals Account to the Profit and Loss Account.	
If the difference is on the debit side of the disposal account, it is a profit on sale.	Debit Machinery Disposals Account Credit Profit and Loss Account
If the difference is on the credit side of the disposal account, it is a loss on sale.	Debit Profit and Loss Account Cr Machinery Disposals Account

YOU SHOULD NOW ATTEMPT EXERCISES 19.7 TO 19.12 BEFORE READING FURTHER.

Bad Debts and Provisions for Bad Debts

If a firm finds that it is impossible to collect a debt then that debt should be written off as a bad debt. This could happen if the debtor simply could not pay the debt.

An example of debts being written off as bad can now be shown in Exhibit 19.14.

Exhibit 19.14

A contract caterer had sold £50 goods to C. Baptiste on 5 January 19-5, but he had become bankrupt. On 16 February 19-5 £240 goods was sold to R. Shaw. He managed to pay £200 on 17 May 19-5, but it became obvious that he would never be able to pay the final £40.

When drawing up final accounts to 31 December 19-5 it was decided to write these off as bad debts. The accounts would appear as follows:

C. Baptiste

19-5		£	19-5		£
Jan	8 Sales	50	Dec	31 Bad Debts	50

R. Shaw

19-5		£	19-5	£
Feb 16	Sales	240	May 17 Cash	200
			Dec 31 Bad Debts	40
		240		240

Bad Debts

19-5		£	19-5	£
Dec 31	C. Baptiste	50	Dec 31 Profit and Loss	90
,,	,, R. Shaw	40		
		90		90

Profit and Loss Account for the year ended 31 December 19-5

	£
Bad Debts	90

Provisions for Bad Debts

The total of the debtors appears in the balance sheet as an asset. If we were certain that all of the debtors would pay their accounts then the figure of debtors would present a true value. However, if some of the debts proved eventually to be bad, then the value of the asset would have been overstated.

To try to bring the value of the debts shown nearer to the true value, a provision should be made to cover the estimated amount of bad debts. This amount should be debited to the profit and loss account as an expense and credited to a Provision for Bad Debts Account.

Such an estimate for a provision could be made:

(*a*) By looking at each debt, and estimating which ones will be bad debts.

(*b*) By estimating, on the basis of experience, what percentage of the debts will prove to be bad debts.

Exhibit 19.15

At the 31 December 19-3 debtors amounted to £10,000. It is estimated that 2 per cent of debts (i.e. £200) will prove to be bad debts, and it is decided to make a provision for these. The accounts would appear as follows:

Profit and Loss Account for the year ended 31 December 19-3

	£
Provision for Bad Debts	200

Provision for Bad Debts

		19-3	£
		Dec 31 Profit and Loss A/c	200

In the balance sheet the balance on the Provision for Bad Debts will be deducted from the total of debtors:

Balance Sheet (extracts) as on 31 December 19-3

Current Assets		£
Debtors	10,000	
Less Provision for Bad Debts	200	
		9,800

Increasing the Provision

Let us suppose that for the same firm as in Exhibit 19.15, at the end of the following year 31 December 19-4, the Bad Debts Provision needed to be increased. This was because the provision was kept at 2 per cent, but the debtors had risen to £12,000. A provision of £200 had been brought forward from the previous year, but we now want a total provision of £240 (i.e. 2 per cent of £12,000). All that is needed is a provision for an extra £40.

The double-entry will be:

Dr Profit and Loss Account
Cr Provision for Bad Debts Account

Profit and Loss Account for the year ended 31 December 19-4

	£
Provision for Bad Debts	40

Provision for Bad Debts

19-4		£	19-4		£
Dec 31	Balance c/d	240	Jan 1	Balance b/d	200
			Dec 31	Profit and Loss	40
		240			240
			19-5		
			Jan 1	Balance b/d	240

The balance sheet as at 31 December 19-4 will appear as:

Balance Sheet (extracts) as on 31 December 19-4

		£
Current Assets		
Debtors	12,000	
Less Provision for Bad Debts	240	
		11,760

Reducing the Provision

The provision is shown as a credit balance. Therefore to reduce it we would need a debit entry in the provision account. The credit would be in the profit and loss account. Let us assume that at 31 December 19-5, in the firm already examined, the debtors had fallen to £10,500 but the provision remained at 2 per cent, i.e. £210 (2 per cent of £10,500). Thus the provision needs a reduction of £30. The double-entry is:

Dr Provision for Bad Debts Account
Cr Profit and Loss Account

Profit and Loss Account for the year ended 31 December 19-5

		£
	Provision for Bad Debts: Reduction	30

Provision for Bad Debts

19-5		£	19-5		£
Dec 31	Profit and Loss	30	Jan 1	Balance b/d	240
,, 31	Balance c/d	210			
		240			240
			19-6		
			Jan 1	Balance b/d	210

The balance sheet will appear:

Balance Sheet (extracts) as on 31 December 19-5

Current Assets		£
Debtors	10,500	
Less Provision for Bad Debts	210	
		10,290

Let us now look at a comprehensive example, Exhibit 19.16.

Exhibit 19.16

A business starts on 1 January 19-2 and its financial year end is 31 December annually. A table of the debtors, the bad debts written off and the estimated bad debts at the end of each year is now given. The double-entry accounts follow, and the extracts from the final accounts.

Year to 31 December	*Debtors at end of year (after bad debts written off)*	*Bad Debts written off during year*	*Debts thought at end of year to be impossible to collect*
	£	£	£
19-2	6,000	423	120
19-3	7,000	510	140
19-4	8,000	604	155
19-5	6,400	610	130

Profit and Loss Accounts for the year ended 31 December (extracts)

		£			£
19-2	Bad Debts	423			
	Provision for Bad Debts	120			
19-3	Bad Debts	510			
	Increase in provision for Bad Debts	20			
19-4	Bad Debts	604			
	Increase in provision for Bad Debts	15			
19-5	Bad Debts	610	19-5	Reduction in provision for Bad Debts	25

Provision for Bad Debts

		£			£
			19-2		
			Dec 31	Profit and Loss	120
19-3			19-3		
Dec 31	Balance c/d	140	Dec 31	Profit and Loss	20
		140			140
			19-4		
19-4			Jan 1	Balance b/d	140
Dec 31	Balance c/d	155	Dec 31	Profit and Loss	15
		155			155
19-5			19-5		
Dec 31	Profit and Loss	25	Jan 1	Balance b/d	155
,, ,,	Balance c/d	130			
		155			155
			19-6		
			Jan 1	Balance b/d	130

Bad Debts

		£			£
19-2			19-2		
Dec 31	Sundries	423	Dec 31	Profit and Loss	423
19-3			19-3		
Dec 31	Sundries	510	Dec 31	Profit and Loss	510
19-4			19-4		
Dec 31	Sundries	604	Dec 31	Profit and Loss	604
19-5			19-5		
Dec 31	Sundries	610	Dec 31	Profit and Loss	610

Balance Sheets as at 31 December (extracts)

		£	£
19-2	Debtors	6,000	
	Less Provision for Bad Debts	120	
			5,880
19-3	Debtors	7,000	
	Less Provision for Bad Debts	140	
			6,860
19-4	Debtors	8,000	
	Less Provision for bad Debts	155	
			7,845
19-5	Debtors	6,400	
	Less Provision for Bad Debts	130	
			6,270

YOU SHOULD NOW ATTEMPT QUESTIONS 19.13 TO 19.16X BEFORE READING FURTHER.

Other Adjustments for Final Accounts

The trading and profit and loss accounts you have looked at have taken the sales for a period and deducted all the expenses for that period, the result being a net profit (or a net loss).

Up to this part of the chapter it has always been assumed that the expenses belonged exactly to the period of the trading and profit and loss account. If the trading and profit and loss account for the year ended 31 December 19-5 was being drawn up, then the rent paid as shown in the trial balance was exactly for 19-5. There was no rent owing at the beginning of 19-5 nor any owing at the end of 19-5, nor had any rent been paid in advance.

However, where on the other hand the costs used up and the amount paid are not equal to one another, then an adjustment will be required in respect of the overpayment or underpayment of the costs used up during the period.

In all of the following examples the trading and profit and loss accounts being drawn up are for the year ended 31 December 19-5.

Underpayment of Expenses

Let us consider the case of rent being charged at the rate of £1,000 per year. It is payable at the end of each quarter of the year for the three months' tenancy that has just expired. It can be assumed that the tenancy commenced on 1 January 19-5. The rent was paid for 19-5 on 31 March, 2 July and 4 October and on 5 January 19-6.

During the year ended 31 December 19-5 the rent account will appear:

Rent

19-5	£		
Mar 31 Cash	250		
Jul 2 ,,	250		
Oct 4 ,,	250		

The rent paid 5 January 19-6 will appear in the books of the year 19-6 as part of the double-entry.

The costs used up during 19-5 are obviously £1,000, as that is the year's rent, and this is the amount needed to be transferred to the profit and loss account. But if £1,000 was put on the credit side of the rent account (the debit being in the profit and loss account) the account would not balance. We would have £1,000 on the credit side of the account and only £750 on the debit side. To make the account balance the £250 rent owing for 19-5, but paid in 19-6, must be carried down to 19-6 as a credit balance because it is a liability on 31 December 19-5. Instead of Rent Owing it could be called Rent Accrued or just simply as an accrual. The completed account can now be shown.

Rent

19-5	£	19-5	£
Mar 31 Cash	250	Dec 31 Profit and Loss A/c	1,000
Jul 2 ,,	250		
Oct 4 ,,	250		
Dec 31 Owing c/d	250		
	1,000		1,000
		19-6	
		Jan 1 Owing b/d	250

Expenses Prepaid

Insurance premiums have been paid as follows:

Feb 28 19-5 £210 for period of three months to 31 March 19-5.
Aug 31 19-5 £420 for period of six months to 30 September 19-5.
Nov 18 19-5 £420 for period of six months to 31 March 19-6.

The insurance account will be shown in the books:

Insurance

19-5	£		
Feb 28 Cash	210		
Aug 31 ,,	420		
Nov 18 ,,	420		

Now the last payment of £420 is not just for 19-5, it can be split as to £210 for the three months to 31 December 19-5 and £210 for the three months ended 31 March 19-6. For a period of 12 months the cost of insurance is £840 and this is therefore the figure needing to be transferred to the profit and loss account. The amount needed to balance the account will therefore be £210 and at 31 December 19-5 this is a benefit paid for but not used up; it is an asset and needs carrying forward as such to 19-6, i.e. as a debit balance.

The account can now be completed.

Insurance

19-5		£	19-5		£
Feb 28	Cash	210	Dec 31	Profit and Loss A/c	840
Aug 31	,,	420	,, ,,	Prepaid c/d	210
Nov 18	,,	420			
		1,050			1,050
19-6					
Jan 1	Prepaid b/d	210			

Prepayment will also happen when items other than purchases are bought for use in the business, and they are not fully used up in the period.

In a 'take away restaurant, packing materials are normally not entirely used up over the period in which it is bought, there being a stock of packing materials in hand at the end of the period. This stock is therefore a form of prepayment and needs carrying down to the following period in which it will be used.

This can be seen in the following example:

Year ended 31 December 19-5
Packing materials bought in the year £2,200
Stock of packing materials in hand as at 31 December 19-5 £400

Looking at the example, it can be seen that in 19-5 the packing materials used up will have been £2,200 – £400 = £1,800 and that we will still have a stock of £400 packing materials at 31 December 19-5 to be carried forward to 19-6. The £400 stock of packing materials will accordingly be carried forward as an asset balance (debit balance) to 19-6.

Packing Materials

19-5		£	19-5		£
Dec 31	Cash	2,200	Dec 31	Profit and Loss A/c	1,800
			,, ,,	Stock c/d	400
		2,200			2,200
19-6					
Jan 1	Stock b/d	400			

The stock of packing materials is not added to the stock of unsold goods in hand in the balance sheet, but is added to the other prepayments of expenses.

Outstanding Revenue other than Sales

Sales revenue outstanding is already shown in the books as debit balances on the customers' personal accounts, i.e. debtors. It is the other kinds of revenue such as rent receivable, etc. which need to be considered. Such revenue to be brought into the profit and loss account is that which has been earned during the period. Should all the revenue earned actually be received during the period, then revenue received and revenue earned will be the same amount and no adjustment would be needed in the revenue account. Where the revenue has been earned, but the full amount has not been received, the revenue due to the business must be brought into the accounts; the amount receivable is after all the revenue used when calculating profit.

Example

Our premises are larger than we need. We rent part of it to another firm for £800 per annum. For the year ended 31 December 19-5 the following cheques were received.

19-5		
Apr	4 For three months to 31 March 19-5	£200
Jul	6 For three months to 30 June 19-5	£200
Oct	9 For three months to 30 September 19-5	£200

The £200 for the three months to 31 December 19-5 was received 7 January 19-6.

The account for 19-5 appeared:

Rent Receivable

			19-5		£
			Apr	4 Bank	200
			Jul	6 Bank	200
			Oct	9 Bank	200

Any rent paid by the firm would be charged as a debit to the profit and loss account. Any rent received, being the opposite, is accordingly eventually transferred to the credit of the profit and loss account. The amount to be transferred for 19-5 is that earned for the twelve months. i.e. £800. The rent received account is completed by carrying down the balance owing as a debit balance to 19-6. The £200 owing is, after all, an asset on 31 December 19-5.

The Rent Receivable Account can now be completed:

Rent Receivable

19-5	£	19-5	£
Dec 31 Profit and Loss A/c	800	Apr 4 Bank	200
		Jul 6 Bank	200
		Oct 9 Bank	200
		Dec 31 Accrued c/d	200
	800		800
19-6			
Jan 1 Accrued b/d	200		

Expenses and Revenue Account Balances and the Balance Sheet

In all the cases listed dealing with adjustments in the final accounts, there will still be a balance on each account after the preparation of the trading and profit and loss accounts. All such balances remaining should appear in the balance sheet. The only question left is to where and how they shall be shown.

The amounts owing for expenses are usually added together and shown as one figure. These could be called Expense Creditors, Expenses Owing, or Accrued Expenses. The item would appear under current liabilities as they are expenses which have to be discharged in the near future.

The items prepaid are also added together and called Prepayments, Prepaid Expenses, or Payments in Advance. Often they are added to the debtors in the balance sheet, otherwise they are shown next under the debtors.

Amounts owing for rents receivable or other revenue owing are usually added to debtors.

The balance sheet in respect of the accounts so far seen in this chapter would appear:

Balance Sheets as at 31 December 19-5

Current Assets	£	*Current Liabilities*	£
Stock		Trade creditors	
Debtors	200	Accrued Expenses	250
Prepayments	610		
Bank			
Cash			

Goodwill

When starting up in business we could start up completely from scratch. On the other hand we could buy someone else's existing business. If we did this the seller of the business may well ask more for the business than the value of the actual physical assets.

Let us suppose that we are going to buy a guest house. The premises are worth £50,000, the equipment £20,000, and stock is worth £12,000. In total that is £82,000. The seller however wants £100,000 for the business. He says that it is worth the extra £18,000 because he has established the guest house as a good, well-run guest house with a regular set of customers. If we were to start from scratch it could well take us a lot of time and a lot of effort to get so well set up. We agree to pay the extra £18,000 for this, and this extra something over and above the value of the physical assets is known as 'Goodwill'.

Until 1985 Goodwill could have been shown as a Fixed Asset in the balance sheet, and could have remained at that same figure for year after year. However, the accounting profession has now changed its practice regarding Goodwill. It can be dealt with in two ways:

(i) It can still be shown as a Fixed Asset, but it must be amortised (depreciated) over the 'economic life' of the asset. This is similar to charging depreciation for any other fixed asset.

(ii) As an alternative to (i) companies could immediately write the asset off, rather similar to charging all the depreciation in one year. A more detailed look at this point will be taken by students who take the subject to a more advanced level.

Goods for Own Use

A caterer will often take items out of his business stocks for his own use, without paying for them. There is certainly nothing wrong about this, but an entry should be made to record the event. This is effected by:

Credit Purchases Account
Debit Drawings Account

Adjustments may also be needed for other private items. For instance, if a proprietor's private insurance had been incorrectly charged to the Insurance Account, then the correction would be:

Credit Insurance Account
Debit Drawings Account

Staff Meals

Many hotels and restaurants allow free meals to staff. This is really an extra cost of staff (labour) and a use of food and beverages at cost. The double entry will be:

CREDIT Purchases Account
DEBIT Staff Meals

If 'staff meals' appears in a Trial Balance it means the above adjustment has been made and the item should be entered in Profit and Loss Account.

In the preparation of final accounts:

CREDIT Trading Account
DEBIT Profit and Loss Account

Vertical Form of Accounts

Throughout this chapter the two-sided presentation of Trading and Profit and Loss Accounts and Balance Sheets is used. For many reasons this is easier to use from a teaching point of view. However, in practice you would not necessarily have to show the final accounts drawn up in that fashion. It would be completely up to the owner(s) of a business to decide on the method of presentation. What really matters is whether or not the presentation still results in the right answer being shown.

Final accounts are often shown in a vertical fashion. This is also referred to as narrative style, or columnar presentation. When this is done the chance is usually taken of displaying 'working capital' as a separate figure. 'Working Capital' is the term for the excess of the current assets over the current liabilities of a business.

Most cafés and restaurants work on a high gross profit % compared with food retailers (grocers). On average this is 60% of sales. This gross profit is necessary to cover the cost of kitchen and service staff which is much more expensive than the staffing costs in a grocery business.

The Trading and Profit and Loss Account is very useful because it will reveal whether or not the expected gross profit % has been achieved. Most owners prefer this information presented vertically.

The Trading and Profit and Loss Account shown as Exhibit 19.2 on page 195 and also the Balance Sheet shown as Exhibit 19.5 on page 200 are now redrafted in a vertical fashion in Exhibit 19.17 – you should note that there is not just one way of presenting these accounts in a vertical fashion, but the one that follows is an example in good style. You will notice that Working Capital £2,660 is thrown up as a separate figure.

Exhibit 19.17

Note 1 **Stephens Café**

Trading and Profit and Loss Account for the year ended 31 December 19-5

	£	£	%
Sales		3,850	100
Less Cost of Food and Beverages			
Purchases	2,900		
Less Closing stock	1,360	1,540	40
Gross Profit		2,310	60
Less Wages *Note 2*		1,000	26
Less Expenses: *Note 3*			
Rent	240		
Lighting and heating	150		
General expenses	60	450	12
Net profit		860	22

Stephens Café

Balance Sheet as at 31 December 19-5

	£	£
Fixed assets		
Furniture and fittings		500
Current assets		
Stock	1,360	
Debtors	680	
Bank	1,510	
Cash	20	
	3,570	
Less Current liabilities		
Creditors	910	
Working Capital		2,660
		3,160
	£	£
Capital		
Cash Introduced		3,000
Add Net Profit for the year		860
		3,860
Less Drawings		700
		3,160

Alternative Terms

Note 1 Revenue Account or Profit and Loss Statement

2 Labour

3 Overheads.

You should not be able to complete the remainder of the exercises at the end of this chapter.

Exercises

19.1. From the following trial balance of B. Charles, who has been in business for one year, extract a trading and profit and loss account for the year ended 31 December 19-6, and a balance sheet as at that date.

Trial Balance as at 31 December 19-6

	Dr	*Cr*
	£	£
Sales		18,462
Purchases	14,629	
Salaries	2,150	
Motor expenses	520	
Rent and rates	670	
Insurance	111	
General expenses	105	
Premises	1,500	
Motor vehicle	1,200	
Debtors	1,950	
Creditors		1,538
Cash at bank	1,654	
Cash in hand	40	
Drawings	895	
Capital		5,424
	25,424	25,424

Stock at 31 December 19-6 was £7,245.

19.2. From the following trial balance of C. Wynter, who has been trading for one year, you are required to draw up a trading and profit and loss for the year ended 30 June 19-4, and a balance sheet as at that date.

Trial Balance as at 30 June 19-4

	Dr	*Cr*
	£	£
Sales		28,794
Purchases	23,803	
Rent	854	
Lighting expenses	422	
Salaries and wages	3,164	
Insurance	105	
Buildings	50,000	
Fixtures and Equipment	1,000	
Debtors	3,166	
Trade expenses	506	
Creditors		1,206
Cash at bank	3,847	
Drawings	2,400	
Motor van	5,500	
Motor running expenses	1,133	
Capital		65,900
	95,900	95,900

Stock at 30 June 19-4 was £12,291.

19.3X. From the following trial balance of F. Chaplin draw up a trading and profit and loss account for the year ended 31 December 19-8, and a balance sheet as at that date. He has been in business for one year only.

Trial Balance as at 31 December 19-8

	Dr	*Cr*
	£	£
General expenses	210	
Rent and rates	400	
Motor expenses	735	
Salaries	3,560	
Insurance	392	
Purchases	18,385	
Sales		26,815
Motor vehicle	2,800	
Creditors		5,160
Debtors	4,090	
Premises	20,000	
Cash at bank	1,375	
Cash in hand	25	
Capital		24,347
Drawings	4,350	
	56,322	56,322

Stock at 31 December 19-8 was £7,660.

19.4X. Extract a trading and profit and loss account for the year ended 30 June 19-4 and a balance sheet as at that date for F. Kidd. The business has been in existence for one year. The trial balance as at 30 June 19-4 was as follows:

	Dr	*Cr*
	£	£
Rent and rates	1,560	
Insurance	305	
Lighting expenses	516	
Motor expenses	1,960	
Salaries and wages	4,850	
Sales		35,600
Purchases	30,970	
Trade expenses	806	
Motor vans	3,500	
Creditors		3,250
Debtors	6,810	
Fixtures and Equipment	3,960	
Buildings	28,000	
Cash at bank	1,134	
Drawings	6,278	
Capital		51,799
	90,649	90,649

Stock at 30 June 19-4 was £16,730.

19.5. From the following trial balance of Contract Caterers draw up a trading and profit and loss account for the year ended 30 September 19-6, and a balance sheet as at that date.

	Dr	*Cr*
	£	£
Stock 1 October 19-5	2,368	
Carriage outwards	200	
Carriage inwards	310	
Returns inwards	205	
Returns outwards		322
Purchases	11,874	
Sales		18,600
Salaries and wages	3,862	
Rent and rates	304	
Insurance	78	
Motor expenses	664	
Office expenses	216	
Lighting expenses	166	
General expenses	314	
Premises and Equipment	5,000	
Motor vehicles	1,800	
Fixtures and fittings	350	
Debtors	3,896	
Creditors		1,731
Cash at bank	482	
Drawings	1,200	
Capital		12,636
	33,289	33,289

Stock at 30 September 19-6 was £2,946.

19.6X. The following trial balance was extracted from the books of The Fine Restaurant on 30 April 19-7. From it, and the notes, prepare his trading and profit and loss account for the year ended 30 April 19-7, and a balance sheet as at that date.

	Dr	*Cr*
	£	£
Sales		18,600
Purchases	8,556	
Stock 1 May 19-6	3,776	
Light and Heat	326	
Carriage inwards	234	
Returns inwards	440	
Returns outwards		355
Salaries and wages	5,447	
Motor expenses	664	
Rent	456	
Rates	120	
Sundry expenses	1,202	
Motor vehicles	2,400	
Fixtures, fittings and equipment	1,600	
Debtors	3,577	
Creditors		3,045
Cash at bank	3,876	
Cash in hand	120	
Drawings	2,050	
Capital		12,844
	34,844	34,844

Stock at 30 April 19-7 was £4,998.

19.7. D. Jones, a hotelier, purchases a billing machine for the sum of £4,000. It has an estimated life of 5 years and a scrap value of £500.

Jones is not certain whether he should use the 'Straight Line' or 'the Reducing Balance' basis for the purpose of calculating depreciation on the machine.

You are required to calculate the depreciation on the machine using both methods, showing clearly the balance remaining in the machine account at the end of each of the five years for each method. (Assume that 40 per cent per annum is to be used for the Reducing Balance Method.)

(Calculations to nearest £.)

19.8. A machine costs £12,500. It will be kept for 4 years, and then sold for an estimated figure of £5,120. Show the calculations of the figures for depreciation for each of the four years using (*a*) the straight-line method, (*b*) the reducing balance method, for this method using a depreciation rate of 20 per cent.

19.9X. A kitchen range costs £12,150. It will be kept in use for 5 years. At the end of that time agreement has already been made that it will be sold for £1,600. Show your calculation of the amount of depreciation each year if (*a*) the reducing balance method at a rate of 33⅓ per cent was used, (*b*) the straight line method was used.

19.10X. A van is bought for £6,000. It will be used for 3 years, and then sold back to the supplier for £3,072. Show the depreciation calculations for each year using (*a*) the reducing balance method with a rate of 20 per cent, (*b*) the straight line method.

19.11. On 1 July 19-2 R. Bryan, purchased a motor van for £4,000. Using the old method only, with calculations to the nearest £, you are required to:

(*a*) Show how the 'Motor Van Account' would appear in the books of R. Bryan for the four years ending 30 June 19-6.

Depreciation is written off at the rate of 20 per cent on a 'Reducing Balance' basis.

(*b*) Explain the difference between the 'Straight-Line' method and the 'Reducing Balance' method of Depreciation.

19.12X. Harvey DaCosta, a cafè proprietor, purchased on 1 November 19-7, a new machine for £18,000. His business year end is 31 October but he cannot decide which method of depreciation he should use in respect of the machine – straight line method or the reducing balance method.

Required:

In order to assist him in making his decision, draw up the Machine Account, and Provision for Depreciation Account, for the three years from 1 November 19-7 using:

(*a*) the straight line method; and

(*b*) the reducing balance method.

Each account must indicate which method is being used and each account be balanced at the end of each of the three years.

Notes (use modern method only):

(i) In both cases the rate of depreciation is to be 10 per cent.

(ii) Calculations should be made to the nearest £.

19.13. On 1 January 19-7 the balances below appeared in the Sales ledger of S. Henry:

	£
D. Fung	200
C. Manley	120

During the year the following events took place:

Feb 1 After negotiation Henry agreed to accept £150 cash from D. Fung and regarded the oustanding balance as irrecoverable.

Mar 10 C. Manley was declared bankrupt. A payment of 30 pence in the £ was received in full settlement.

Show how these matters would be dealth with in Henry's ledger assuming that the financial year ends on 30 June.

19.14. On 30 September 19-7 B. Fraser's debtors totalled £12,000. He decided to write off the following as bad debts:

	£
G. Green	60
H. Winston	80

He further decided to make a provision for Bad Debts of 10 per cent on the remaining debtors.

Debtors on 30 September 19-8 totalled £10,000 when Fraser decided to maintain the provision at 10 per cent.

You are required to show for each of the years ended 30 September 19-7 and 19-8:

(*a*) provision for Bad Debts Account;
(*b*) the appropriate entries in the Profit and Loss Account; and
(*c*) the necessary Balance Sheet entries on each of the above dates.

19.15X.

Date: 31 Dec	*Total Debtors*	*Profit and Loss*	*Dr/Cr*	*Final Figure for Balance Sheet*
	£	£		£
19-3	7,000			
19-4	8,000			
19-5	6,000			
19-6	7,000			

The above table shows the figure for debtors appearing in a trader's books on 31 December of each year from 19-3 to 19-6. The Provision for Doubtful Debts is to be 1 per cent of debtors from 31 December 19-3. Complete the above table indicating the amount to be debited or credited to the profit and loss account for the year ended on each 31 December, and the amount for the final figure of debtors to appear in the Balance Sheet on each date.

19.16X. A business started on 1 January 19-5 and its financial year end is 31 December annually. A table of the debtors, the bad debts written off and the estimated bad debts at the end of the year is now given.

Year to 31 December	*Debtors at end of year (after bad debts written off)*	*Bad Debts written off during the year*	*Debts thought at end of year to be impossible to collect*
	£	£	£
19-5	12,000	298	100
19-6	15,000	386	130
19-7	14,000	344	115
19-8	18,000	477	150

You are required to show the above in the double-entry accounts, as well as the extracts from the Profit and Loss Account for each year and the Balance Sheet extracts.

19.17. The financial year of J. Thomas ended on 31 December 19-6. Show the ledger accounts for the following items including the balance transferred to the necessary part of the final accounts, also the balances carried down to 19-7:

(*a*) Motor Expenses: Paid in 19-6 £744; Owing at 31 December 19-6 £28.
(*b*) Insurance: Paid in 19-6 £420; Prepaid as at 31 December 19-6 £35.
(*c*) Rent: Paid during 19-6 £1,800; Owing as at 31 December 19-5 £250; Owing as at 31 December 19-6 £490.
(*d*) Rates: Paid during 19-6 £950; Prepaid as at 31 December 19-5 £220; Prepaid as at 31 December 19-6 £290.
(*e*) Thomas sub-lets part of the premises. Receives £550 during the year ended 31 December 19-6. Tenant owed Thomas £180 on 31 December 19-5 and £210 on 31 December 19-6.

19.18X. J. Persad's year ended on 30 June 19-4. Write up the ledger accounts, showing the transfers to the final accounts and the balances carried down to the next year for the following:

(*a*) Stationery: Paid for the year to 30 June 19-4 £855; Stocks of stationery at 30 June 19-3 £290; at 30 June 19-4 £345.
(*b*) General expenses: Paid for the year to 30 June 19-4 £590; Owing at 30 June 19-3 £64; Owing at 30 June 19-4 £90.
(*c*) Rent and Rates (combined account): Paid in the year to 30 June 19-4 £3,890; Rent owing at 30 June 19-3 £160; Rent paid in advance at 30 June 19-4 £250; Rates owing 30 June 19-3 £205; Rates owing 30 June 19-4 £360.
(*d*) Motor Expenses: paid in the year to 30 June 19-4 £4,750; Owing as at 30 June 19-3 £180; Owing as at 30 June 19-4 £375.
(*e*) Percival earns commission from the sales of one item. Received for the year to 30 June 19-4 £850; Owing at 30 June 19-3 £80; Owing at 30 June 19-4 £145.

19.19. On 1 January 19-6 the following appear in M. Nelson's Balance Sheet: Rates in advance £150.
During the year the following rates payments were made: 11 May 19-6 £400; 23 November 19-6 £400. The second £400 covers the period from 1 October 19-6 to 31 March 19-7.

Write up the account for the year ended 31 December 19-6, showing clearly the amount to be charged to the Profit and Loss Account for the year ended on that date.

Write down the amount which should appear in Nelson's Balance Sheet on 31 December 19-6, and indicate whether the amount is an asset or a liability.

19.20X. N. Roberts is a hotelier who heats his premises by oil-fired central heating.

On 1 January 19-5 the Stock of Oil in hand was £35 and £50 was in hand on 31 December 19-5. Reeves owed £60 to the Oil Suppliers on 1 January 19-5 and there was an invoice for oil supplied during 19-5, unpaid on 31 December 19-5 of £145. During the year 19-5 payments made to the Oil Suppliers amounted to £260.

Write up Reeves' Fuel Account for the year ending 31 December 19-5 showing the appropriate transfer to Profit and Loss Account and bringing down any remaining balances.

19.21. From the following Trial Balance of John Brown, restaurateur, prepare a Trading Account and Profit and Loss Account, taking into consideration the adjustments shown below:

Trial Balance as at 31 December 19-7

	Dr. £	*Cr.* £
Sales		40,000
Purchases	15,000	
Sales Returns	500	
Purchases Returns		620
Opening Stock at 1 January 19-7	10,000	
Provision for Bad Debt		80
Wages and salaries	13,000	
Rates	600	
Telephone	100	
Fittings and Equipment at cost	14,000	
Van at cost	3,000	
Debtors and creditors	980	700
Bad Debts	20	
Capital		17,900
Bank balance	300	
Drawings	1,800	
	59,300	59,300

Adjustments:
(i) Closing stock at 31 December 19-7 £12,000.
(ii) Accrued wages £500.
(iii) Rates prepaid £50.
(iv) The Provision for Bad Debts to be increased to 10 per cent of Debtors.
(v) Telephone Account outstanding £22.
(vi) Deprreciate shop fittings at 10 per cent per annum, and van at 20 per cent per annum, on cost.
(vii) Staff meals £1,000.
A Balance Sheet is not required.

19.22. J. Graham drew up the following trial balance as at 30 September 19-8. You are to draft trading and profit and loss accounts for the year to 30 September 19-8 and a balance sheet as at that date.

	Dr.	Cr.
	£	£
Loan from P. Parkin		5,000
Capital		25,955
Drawings	8,420	
Cash at Bank	23,115	
Cash in Hand	295	
Debtors	12,300	
Creditors		9,370
Stock 30 September 19-7	3,910	
Motor Van (Cost £6,000)	4,100	
Office Equipment (Cost £8,000)	6,250	
Sales		130,900
Purchases	62,100	
Returns Inwards	550	
Carriage Inwards	215	
Returns Outwards		307
Carriage Outwards	309	
Motor Expenses	1,630	
Rent and Rates	2,970	
Telephone Charges	405	
Wages and Salaries	42,810	
Insurance	492	
Office Expenses	1,377	
Sundry Expenses	284	
	171,532	171,532

Notes at 30 September 19-8:

(*a*) Prepaid expenses: Insurance £105; Rates £405.
(*b*) Expenses owing: Rent £300; Telephone £85.
(*c*) Stock £27,475.
(*d*) Depreciate Motor Van and Office Equipment at the rate of 20 per cent on original cost.

Keep your answer. It will be used as the basis for 19.24X.

19.23X. The following trial balance was extracted from the records of J. Jordan, a restaurant proprietor, as at 31 December 19-1:

	Dr.	*Cr.*
	£	£
Discounts Allowed	410	
Discounts Received		506
Carriage Inwards	309	
Carriage Outwards	218	
Returns Inwards	1,384	
Returns Outwards		810
Sales		120,320
Purchases	44,290	
Stock 31 December 19-0	10,816	
Motor Expenses	4,917	
Repairs to Premises	1,383	
Salaries and Wages	36,184	
Sundry Expenses	807	
Rates and Insurance	2,896	
Premises at Cost	40,000	
Motor Vehicles at Cost	11,160	
Provision for depreciation motors as at 31.12.19-0		3,860
Debtors and Creditors	31,640	24,320
Cash at Bank	4,956	
Cash in Hand	48	
Drawings	12,736	
Capital		50,994
Loan from P. Holland		4,000
Bad Debts	1,314	
Provision for bad debts at 31 December 19-0		658
	205,468	205,468

The following matters are to be taken into account at 31 December 19-1:

(i) Stock £16,420.

(ii) Expenses owing: Sundry Expenses £62; Motor Expenses £33.

(iii) Prepayment: Rates £166.

(iv) Provision for bad debts to be reduced to £580.

(v) Depreciation for motors to be £2,100 for the year.

(vi) Part of the premises were let to a tenant who owed £250 at 31 December 19-1.

(vii) Loan Interest owing to P. Holland £4,000.

You are required to prepare a Trading and Profit and Loss Account for the year ended 31 December 19-1, and a Balance Sheet as at that date.

19.24X. Redraft 19.22 in vertical form with % column.

19.25X. Harvey Brown is a caterer. From the following information prepare a Trading and Profit and Loss Account for the year ended 31 December 19-4 and a Balance Sheet on that date.

Trial Balance – 31 December 19-4

	£	£
Capital 1 January 19-4		6,400
Land and buildings	5,000	
Motor vehicles (cost £1,200)	600	
Drawings	1,400	
Stock	910	
Bank overdraft		96
Sales		14,260
Purchases	6,100	
Motor expenses	310	
Sundry expenses	106	
Wages	6,560	
Debtors	820	
Creditors		1,210
Rates and insurance	160	
	21,966	21,966

The following items should be taken into consideration:

(*a*) Stock at 31 December 19-4 £1,820.
(*b*) A provision for doubtful debts of 5 per cent on the debtors at 31 December 19-4 is to be created.
(*c*) Depreciation is to be provided on motor vehicles at 20 per cent on cost.
(*d*) Rates prepaid at 31 December 19-4 £12.
(*e*) Motor expenses bill for December £26 is owing at 31 December 19-4.
(*f*) Sundry expenses includes £15 for a private telephone bill of Angus Brown.
(*g*) A cheque for £250 was paid to a creditor on 31 December 19-4 but had not been entered in the books at the time of extracting the trial balance.

(Keep your answer. It will be used as a basis for question 19.27X.)

19.26X. On 31 October 19-9 the financial position of J. Frost was as follows: Cash at bank £900; Trade creditors £1,750; Motor vehicles (cost £1,000) £750; Sundry debtors £1,200; Cash in hand £50; Stock-in-trade £2,000; Drawings £2,000; Capital at 1 November 19-8 £2,600.

During the year ended 31 October 19-9 Frost earned a Net Profit of £2,550.

You are required to:

Prepare J. Frost's Balance Sheet as at 31 October 19-9 in a vertical form, showing clearly all the totals and sub-totals normally found in a Balance Sheet including 'Working Capital'.

19.27X. From your answer to question 19.25X, draw up the final accounts in a vertical form, taking into account Staff Meals of £1,500 and food used by Brown for private use £500.

20

The Hotel Tabular Ledger

Learning Objectives

At the end of this chapter you should be able to:

20A **Apply accountancy principles to the preparation of the Visitors' Ledger (Tabular Ledger).**

Hoteliers with over 20 rooms usually decide to operate a hotel tabular ledger or visitors' ledger for the accounts of their guests. Many establishments with less than 20 rooms will also operate the system.

The proprietor or manager has three choices:

1. Operate a manual ledger which may be a 3 in 1 system.
2. Mechanise the operation using a hotel billing machine.
3. Computerise the system.

This chapter will consider only the basic manual tabular ledger, as this illustrates all the basic principles involved. All entries in the ledger in Exhibit 20.1 are inclusive of VAT and should be self explanatory. The number of sales categories has been kept to a minimum. Each hotel must decide on the amount of analysis required for control purposes.

Notes to Exhibits 20.1, 20.2, 20.3 and 20.4

1. The tabular ledger forms part of the double entry but deviates from the normal practice. Usually the book-keeper makes a day book entry from a voucher and then completes the double entry in the ledgers later.

In the tabular ledger system the receptionist enters into the ledger direct from the voucher but only completes one step of the double entry. It should be understood that the tabular ledger is a ledger of personal accounts used for credit transactions and later money settlements and is really a sales ledger. The next step is to make the daily entry in the monthly summary sheet (Exhibit 20.4) which is a day book and at the month end the double entry will be completed in the various accounts in the general ledger. It is also possible to operate a control account and make the tabular ledger self balancing. This is shown in Exhibits 20.2, 20.3.

2. *Visitors' Paid Out (VPO)*

This is not a sale by the hotel. It means that the hotel is prepared to pay a supplier on the guest's behalf and charge the payment to the guest's account in the tabular ledger (abbreviated in following examples as Tab. L).

If we take the item in Exhibit 20.1 room 5 £4 to be a taxi fare paid on behalf of Miss May by the receptionist using petty cash the double entry would be

1. DR VPO
   CR Petty Cash
2. DR Room 5
   CR VPO

The VPO account would appear as follows:

VPO

1st May	Petty Cash		£4	1st May	Tab. L	Room 5	£4

3. *Advance Bookings*

Suppose Miss May has paid a £10 deposit on 31st March the double entry would have been debit cash book credit advanced deposits. If she left on 2nd May owing £40 she would only pay £30 and the balance on the advance deposit account would be transferred to the tabular ledger.

Advanced Deposits

2nd May	Tab. L	Room 5	£10	31st March	Cash Book	£10

Exhibit 20.1

Tabular Ledger
1 May 19-5

Tariff	£
Double Room	10
Single	7
Breakfast	1
Lunch	3
Dinner	4

Transactions 1st May 19-5

1. Balance b/F 30th April 19-5.
   Room 1 £100, Room 2 £58, Room 3 £80.
   Room 4 £30, Room 5 £12, Total £280.
2. Charge accommodation for the day.
   Room 1 double, Room 2 single, Room 3 double, Room 4 single, Room 5 single.
3. All residents take breakfast.

4. Lunches are served as follows:
   Room 1 Mr. & Mrs. Brown Chance trade £9.
   3 Mr. & Mrs. Green
   5 Miss May.
5. Other charges including VAT for the day:
   Room 1 £4 Room 3 £1
6. Other charges:
   Room 3 Books & Newspapers £4 } No VAT
   Room 4 Newspapers £2 }
7. VPO:
   Room 3 Taxi £7
   5 Theatre tickets £4
8. Afternoon departures.
   Room 3 settled in cash.
   4 Transfer to Sales Ledger A/c Gray Bros. Ltd.
9. Allowance Room 5 £1 for noisy room.
10. Dinners served:
   Room 1 Mr. & Mrs. Brown, Room 2 Mr. Smith, Room 5 Miss May.

		Debit									*Credit*					
Room No.	*Guest*	Bal. b/f	Room	Breakfast	Lunch	Dinner	Other inc. VAT	Non VAT	V.P.O.	Total	Allow. inc VAT	Allow. non VAT	Cash	Ledger	Bal. c/f	Total
1	Mr. & Mrs. A. Brown	100	10	2	6	8	4			130					130	130
2	Mr. J. Smith	58	7	1		4				70					70	70
3	Mr. & Mrs. F. Green	80	10	2	6		1	4	7	110			110			110
4	Mr. J. Jones of Gray Bros. Ltd.	30	7	1				2		40				40		40
5	Miss I. May	12	7	1	3	4			4	31	1				30	31
	Chance				9					9			9			9
	Total	280	41	7	24	16	5	6	11	390	1		119	40	230	390

Exhibit 20.2

Trial Balance 30/4/19-5

Room	*Dr*	*Cr*
1	100	
2	58	
3	80	
4	30	
5	12	
Control		280
	280	280

Trial Balance 1/5/19-5

1	130	
2	70	
3	30	
Control		230
	230	230

Exhibit 20.3

Control A/c in Tab. Ledger

1/5	Cash	119	30/4	Bal. B/d	280
	Sales Ledger	40	1/5	Total Sales	110
	Allow.	1			
	Bal. C/d	230			
		390			390

Control A/c in General Ledger

30/4	Bal. B/d	280	1/5	Cash	119
1/5	Total Sales	110		Sales Ledger	40
				Allow.	1
				Bal. C/d	230
		390			390

Exhibit 20.4

Monthly Summary Sheet

Date 19-5	Rooms	Breakfast	Lunch	Dinner	Other inc. VAT	Allowing VAT	VAT *	Non VAT Items	Allow Non VAT	VPO
May 1	41	7	24	16	5	(1)	12	6	–	11
Etc										
May 31	2,000	1,500	1,000	1,500	1,000	(100)	900	300	(100)	200

Note: Brackets indicate DEBITS. All other entries are credits i.e. sales. The totals are posted to the general ledger at the month end.

*VAT Calculation

VAT Outputs

$$41 + 7 + 24 + 16 + 5 - 1 = £92$$

$$\text{VAT} \quad \frac{15}{115} \times 92 = £12.$$

Exercises

20.1X. Write up the Hotel Tabular Ledger from the following:

Tariff for the Beach Hotel

Room and Breakfast	£3.50 (inc. of Bft. 50p) per person
Inclusive Terms	£6.00 (inc. of Board £3.00) per person
Private bathroom	£2.00 per room per night
Early morning beverage	10p per person
Morning coffee	15p per person
Table d'hote lunch	£1.00 per person
Meal beverage	10p extra per person

N.B. Terms are charged, in this hotel, in advance or for new arrivals immediately upon on arrival. Inclusive terms cover room, breakfast, lunch, afternoon tea and dinner only.

List of guests in residence:

Type	*Terms*	*Room No.*	*Name*	*Amount b/f*
Double & bath	Inc.	12A	Mr/s. Gough-Davies	£14.35
Single & bath	R & B	15	Miss Lyall	£11.54
Single	R & B	16	Mr. E.C.E. Smith	£22.15
Twin-bedded	R & B	17	Mr/s. E. Cullinane	£13.51

List of transactions:

0730 Early morning beverages to all residents.
Newspapers: 12A – 10p; 15 – 5p; 16 – 8p; 17 – 10p.
0745 Telephones: 12A – £1.75; 17 – 90p.
0815 Disbursements: 17 – 75p for taxi; 16 – 80p for dry cleaning.
0830 Breakfasts served to all residents.
0845 Chance breakfasts £4.
0900 Departure: 17 checks out and the account, less an advance deposit of £3, is sent for payment to the Sea Angling Club (S/11).
0930 Room 12A checks out and pays account by cheque.
1000 Mr. Smith pays £10 on account.
1100 Arrivals: Mr. & Mrs. Henry – Room 17 on inclusive terms
Mr. & Mrs. M. Steele given room 12A on inclusive terms.
1130 Morning coffees to all residents.
1145 Chance morning coffees £3.15.
1200 Arrival: Capt. Blossom. Given rooom 14 (Single and bath) on R & B.
1215 Change of room – 14 to 18 (single).
1230 Lunches: 12A – two lunches, coffee for 2, wine £1.75.
15 – £1, coffee 10p, gin and tonic 29p.
16 – £1, wine 39p, cigar 27p.
17 – two lunches, 1 coffee, brandy 90p.
18 – £1, 1 cigar 35p.
Chance lunches – £13.80; beverages – £1.30; wines – £3.80; spirits and liqueurs – £2.70; minerals – 18p; tobacco – 87p.
1430 Allowances and adjustments (for the correction of errors in yesterday's tab):
Omission of 50p VPO (taxi) for Room 16.
Overcharge of 10p for EMT for Room 15.
1500 Meeting in the Westbourne Room for Green Fingers Club: Room £5; Private bar £18.13; Buffet £11.50: a/c transferred to ledger.
1515 Lounge bar pays in £35.70 for liquor and £6.80 for tobacco.

20.2X. Write up the Hotel Tabular Ledger from the following:

Tariff for the Resthaven Hotel

Room and Breakfast	£6.75 (inc. of Bfst. 75p) per person
Full Board	£10.75 (inc. board £4.75) per person
Private Bathroom	£3.00 supplement per room
Early Morning Tea	15p per person
Morning coffee	20p per person
Table d'hôte lunch	£2.00 per person
Meal beverage	20p per person

N.B. (i) Terms are charged, in this hôtel, in advance, or for new arrivals immediately on arrival.
(ii) Full Board covers bed, breakfast, lunch and dinner.
(iii) All charges are fully inclusive of service charge and VAT.

List of guests in residence:

Type	*Terms*	*Room No.*	*Name*	*Amount b/f*
Double & bath	F.B.	206	Mr/s. J. Davey	£31.26
Single	R & B	211	Mr. D. Adey	£11.54
Twin	R & B	214	Mr/s. S. Miller	£13.42
Single & bath	F.B.	218	Miss J. Johnson	£24.60

List of transactions:

0730 Early morning beverages to all residents.
Newspapers: Room 206 – 7p; Room 211 – 10p; Room 214 – 7p; Room 218 – 15p.

0800 Telephone: Room 211 – £1.22.
Disbursements: Room 218 Dry Cleaning 80p; Room 206 Flowers £2.50.

0830 Breakfast to all residents.
Chance breakfasts £4.50.

0900 Departures:
Room 211 – signs his bill for forwarding to Computerix Ltd. (folio L24).
Room 214 – pays by cheque.

1000 Room 206 Mr. Davey pays £30 on account.

1030 Morning coffee to all residents. Chance morning coffees £2.00.

1115 Arrival: Mr. J. Cross, Room 112, single with bath, R & B terms.

1130 Arrival: Mr/s. Dupont, Room 214, R & B terms.

1230 Lunches: Rooom 206 – 2 lunches, 2 coffees, wine £3.25.
Room 218 – 1 lunch, lager 32p.
Room 214 – 2 lunches, 2 coffees, wine £2.80, Vichy Water 60p.
Chance lunches: Food £22.00, coffee £1.80, wine £11.30, spirits and liqueurs £3.26, cigars £1.60.

1430 Allowances and adjustments:
Room 206 – charged 7p for newspaper in error.
Room 218 – not charged £1.25 for wine with last night's dinner.

1500 Function Charge: The Rockford Room – S.W. Marketing Services Ltd. – Room hire £25.00, 90 lunches @ £3.25, bar £68.00, wine £120.00, tobacco £8.25. Account to ledger L.6, less advance deposit £100.

1530 Lounge bar pays in £42.00 drinks, £7.40 tobacco, £18.50 bar snacks.

21

Purchasing Practice

Learning Objectives

At the end of this chapter you should be able to:

21A Recognise the significance of purchasing research as an aid to managerial planning.

21B Apply the principles of stock management.

The buyer's motto is to obtain the goods and services requested at the right quality, the right price, and the right time.

Purchasing research should take place in the following areas:

1. Research into Food and Beverage Materials

Price trends should be watched and if necessary statistical method should be used to produce information not available from trade magazines or other published material.

The prices paid for food and beverage materials should be kept in relationship to the prices charged to customers. This is necessary to achieve the gross profit percentage.

Continuity of supply should be ensured by entering into a contract if the trend shows a commodity becoming scarce or costly.

Finding the Trend by Statistical Method

The buyer needs to know how prices are changing with time. Are prices for a particular commodity increasing, decreasing or remaining the same? Is there seasonal variation?

Let us take an example of a long term contract where the catering firm takes a given quantity per quarter of food item 'X'.

(1) Year	(2) Quarter	(3) £'00 Cost	(4) Moving Annual Total (MAT)	(5) Moving Average of Fours (MA)
1	1	73		
	2	71		
			287	71.75
	3	70		
			289	72.25
	4	73		
			291	72.75
2	1	75		
			292	73.00
	2	73		
			295	73.75
	3	71		
	4	76		

Column (4) Moving Annual Total is calculated by adding up the costs in column (3) for the first full year, i.e. $73+71+70+73 = 287$. This is put in column (4) on a level in between the figures in column (3) for the 2nd and 3rd quarters. The next figure in column (4) i.e. 289 is calculated by dropping off the figure for the 1st quarter of year 1 and adding the figure for the 1st quarter of year 2, i.e. $287-73+75 = 289$. By doing this it becomes a 'moving' annual average. When each of the figures in column (4) is divided by 4 it becomes the moving average of fours, i.e. it is the moving quarterly average, as shown in column (5).

Columns (3) and (5) can be plotted on a time series graph. Note that the time scale is always on the *horizontal* axis. See Exhibit 21.1.

If you were to simply look at the figures in column (3), quarter by quarter, it is not too evident what the trend is. If however the trend line, as shown by the moving average of fours (5) on the graph is looked at then the fact that the trend is very much an upward one can be clearly seen. This is the great advantage of showing data in a trend presentation rather than just the actual costs of each period.

The trend line enables the buyer to answer the question 'how are costs and prices for item 'X' generally'. The answer is clear – upwards.

Exhibit 21.1

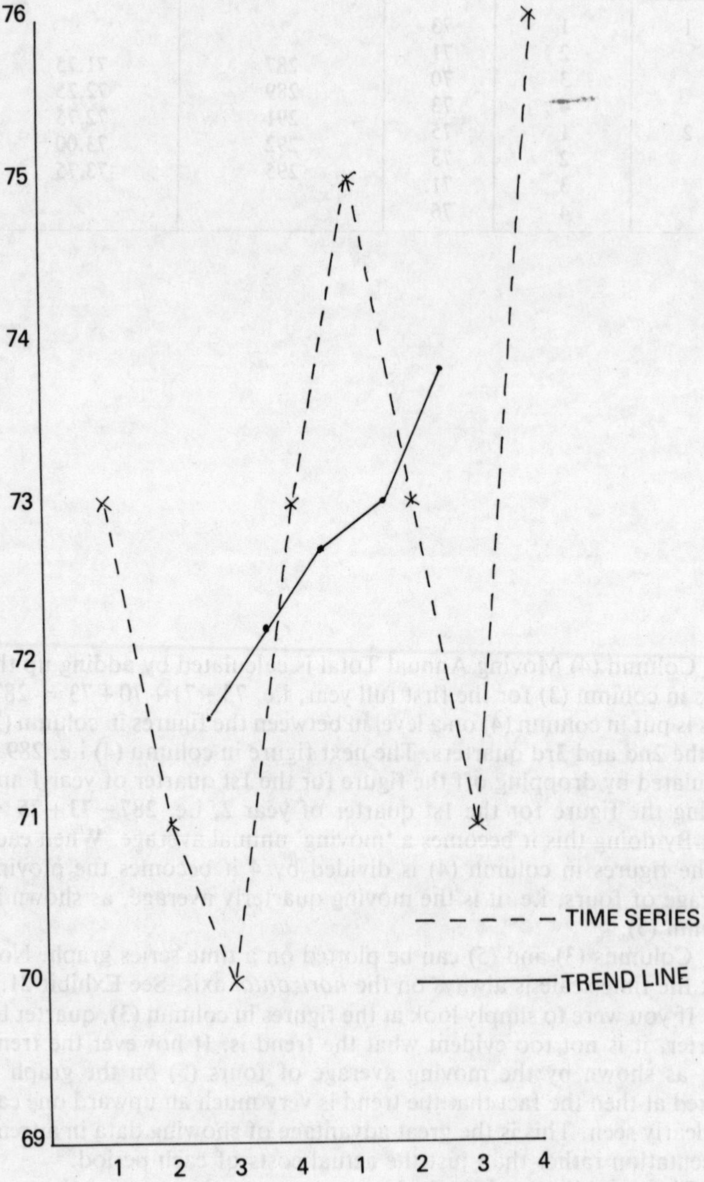
76
75
74
73
72
71
70
69
1
2
3
4
1
2
3
4
Year 1
Year 2
TIME SERIES
TREND LINE

Periodic Variations

The buyer may wish to know if the costs vary according to the time of year irrespective of the general trend. Two year's data may not be sufficient to answer the above question. The following is an example taking 5 years figures.

Year	*Quarter 1*	*Quarter 2*	*Quarter 3*	*Quarter 4*
1	73	71	70	73
2	75	73	71	76
3	77	74	76	78
4	78	77	76	79
5	79	78	76	79
Totals	382	373	369	385
Averages (a)	76.4	74.6	73.8	77.0
Overall Average (b)	75.45	75.45	75.45	75.45
Periodic Variations (a) – (b)	+0.95	−0.85	−1.65	+1.55

The overall average is obtained, of course, by dividing the total of all the figures (382 + 373 + 369 + 385 = 1,509) by the number of items (20). Look at the periodic variations, and particularly the + and − signs; they tell us that:

(*a*) In any year, first quarter sales can be expected to be 0.95 (i.e. £95) *above* average.

(*b*) In any year, second quarter sales can be expected to be 0.85 (i.e. £85) *below* average.

(*c*) In any year, third quarter sales can be expected to be 1.65 (i.e. £165) *below* average.

(*d*) In any year, fourth quarter sales can be expected to be 1.55 (i.e. £155) *above* average.

You can always check the correctness of your calculations, because the positive variations should add up to the same as the negative variations, thus: –

0.95 + 1.55 should equal 0.85 + 1.65
i.e. 2.50 should equal 2.50 which it does!

2. Cost Analysis

The buyer should be aware of developments in food technology, and receive the full co-operation of the production departments in comparing portion prices bought out with the cost of similar portions produced internally. This is usually referred to as a 'make or buy decision'. Obviously there are lots of examples among food items where a decision has to be taken:

Frozen vegetable	v	fresh vegetables
Preportioned meat	v	meat prepared from raw weight (see Yield Testing.)
Frozen gateaux etc.	v	Prepared gateaux etc.

It is important to compare quality as well as cost before taking a decision.

Stock Management

A periodic physical stocktaking is necessary for the following reasons.

1. To check the stores records for receipts and issues and the book value of stock. Any discrepancy should be entered in the stores record card and/or bin card. Any corrective or disciplinary action should be taken to avoid repetition of the variance.
2. A correct food and beverage stock is required every time a trading account is prepared. This will ensure the accuracy of the cost of food and beverage and the correct gross profit percentage which is a very important yardstick in hotel and catering operations.

Stocktaking should be undertaken by senior staff from the accounts, food and beverage and buying departments. Smaller firms may place this responsibility on the manager or employ an outside professional stock taker. The time of the stocktaking is very important and it usually coincides with the date of the accounting period in question i.e. quarter ended or year ended. Business should not be undertaken when stocktaking takes place therefore it is common, especially in hotels, for the stocktaking to be undertaken during the night. This may require several members of staff. The ideal situation would be to have 13 accounting periods of 28 days but many firms stocktake only each quarter and others only once each year.

Rate of Stock Turnover

This provides a useful guide to the buyer. Guide lines should be established by the management to indicate the value of stock to be held at any one time and the rate of stock turnover.

The formula for rate of stock turnover (RST) is:

$$\frac{\text{COST OF FOOD AND BEVERAGES}}{\text{AVERAGE STOCK}}$$

The average stock in a firm with 13 accounting periods would be:

$$\frac{\text{Total of each stocktaking in a year}}{13}$$

If we look at one 28 day trading period the accounting system will provide:

The opening stock say	£800
closing stock	£600
purchases of Food and Beverages	£2,600

therefore Cost of F & B would be: £800 + £2,600 − £600 = £2,800

Average stock $\frac{£800 + £600}{2} = £700$

,, Rate of Stock Turnover (RST) = $\frac{£2,800}{£700}$ = 4 times

,, If in a four week period stock is turned over 4 times, the amount actually kept in stock at any time should equal 4 weeks ÷ 4 (Stock turnover rate) = 1 weeks stock. In other words these should always be enough in stock to be able to service the next 1 week's use of it.

A firm with a relatively low rate of stock turnover will have the following problems.

1. Capital is tied up in slow moving stock which could have been invested elsewhere. For instance, suppose that stock is to be bought to last for a month. A sensible figure might be £50,000 and that cash would come out of the bank. Suppose instead that far too much stock was bought, quite unnecessarily, and that £74,000 was spent instead. For the whole of the month an extra £24,000 was kept. Not only would it take up extra space, and give other problems, but there would not be any financial return on that £24,000. If instead of spending it on stock it had been invested elsewhere at (say) 10 per cent per annum then it would have earned £24,000 × 10% p.a. for one month = £200. The firm would therefore have been £200 better off if the extra stock had not been bought, just in terms of interest earned, but it might have also cost extra money to keep it stored as well, e.g. electricity for freezers and so on.
2. Risk of spoilage.
3. Cost of staff in store administration will be relatively high.
4. The stock will have to be insured therefore the premium will be unnecessarily high.

Stock Levels

Each item of stock should have a maximum and minimum level (see chapter 3). These levels are difficult to determine but the following guidelines should be used:

1. The maximum and minimum forecast of stock usage figures for the trading period are based on past records and forecast sales volume.
2. The re-ordering time for each stock item.
3. The economic ordering quantity.
4. Any changes in delivery times.
5. Any changes in cost prices
6. Periods of time when a particular item is scarce.
7. The storage space available.
8. The shelf life of stock items, obviously many food items will go bad if kept beyond a certain time.
9. Details of the purchasing or cost of sales budget.

The following points should be determined for each stock item:

(*a*) The safety stock (buffer stock). This is the lowest stock which will exist if purchasing follows the plan. If it is not possible to purchase according to plan then the buffer stock will have to be used. This can only happen in the short term, as constantly using buffer stocks means that stock have constantly been kept at too low a level.

(*b*) The working stock i.e. the stock in use which rises and falls with stores receipts and issues.

(*c*) The re-order level i.e. the level where it is necessary to re-order to ensure that the stock of any item will not run out. This level will need constant attention from the buyer, especially for fresh food items. Re-order level should include the buffer stock to give protection against a stop in production, due to lack of a stock item.

There is a useful formula:

Re-Order Level =

$$ROL = PL + B$$

P = future demand of an item per period.
L = expected obtainment time in periods.
B = buffer stock.

The use of the above formula can be illustrated by an example of a vintage wine using a weekly period:

Suppose the expected demand for the vintage wine is 10 bottles per week and it takes 2 weeks to obtain. The buffer stock is 15 bottles.

The re-order level would be:

$$\begin{aligned} ROL &= PL + B \\ &= (10 \times 2) + 15 \\ &= 20 + 15 \\ &= 35 \text{ bottles.} \end{aligned}$$

Pareto Analysis

Pareto was an eighteenth century economist who established what has become known as the '80/20 rule', which can be applied to stock holding in industry. Basically the rule means that the value of 80% of sales are accounted for by only 20% of the range of items for sale.

For a lot of firms in certain industries, it will be found on investigation that the bulk of the stock used consists of a relatively few items. Take a publisher as an instance who has 1,000 different titles which he publishes. Of these titles 50 may be best-sellers accounting for, say, a total of 2 million sales per annum, whilst the other 950 titles may sell only ½ million copies between them. It is obvious therefore that in this firm the highest priority be given to stocking the best-sellers. If a best-seller runs out of stock at a peak time, e.g. before Christmas in the case of novels bought as Christmas presents, the sales lost forever could be considerable. If a low-selling book ran out of stock the loss would normally be relatively small.

Similarly, in the case of a restaurant it may be found that red wine X sales consist of 2,000 per annum, whilst red wine Y sells only 10 bottles a year. Obviously the restaurant is going to pay far more attention to ensuring that it has stock of wine X than it will of wine Y.

If therefore, stock control is to be properly carried out, most of the attention should be focussed on the items which constitute the major part of sales. In firms where it is not possible to have full stock control, at least these items should have some sort of control imposed upon them, and lack of stock control falling on the other items.

Exercises

21.1X. Distinguish between buffer stock and working stock.

21.2. Calculate the re-order level from the following data:
Budgeted future demand per month (4 weeks) 1,000 units.
Delivery time after order 2 weeks.
Buffer stock 50 units.

21.3X. How can Pareto's theory be applied to stock management?

21.4X. Calculate the buffer stock if:
Re-order level is 400 units.
Budgeted purchasing per month is 200 units.
Delivery time after order is 6 weeks.

21.5X. In the past many hospitals and other institutions, as well as hotels, maintained their own upholstery departments in order to make their own soft furnishings, uniforms, and upholstery. This practice declined but is now re-emerging.

You are required to:

(*a*) Discuss the considerations to be borne in mind when deciding whether to "make or buy", illustrating your answer with the above example, or any other relevant area with which you are familiar.

(*b*) Briefly describe other "make or buy" areas in the Industry.

(HCIMA)

22

Budgetary Control Part I

Learning Objectives

At the end of this chapter you should be able to:

22A **Appreciate the difference between forecasting and budgeting.**

22B **Distinguish between flexible and fixed budgets.**

22C **Prepare capital and operating budgets.**

22D **Prepare a master budget.**

Accounting for Management Control

Introduction

The recording function of accounting, often called book-keeping, and the drafting of the final accounts is called Financial Accounting. Much of it is concerned with legal requirements, such as complying with the provisions of the Income Tax Laws when drafting final accounts, or keeping an accounting record of a customer's legal indebtedness, i.e. a debtor's account. These accounts are also given to other interested parties such as the bankers to the firm, creditors, Inspectors of Taxes etc.

Whilst Financial Accounting is necessary from a legal point of view, it cannot be said to be ideal from the point of view of controlling the activities of a firm. The use of accounting for controlling the activities of a firm is probably more important, therefore we will now look at accounting for "Management Control" purposes. The word "management" does not necessarily mean that the concern is a limited company, although most of the larger organizations in the private sector of industry would in fact be limited companies. It means instead the people who are managing the affairs of the organisation, whether they are directors, partners, sole traders or "managers" classified as those employees who are in charge of other employees.

Before starting to examine Accounting for Management Control let us look first at the deficiencies of Financial Accounting when we want to control the activities of an organization. Its first deficiency is that it deals with operations that have already occurred: it deals with the past, not the future. It is possible to control something whilst it is happening, and control can be arranged for something that is going to happen, but when it has already happened without being controlled then the activity has ended and we are too late to do anything about control. In this way if a firm incurs a loss and we do not realize it until long after the event then the loss cannot be prevented. What we really want to do is to control affairs so that a loss is not incurred if at all possible, and we should be able to call on accounting techniques to help in the control of activities. However, it certainly does not mean that we are not interested in the past. We can learn lessons from the past which can be very useful in understanding what is going on now, and what is likely to be happening in the future.

The second deficiency of Financial Accounting is that it is concerned with the whole of the firm. Thus the Trading Account of a firm may show a gross profit of £60,000, and whilst it is better to know that than to have no idea at all of what the gross profit is, it does not tell management much about past transactions.

This means that Financial Accounting is of little use by itself for Management Control purposes. It does not mean that it is of no use at all for control purposes, as for instance the Financial accounting system may reveal that the debtors at a point in time are £50,000. Management need to know this if they are to control their finances properly, but although this is true of some accounting figures in Financial Accounting many of the other accounting figures may not be much use in controlling the business. For example if a building was bought in 1930 for £20,000 it may well be worth £200,000 today, whilst if we rented a similar building now it might cost us £30,000 a year. We would surely not use the original cost of £20,000 as the deciding factor as to what we will do now with the building.

Objectives of the Firm

Before we can discuss Management Control we have to ask ourselves what it is for, we cannot really have control unless it is for a purpose. It would be generally agreed that Management Control is needed in guiding the firm so that it achieved its objectives. Before any plans can be drawn up in financial terms the objectives of the firm should be defined quite clearly by the directors or owners of a firm. It must not be thought that to make as much profit as possible is the objective of every firm. It would still beg the question of whether it was maximum profit in the long term or the short term that was most important.

In fact it is very rare for the objectives of a firm to be spelled out clearly and unambiguously. Just because in theory it would be a good idea if all firms were to write down their objectives, so that misunderstandings could be cleared up more easily does not mean that it is done. In every walk of life there is a great deal of muddled thinking, and boards of directors and owners of firms are no exception to the general rule. There is a great deal of "muddling through'' without any really clear ideas in which direction the firm is heading. If the objectives are uncertain then management control must also be uncertain, and the muddled thinking will penetrate downwards from the board of directors to the kitchen.

Objectives could be expressed in terms of profit and in addition other factors could be brought in. Instances could be the size of the share of the market the firm wished to achieve, the quality of the service, the sense of obligation to its employees or the duty of the firm to the community at large. As to whether or not a firm has good management control this can only be found by looking at how effective the management control system was in guiding the firm towards its objectives. Thus a firm making artificial limbs might conceivably set itself a much lower profit target than it could make, because the directors put product quality before profit. The management control system in that case is concerned more with quality than it would be with profit. But the directors may well have stipulated a profit figure they must achieve, even though it is lower than they could manage if they let quality slide, and therefore the management control system would have as its task the maintaining of the highest quality product possible while still achieving the profit target.

Accounting and Management Control

It must not be thought that accounting of any form is the Management Control System. Instead it is part of it. A great deal of information is required by managers at every level if they are to be able to tackle their jobs effectively. Depending on which manager it is, they will need information on orders, manpower, equipment and materials. To take orders as an example some of them will need to know details of orders received, orders completed, orders uncompleted, orders given to sub-contractors and orders withdrawn by customers because of the firm's inability to meet their requirements. Much of this information will be in non-accounting terms, as accounting deals only with items which can be expressed in monetary terms.

People and Management Control

It is also to point out that the most important resource of any firm are the people who work in it. A danger exists that a great deal of care and attention may be given to designing a management control system and operating it, but this is absolutely of no use to management if it does not result in action by the human beings in the firm. Systems and figures do not themselves do anything, instead it is the people in the firm who take (or do not take) the necessary action.

You must bear in mind that figures thrown up by accounting systems are only part of the evidence available when a decision has to be made as to the necessary action. A particular department may be incurring losses now, but the sales manager may give as his considered opinion that sales will increase soon and that the department will become profitable. If people accepted accounting figures as the only criteria on which action should be based then there would be some very bad actions by management. Many of the now very successful catering services have started off by incurring losses in the early stages, and have been eventually successful because the firm has persevered with the service because they had the faith that it would eventually make the grade.

If it was possible to have exactly the same system of management control in three different firms, it might be found in firm A that the control system was useless because no one acted on the data produced. In firm B the control system might result in damage being done to the firm because management used the data as though it was the only criteria in gauging the actions it should take. In firm C it might be an extremely good system because the management saw the data as a useful guide in the planning and control of the firm, and had also made certain that the rest of the organization took the same view.

How human beings reacted to a management control system is therefore right at the heart of the problem of ensuring that an effective management control system is in use.

The Accountant and Management Control

As far as accounting and its use in management control is concerned, it must be stressed that the role of the accountant should not be pre-determined by any fixed ideas. Instead it is determined by the needs of the business in accordance with its objectives. The accounting question which should be asked is what does management need from the accountant to enable it to perform its task. An accountant in management should not just be someone who has learned certain techniques which he will apply. It is in catering for the needs of management where his role lies. This often means devising solutions to problems or of obtaining data which is well outside his previous experience and which he has never learned in his studies.

Divisions of Management Control

This can be divided between:

(1) *Planning* what the business is going to do. When this is put into accounting terms, i.e. monetary values placed on the plans, the statement of the plans is called a budget.

(2) *Operations.* Ensuring that specific tasks are carried out efficiently.

(3) *Measuring and Evaluating Performance.* Accounting has a major part to play in the measurement of what has been done and establishing how well it has been done.

This means that Management Control
states WHAT shall be done
sees that it IS done
checks HOW it has been done.

Before it is possible to draw up a plan in financial terms, i.e. a budget, the firm must know the costs of all the various operations in a business. For instance, if you were planning to buy a car and use it to travel 10,000 miles in the next year, you would need to know the cost of petrol and oil, insurance, motor tax, miles per litre obtained, and the probable cost of repairs, to be able to budget for the use of the car. The same applies to the costs of a business. A study of costs is also needed for many other purposes than drawing up budgets. The study of costs for accounting purposes is called "Cost Accounting".

Budgeting and Budgetary Control

Management control is needed to try to ensure that the organisation achieves its objectives. Once the objectives have been agreed, plans should be drawn up so that the progress of the firm can be directed towards the ends of specified in the objectives. Now it must not be thought that plans can be expressed only in accounting terms, or social objectives shown in a plan concerned with employee welfare. But some of the objectives, such as the attainment of a desired profit, or of the attainment of a desired growth in assets can be expressed in accounting terms. When a plan is expressed quantitavely it is known as a "budget" and the process of converting plans into budgets is known as "budgeting". In this book we are concerned primarily with budgets shown in monetary terms, i.e. financial budgets.

The budgeting process may be quite formal in a large organisation with committees set up to perform the task. On the other hand in a very small firm the owner may jot down his budget on a piece of scrap paper or even on the back of a used envelope. Some even manage without writing anything down at all, they have done the budgets in their heads and can easily remember them. This chapter is concerned with budgeting in a formal manner.

Studies have shown that the more that managers are brought into the budgeting process, then the more successful budgetary control is likely to be. A manager on whom a budget is imposed, rather than a manager who had an active part in the drafting of his budget, is more likely to pay less attention to the budget and use it unwisely in the control process.

Having sounded the warning that needs to be borne in mind constantly when budgeting, we can now look at the positive end of budgeting – to see the advantages of a good budgetary control system.

Budgets and Profit Planning

The methodology of budgetary control is probably accountancy's major contribution to management. Before we get down to the mechanics of constructing budgets we should first of all look at the main outlines of drafting budgets.

When the budgets are being drawn up the two main objectives must be uppermost in the minds of top management, that is that the budgets are for:

(*a*) Planning. This means a properly co-ordinated and comprehensive plan for the whole business. Each part must interlock with theother parts.

(*b*) Control. Just because a plan is set down on paper does not mean that the plan will carry itself out. Control is exercised via the budgets, thus the name budgetary control. To do this means that the responsibility of managers and budgets must be so linked that the responsible manager is given a guide to help him to produce certain desired results, and the actual achieved results can be compared against the expected, i.e. actual compared with budget.

Preparation of Estimates

The first thing to establish is what the limiting factors are in a firm. It may well be the fact that sales cannot be pushed above a certain amount, otherwise it might be the fact that the firm could sell as much as it can produce, but the productive capacity of the firm sets a limit. Whatever the limiting factor is, there is no doubt that this aspect of the firm will need more attention than probably any other. There would not, for instance, be much point in budgeting for the sale of 1,000 meals if production in the kitchen was not more than 700, or to produce 2,000 if only 1,300 of them could be sold.

There is no doubt that usually the most difficult estimate to make is that of sales revenue. This can be done by using one of two methods:

(i) Make a statistical forecast on the basis of the economic situation, conditions applying with reference to the foods sold by the company, and what is known about the actions of competitors.

(ii) The opposite is to make an internal forecast. This is usually done by asking each department to estimate the sales in their own areas, and then total the estimates. Sometimes the salesmen are not asked at all.

Now we should remember that much of the subject matter that you have read about, or are currently reading in Economics, is very relevant here. A knowledge of elasticity of demand, whether the product is a complementary product, e.g. the price of egg cups is linked to the demand for eggs, whether it is a substitute, e.g. that a rise in the price of butter may induce housewives to turn to other commodities instead, is very relevant in this area. Factors such as whether the firm has a monopoly, whether the firm has many small customers, a few large customers, or even one large customer, are of crucial importance. Estimating sales revenue is very much a matter of taking all the economic factors into account allied to other factors.

The sales budget is, however, more than just a sales forecast. Budgets should show the actions that management is taking to influence future events. If an increase in sales is desired the sales budget may show extra sales, which may well be an indication of the action that management is going to take by means of extra advertising, giving a better service, or changing profit margins to push up sales in that way.

Budgeting can be "fixed" or "flexible". Fixed budgeting is based on one sales figure. Flexible budgeting is based on a range of sales. This will be discussed in Chapter 23.

Operating and Capital Budgets

The sales budget is the main operating budget. Once it has been formulated the other operating budgets follow i.e. cost of sales, labour and overheads.

Other financial budgets will be capital in nature because they are concerned with the balance sheet. Examples are budgeting for replacing or improving fixed assets which in turn usually require medium or long term finance. A working capital budget is vital and the most important part of this is a cash budget.

The budgeting could be summarised in a diagram.

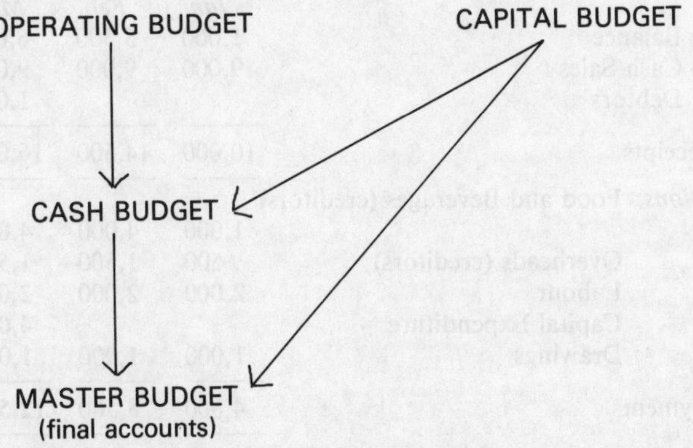

A practical example is shown in Exhibit 22.1.

Exhibit 22.1

The Downs Restaurant

Balance Sheet as 31.12.19-8

Fixed Assets at cost			10,000
Current Assets			
Stock	5,500		
Cash & Bank	1,000	6,500	
less Current Liabilities			
Creditors: –			
Food & Beverages	1,000		
Overheads	500	1,500	5,000
			£15,000
Capital			12,000
Loan for 3 years			3,000
			£15,000

Budget Details 19-9

1. Sales £120,000 p.a. 10% of which are on CREDIT. Average collection period 2 months.
2. Food & Beverages costs 40% of Sales. All on CREDIT. Average payment period 1 month.
3. Stock 31.12.19-8 to be the AVERAGE STOCK for the year 19-9.
4. LABOUR £24,000 p.a. OVERHEADS £18,000 p.a.
5. AVERAGE payment period for OVERHEADS 1 MONTH. (overheads do not include loan interest or depreciation)
6. LOAN INTEREST 16% p.a. PAID half-yearly, June and December.
7. CAPITAL EXPENDITURE £4,000 to be paid 31.3.19-9.
8. DEPRECIATION OF FIXED ASSETS £180 for the three months.
9. Cash drawings £1,000 per month.

Prepare

1. Cash budget for 3 months January to March 19-9.
2. Budgeted revenue account for 3 months ending 31.3.19-9.
3. Expected balance sheet as at 31.3.19-9.

Cash Budget

	19-9 Jan.	*Feb.*	*Mar.*
Opening Balance	1,000	5,500	6,000
Sources: Cash Sales	9,000	9,000	9,000
Debtors			1,000
Total Receipts	10,000	14,500	16,000
Applications: Food and Beverages (creditors)	1,000	4,000	4,000
Overheads (creditors)	500	1,500	1,500
Labour	2,000	2,000	2,000
Capital Expenditure			4,000
Drawings	1,000	1,000	1,000
Total payments	4,500	8,500	12,500
Closing balance	5,500	6,000	3,500

Budgeted Revenue Account for three months ending 31st March 19-9

			%
Sales		30,000	100
Cost of Sales 40%		12,000	40
Gross profit		18,000	60
Labour		6,000	20
Overheads	4,500		
Loan Interest	120		
Depreciation	180	4,800	16
Net profit		7,200	24

Budgeted Balance Sheet as at 31st March 19-9

Fixed assets	14,000		
less depreciation	180		13,820
Current assets stock	5,500		
debtors	2,000		
cash	3,500	11,000	
Current Liab. Creditors Food & Beverages	4,000		
Overheads	1,500		
Loan Interest	120	5,620	5,380
			19,200
Capital			
Balance as at 31.12.19-8	12,000		
Add: Net Profit	7,200		
	19,200		
Less: Drawings	3,000		16,200
Loan			3,000
			16,200

When the actual results are available they should be compared with the master budget. Any significant difference, i.e. a variance, should be investigated and corrected if possible. Variance analysis is discussed in Chapter 23.

Exercises

22.1X.(*a*) Who would you regard as essential members of a budget committee, and why?

(*b*) What factors would you consider when preparing the sales budget for a restaurant?

(HCIMA)

22.2. From the following forecasts of income and expenditure prepare a cash budget for the four months commencing 1st April 19-3.

Notes:

(*a*) Assume that all sales are on a cash basis.
(*b*) The time lag in the payment of suppliers accounts is two months.
(*c*) The time lag in the payment of overheads is one month; in the case of labour it is nil.
(*d*) New furniture costing £3,000 will be purchased in June and paid on delivery.
(*e*) The annual interest on the company's investments will be received in July; the amount is £1,000.

Month	*Sales*	*Purchases*	*Labour*	*Overheads*
February	10,000	4,000	3,000	4,000
March	11,000	10,000	3,000	3,000
April	12,000	8,000	4,000	2,000
May	14,000	6,000	4,000	6,000
June	16,000	7,000	5,000	5,000
July	12,000	7,000	3,000	4,000

You are informed that the company's bank balance on the 1st April 19-3 was £1,000.

22.3. (*a*) Define a budget and distinguish between capital budgets and revenue budgets giving two examples of each type.

(*b*) From the following information prepare a Profit Budget Statement for the year ending 28th February 19-3 and for each quarter.

Sales last year (19-1 – 19-2) amounted to £126,500 and for the year 19-2/3 are estimated at £16,500 above last year. The sales vary during the year and the amounts for the quarters to May, August, November and February are expected to conform to the ratio of 2:7:12:5.

Gross profit is estimated at 57% of sales.

Wages has traditionally been fixed at 31% of sales but it is planned this year to reduce the cost by 0.5% of sales.

Fixed expenses amount to £15,000 per annum, and other sundry variable expenses are estimated at 9% of sales.

Show on your budget statement the net profit percentages on sales for each quarter, and the year to two places of decimals.

22.4X. From the following information prepare a Cash Budget for the 3 months commencing 1st April 19-4.

Month	£ *Food Sales*	£ *Drink Sales*	£ *Food Purchases*	£ *Drink Purchases*	£ *Labour*	£ *Overheads*
Feb	15,000	4,500	6,000	2,200	6,000	5,200
Mar	15,500	4,800	6,100	2,400	6,200	5,200
April	17,000	5,400	6,800	2,700	6,500	5,400
May	17,800	6,300	7,000	3,200	6,900	5,600
June	23,000	6,900	7,300	3,400	7,500	5,800

Notes:
1. Assume all sales are cash sales.
2. £800 annual interest on investments will be received on May 15th.
3. The time lag in the payment of suppliers is 2 months: in the payment of overheads is one month; in the case of labour costs it is nil.
4. New kitchen plant costing £5,000 will be purchased in May and paid for in June.
5. The bank balance of the company on 1st April 19-2 is estimated to be £15,000.

22.5. Discuss the purpose and advantages of a cash budget, and prepare such a budget for the months of July, August and September, 19-9 on the following information:

		£
Bank and cash balance at 1st July		23,609
Sales for May		18,405
Estimated sales for June		19,811
	July	15,402
	August	17,663
Purchases for May		4,976
Estimated purchases for June		5,086
	July	5,023
	August	4,982
Estimated expenses payable in July		3,842
	August	4,185
	September	3,976
One quarter's rent at £3,600 p.a. on 1st July		
Half year's rates at £1,200 p.a. payable on 1st July		
Interim dividend of 5 per cent on capital of £60,000 due to be paid 2nd July (ignore taxation)		
Investment income expected 5th July		2,000
Estimated wages to be paid in July		4,061
	August	5,004
	September	3,896

Sales accounts are settled, on average, six weeks after the end of the month in which the sales were made.

Purchase accounts are settled on the 20th of the month following the end of the month in which the purchases were made.

22.6. A company, West Lodge Ltd., has been formed to take over an existing resort guest house as from 1st August 19-3. The capital of this company amounts to £100,000. The purchase price of the guest house will be £97,000, which represents the fixed assets only. The following targets have been set:

1. Net profit for the year, after charging £5,000 depreciation on fixed assets, to be £12,000.
2. Gross Profit will be 60% of *all* sales.
3. Labour costs will be 30% of sales with other overheads absorbing another 20% of sales. (Depreciation is included in this figure.)
4. 75% of all sales will be received in cash in the month of sale with the balance being received a month later. (Sales to be evenly spread over the year.)
5. Stock will be maintained at the level of two months' trading requirements.
6. Trade creditors will amount to £4,000 as at 31st July 19-4.

You are required to:

(*a*) Calculate the cash requirement for the year to 31st July 19-4, and draw up a budgeted Trading and Profit and Loss Account for the year followed by a budgeted Balance Sheet.

(*b*) Make appropriate comments on the results you have produced including, where relevant, the assumptions on which they are based.

(HCIMA)

22.7X. G. Rill plans to open a restaurant on 1st July, 19-9. He will invest capital of £40,000 in cash immediately and any additional needs will be met with the aid of a bank overdraft.

His initial requirements are furniture and equipment £38,000 (depreciated at 10% per annum) and food stocks £2,000. Meals are expected to be sold at 150% above food cost and 20% of the sales will be on credit, the remainder being for cash. Expected sales are £5,000 per months for the first three months and £6,000 per month thereafter. One month's credit is expected from suppliers of food and equipment. Monthly wages and other expenses paid out in cash will be £1,600. This does not include rent and insurance of £3,000 for the first year, which will be paid in July, and initial advertising of £600 for the first six months, to be paid in August. It is intended to replace food stocks during the month in which the food is used.

You are required to prepare:

(*a*) a monthly cash budget for the six months ending 31st December, 19-9;

(*b*) a budgeted profit and loss statement for the half-year ending 31st December, 19-9; and

(*c*) a budgeted balance sheet as at that date.

(*d*) The average collection period is 2 months.

(HCIMA)

22.8. S. Simon owns a Restaurant and he produces a very abridged Balance Sheet at 1st January, 19-1.

	£		£
Capital	4,000	Fixed Assets	
		(less depreciation of £1,600)	2,000
		Stock	1,200
Creditors	1,000	Debtors	500
		Bank	1,300
	£5,000		£5,000

S. Simon has made a forecast of his business activities during 19-1.

	£	
Equipment		
To be disposed for	200	(Book value nil)
To be bought for	1,600	
Sales	7,500	
Purchases	6,000	
Business Expenses (all paid by cheque)	1,000	
Withdrawn for own use	520	
Depreciation for year	500	
Year end balances		
Debtors	1,000	
Creditors	1,500	
Stock (at cost)	2,000	

(1) Using the figures supplied by S. Simon prepare statements to show: –
(*a*) The expected cash position at the end of 19-1.
(*b*) The projected Profit or Loss for 19-1.
(*c*) A forecast Balance Sheet as at 31st December, 19-1.

(HCIMA)

22.9X. The South View Hotel Ltd., which is a non-seasonal, unlicensed private hotel with accommodation for 100 guests, has appointed a new Manager who intends to operate a system of budgetary control using monthly budgets.

The Balance Sheet as at 31st December 19-9 was:

	£	£	£
Goodwill			20,000
Premises			90,000
Other Fixed Assets	20,000	6,000	14,000
			124,000
Current Assets			
Food Stocks	500		
Debtors	2,500		
		3,000	
Current Liabilities			
Creditors for food	1,800		
Overdraft	200		
		2,000	
Working Capital			1,000
			£125,000

Finance:	
Authorised and Issued Capital	100,000
Reserves Unappropriated Profit	15,000
	115,000
Bank Loan	10,000
	£125,000

Budget details for first three months of 19-0: –

1. Occupancy 50%. Average inclusive terms per person per week of £50 split – 50% Room charge, 50% food. (Assume each month to be exactly four weeks).
2. 75% Sales cash, 25% credit to be received in following month.
3. Food purchases are budgeted 40% of food sales and will be paid in following month.
4. Wages (30% of total sales) and Operational Expenses (20% of total sales) will be paid with not time lag.
5. Interest on bank loan is 20% p.a. (to be treated as an accrual).
6. Depreciation of other Fixed Assets will be 10% p.a. on cost.
7. Advanced bookings for July/August to be received in March are expected to be £500.
8. Food stocks expected 31st March 19-0 £300.
9. A motor vehicle is to be purchased for cash (£2,000) on 31st March 19-0.

You are required to prepare: –

1. A cash budget for each of the three months.
2. A budgeted revenue account for three months ending 31st March 19-0 (with a Departmental Trading Account).
3. The expected Balance Sheet as at 31st March 19-0.

22.10X. The Carlton Private Hotel Ltd., an old established business, has a financial year 1st April to 31st March and divides it into two 6 monthly budget periods.

Prepare the Budgeted Revenue account (with Departmental Trading account) for half year ending 30th September 19-2, and a Working Capital Budget as at 30th September 19-2.

Balance Sheet as at 31st March 19-2

Fixed assets	13,000	
Stock	1,000	
Prepaid rates	500	
Cash and Bank	1,500	16,000
Less: Creditors for food and beverages	1,000	
Accrued rent	700	
Advanced bookings	300	2,000
Net assets		£14,000
Finance:		
Ordinary share capital		10,000
Profit & Loss account		4,000
		£14,000

Cash Budget for 6 months ending 30th September 19-2

Balance b/f		1,500
Receipts from rooms		24,700
Receipts from restaurant		24,500
		50,700
Less: Food and beverage creditors	11,000	
Wages and salaries	15,000	
Overheads	7,400	33,400
Balance c/f		17,300

Other Forecasts

1. Sales will be divided equally between Rooms and Restaurant.
2. A banquet £500 ordered for September 19-2 will not be paid for until October 19-2.
3. Cost of sales will be 40% of Restaurant sales.
4. Average stock £2,000.
5. The food and beverage purchases will be on monthly credit.
6. Prepaid rates £700 as at 30th September 19-2.
7. Accrued rent £500 as at 30th September 19-2.
8. Depreciation for 6 months ending 30th September 19-2 £1,000.

Comment on the working capital position as at 30th September 19-2 taking into account the following:

(*a*) a contract for a central heating installation will be completed in October 19-2 at a cost of £10,000.

(*b*) the two Directors award themselves Directors Fees of £10,000 each for the year at the annual general meeting which usually takes place in April.

(*c*) over the last few years 85% of the annual net profit is earned in the period 1st May to 30th September (the net profit does not take into account director fees).

23

Budgetary Control: Part II

Learning Objectives

At the end of this chapter you should be able to:

23A **Compare a budgeted Trading Account with an actual one.**

23B **Analyse the variances.**

23C **Describe the functions of a budget committee.**

Variance Analysis

Budgeted final accounts are compared with the actual results when they are known, and any difference is a *variance*. Variances should be analysed, and in a budgetary control system there can be sales, materials (food and beverages) labour and overhead variances.

Variance analysis is possible in food and beverage operations which are usually controlled at Gross Profit level only. This means variance analysis in sales and materials (cost of sales) only. The control system should be based on flexible budgeting and on standard food and beverage costs. Fixed budgeting considers only one level of output – sales e.g. 1,000 covers in a given period. Flexible budgeting would consider a range of, say, 750 to 1,250 covers.

In a Gross Profit control system four variances will be calculated:

1. Sales Price i.e. Actual quantity × Difference in price (Budgeted price – Actual price). This is often referred to as 'Average Spending Power Variance' (ASP).
2. Sales Volume i.e. Standard gross profit per unit × Difference in quantity (Budgeted quantity – Actual quantity).
3. Ingredient Price Variance i.e. Actual usage or quantity × Difference in cost price (Standard cost price – Actual cost price).
4. Ingredient Usage or Quantity Variance i.e. Standard cost price × Difference in quantity (Usage in Flexible Budget – Actual usage or quantity).

If a variance increases gross profit it is a *favourable* (F) variance.

If a variance reduces gross profit it is *adverse* (A).

A 'controllable' variance is within the scope of the food and beverage manager's responsibility. For instance, if a greater weight of an ingredient is used than the standard weight already specified. This can be controlled by checking that this does not happen in future.

Some variances are outside the scope of his responsibility and therefore not controllable. An instance of this would be a general increase in an ingredient, e.g. tea prices rise sharply.

GROSS PROFIT CONTROL by variance analysis will now be illustrated:

Exhibit 23.1

A restaurant expects to sell 1,000 covers in a given period at £4 each. The actual sales were 1020 at £3.80.

The standard cost is:

500g of A @ £2 per kg =	1.00
250g of B @ 2.4 per kg =	.60
STANDARD COST OF 1 cover	1.60

The actual costs from the control office were

A 530 kg @ 1.90 =	£1007
B 250 kg @ 2.60 =	650
	£1,657

Comparative Trading Accounts

	Fixed			*Flexible*			*Actual*		
	P	Q	£	P	Q	£	P	Q	£
Sales	4	1000	4000	4	1020	4080	3.8	1020	3876
A	2	500	1000	2	510	1020	1.9	530	1007
B	2.4	250	600	2.4	255	612	2.6	250	650
Cost	1.6	1000	1600	1.6	1020	1632			1657
Gross Profit	2.4	1000	2400	2.4	1020	2448			2219

1.	Sales Price	1020×0.2	=	204	A
2.	Sales Volume	2.4×20	=	48	F
3.	Cost Price A	530×0.1	=	53	F
	B	250×0.2	=	50	A
4.	Cost Usage A	2.0×20	=	40	A
	B	2.4× 5	=	12	F

Reconciliation

Standard Gross Profit (Fixed Budget)			2,400
+ Favourable Variances –			
	Sales Volume	48	
	A price	53	
	B Usage	12	113
– Adverse Variances			2,513
	Sales price	204	
	B price	50	
	A usage	40	294
Actual Gross Profit			2,219

The reasons for each variance should be investigated by management and corrected if possible.

The above is only one approach to variance analysis. More sophisticated system are beyond the scope of this book.

The Budget Committee

Small catering organisations may be able to forecast future activity but are unlikely to operate an adequate system of budgetary control. If budgeting is attempted it may well be the responsibility of only one person. The distinction between forecasting and budgeting is important:

Forecasting is the planning of a catering organisation's activity in advance. Budgeting is an expression of the forecasted activity in terms of revenue and expenditure (i.e. a Financial Plan).

A larger organisation wishing to operate budgetary control should appoint a budget committee. This should consist of the senior executives of the business. An example of a committee can be given by referring to the organisation chart of a hotel in Exhibit 2.1.

The committee may be: –

General Manager – Chairman

Accountant or Office Manager – Secretary

Food and Beverage Manager

Chief Buyer

Front Office or Reception Manager

Before any budgets are drawn up the committee must decide how the system will fit into the existing structure. Each departmental manager's authority and responsibility should be clearly defined including the duty of setting the budget for his/her department.

The main function of the committee is to prepare draft budgets for the board of directors or top management.

The following are important in preparing budgets:

1. Past performance – i.e. analysis of income and expenditure.

2. Current trends.
3. Other relevant information such as local conditions, unemployment, degree of competition etc.

Other functions are:

(*a*) Choice of budget period for operating budgets. For most the appropriate period should be a financial year. It is difficult to forecast accurately for a longer period. Some catering businesses are seasonal therefore a budget period of less than one year is advisable. Capital budgets for fixed assets may be for five years.

(*b*) The Review period (control period)
This means comparing budget with actual results as soon as possible after the actual results are known. The period may be weekly, monthly or, exceptionally, quarterly. Any longer periods would make control impossible as prompt action is the only way to effective control.

(*c*) The preparation of a budget manual to be made available to all staff involved in the system. This give full and detailed instruction thus avoiding misunderstandings, and ensures that data is suitable for the task of budgeting.

Exercises

23.1. Complete the variance analysis from the data below and comment on the results.

	Budget	*%*	*Actual*	*%*	*Variance*	*%*
Sales	6,250	100	5,900	100		
Cost of materials	2,350		2,750			
Gross Profit	3,900		3,150			
Labour	1,750		1,790			
Overheads	1,000		1,090			
Profit	1,150		270			

23.2. The Catering Dept. of an engineering firm operates a system of standard dish-costing. The standard recipe for dish A with the budgeted ingredient prices is:

250g of ingredient x at £2 per kg
200g of ingredient y at £1 per kg

The factory operates a five day week and its financial year is split into thirteen periods of four weeks each. The catering manager intends to prepare and sell 100 dishes a A per day.

At the end of accounting period one the actual costs were 510kg of x at £1.90 per kg. and 390kg of y at £1.20 per kg.

(1) Prepare a standard dish cost card for one portion of A.
(2) Calculate the price and usage variances for each ingredient at the end of accounting period one and reconcile the total standard cost of the dishes of A produced with the actual cost.

23.3. A steak bar sells 200g (approx. 6oz) rump steaks. The sales budget for a given period is 10,000 @ £2 each exclusive of VAT.

The current cost of the meat is £3 per kg. (assume this to be the standard).

The actual sales were 9,000 @ £2.20, exclusive of VAT.

The cost records show that 2,000 kg. were used @ £2.80 per kg.

Prepare:

(i) A fixed/flexible/actual trading account, and

Calculate:

(ii) (*a*) Sales price variance

(*b*) Sales volume variance

(*c*) Meat cost price variance

(*d*) Meat cost usage variance

Reconcile:

(iii) The fixed budgeted (standard) gross profit with the actual gross profit.

23.4X. A restaurant prepares a budget from which standards are established. For May 19-3 the budgeted standards set, and the actual results achieved, are as follows:

	Budgeted		*Actual*	
Sales:		£		£
	750 dishes at 0.53p	397.50	780 dishes at 0.53p	413.40
	Less cost of sales	198.75		197.60
Gross profit		£198.75		£215.80

The standard cost per dish (only two ingredients are used) were calculated as follows:

		Standard cost per dish
Ingredient A	8 oz at £0.25 per lb	£0.125
Ingredient B	4 oz at £0.56 per lb	£0.140

The actual costs were as follows:

	Actual price	*Actual Food Used*
Ingredient A	£0.26 per lb	400 lbs
Ingredient B	£0.52 per lb	180 lbs

You are required to:

(*a*) calculate the following variances: –

(i) sales volume variance

(ii) ingredient price variances and

(iii) ingredient usage variances.

(*b*) reconcile the budgeted profit with the actual profit, and

(*c*) briefly comment on the significance of the variances.

(HCIMA)

23.5X. The Restview Restaurant prepared a budget from which standards are established. For a week in June 19-8 the budgeted standards set, and the actual results achieved are as follows:

	Budgeted		*Actual*	
Sales:		£		£
	1,500 dishes at £1.06	1,590.00	1,560 dishes at £1.10	1,716.00
Less cost of sales		795.00	Less cost of sales	783.20
Gross profit		£795.00		£932.80

The standard cost per dish (only two ingredients are used) were calculated as follows:

		Standard cost per dish
Ingredient A	8 oz at £0.50 per lb	£0.25
Ingredient B	4 oz at £1.12 per lb	£0.28

The actual costs were as follows:

	Actual price	*Actual Food Used*
Ingredient A	£0.52 per lb	800 lbs
Ingredient B	£1.02 per lb	360 lbs

You are required to:

(*a*) calculate the following variances: –
(i) Sales variances,
(ii) ingredient price variances, and
(iii) ingredient usage variances.

(*b*) reconcile the budgeted profit with the actual profit, and

(*c*) briefly comment on the significance of the variances.

(HCIMA)

23.6X. (*a*) The Limited Menu Restaurant provides one basic main courses. It has a system of budgetary control which has a weekly fixed budget as follows:

Sales 4,000 meals at £1.50		£6,000
Ingredient A 1 lb per meal at 50p per lb.	£2,000	
Ingredient B ½ lb per meal at 20p per lb.	400	
Cost of sales		2,400
Gross profit		3,600

The actual results for the week ending Sunday, 15th March 19-1 are:

Sales 4,200 meals		£6,720
Ingredient A	£2,460	
Ingredient B	396	
Cost of sales		2,856
Gross profit		3,864

Ingredients used:
A 4,100 lbs at 60p per lb
B 2,200 lbs at 18p per lb.

Calculate *and comment on* the sales and cost of sales variances.

(*b*) Discuss the usefulness of variance analysis in the hotel and catering industry.

(HCIMA)

23.7X. A popular restaurant offers both red and white wine by the glass.

In a given budget period the expected sales were 2,000 glasses @ 50p each (ASP).

The standard wine cost is 12½p per glass.

The actual sales were 1,900 glasses and due to increased labour and overhead costs, 20% was added to budgeted selling prices.

The actual cost was 13p per glass.

All prices are exclusive of VAT.

1. Prepare a fixed (original) budgeted, flexible (control) budgeted and actual trading account.
2. Compute
   (*a*) sales variances
   (*b*) cost variances.
3. Reconcile the fixed budgeted gross profit with the actual.

24

Statement or Trading Accounts

Learning Objectives

At the end of this chapter you should be able to:

24A Understand the use of Operating Statements.

24B Understand the concept of inclusive cost of labour.

24C Understand the treatment of overheads.

There are several examples of operating statements or Trading and Profit and Loss accounts in earlier chapters.

A trading account should show the gross profit for each operated department. An adaptation of the accounting system (see chapter 18) should be able to provide a suitable analysis of sales, opening stock, closing stock and purchases (cost of sales).

Two appropriate examples are provided.

Departmental Trading Accounts

Exhibit 24.1 is a typical example of a restaurant and Exhibit 24.2 is a similar presentation for a hotel.

Exhibit 24.1

The Fine Restaurant

Trading & Profit & Loss Account for the year ended 31st December 19-5

	Food		**Beverages**		**Cigs etc**		**Total**	
	£	%	£	%	£	%	£	%
Sales	55,000	100	35,000	100	10,000		100,000	100
Stock 1st Jan. 19-5	2,000		3,000		500		5,500	
Purchases	21,000		16,500		9,500		47,000	
less stock 31st Dec. 19-5	(1,000)		(2,000)		(1,000)		(4,000)*	
Cost of sales	22,000	40	17,500	50	9,000	90	48,500	48.5
Gross Profit	33,000	60	17,500	50	1,000	10	51,500	51.5
less labour							24,000	24
overheads							18,000	18
Net Profit							9,500	9.5

*Note that figures shown in brackets represent deductions.

Gross Profit percentages or margins are very important determinants of profitability in commercial catering. They should be produced and reviewed carefully as frequently as possible, certainly more than once a year, and preferably monthly.

The term 'sales mix' percentage is often used and in the above exhibit it can be stated thus:

Sales	£	%
Food	55,000	55
Beverages	35,000	35
Cigs. etc.	10,000	10
Total	100,000	100

Exhibit 24.2

Revenue Account for Six Months ending 30th September 19-2

		Rooms		*Restaurant*			*Total*	
		£	%		£	%	£	%
Sales		25,000	100		25,000	100	50,000	100
Less: Cost								
Stock 1 April 19-2					1,000			
Purchases					12,000			
					13,000			
Less Stock 30 September 19-2					3,000			
					10,000	40	10,000	20
Gross Profit		25,000	100		15,000	60	40,000	80
Less: Labour				15,000				
Overheads				7,000				
Depreciation				1,000			23,000	46
Net Profit							17,000	34

The standard system of hotel accounts suggests departmentalisation of some labour and overhead items.

The Standard System of Hotel Accounts

Uniform accounting systems are well established in some industries and an attempt was made to introduce a uniform accounting system for the Hotel and Catering Industry in 1969 when the economic development committee for hotels and caterers published 'the standard system of hotel accounts'.

This has not been very successful to date and some argue that the industry is being denied the benefits that a system of this kind can bring.

Standard System of Hotel Accounting

The standard system provides for a basic classification of accounts as follows:

(*a*) classification of profit and loss accounts;
(*b*) classification of balance sheet accounts.

In addition the manual gives examples of operating statements and there is an alphabetical list of accounts in the basic classification.

Profit and Loss Accounts

The system distinguishes three 'operated departments':

(i) rooms;
(ii) food;
(iii) liquor and tobacco.

These are departments which 'with a measurable use of labour, engage directly in the services and commodities provided for hotel guests'.

In order to control the financial operation of the hotel several 'control levels' are suggested by the system. These are illustrated below.

Operated Department's Net Sales
  Less Cost of Sales
  Equals Department GROSS PROFIT
Gross Profit
  Less Wages and Staff Costs
  Equals Departmental NET MARGIN
Net Margin
  Less Allocated Expenses
  Equals Departmental OPERATING PROFIT
Departmental Operating Profit
  Plus Other Income
  Equals Hotel OPERATING INCOME
Hotel Operating Income
  Less Service Departments and General Expenditure
  Equals Hotel OPERATING PROFIT
Hotel Operating Profit
  Less Repairs, Plant and Property Expenses
  Equals Hotel NET OPERATING PROFIT

The Sandown Hotel, in 19-2, had a total turnover of £70,000 of which room sales accounted for £30,000, food sales £30,000 and bar sales £10,000.

The hotel achieved its budgeted cost of sales figures of 40% on sales in respect of both food and bar departments. Wages were paid as follows:

	£
Rooms	6,600
Food	7,800
Bar	1,600

Some staff lived in the hotel and the estimated cost of this accommodation was allocated as follows:

	£
Rooms Dept. Staff	1,800
Food Dept. Staff	2,000
Bar Dept. Staff	600

Other departmental expenses, as a % of departmental sales, amounted to:

Rooms	11%
Food	10%
Bars	12%

Income from guests' laundry and telephones came to £1,100.
Other costs for 19-2 were:

		£
(i)	Administration	4,400
(ii)	Property repairs	3,200
(iii)	Rates and insurance	2,600
(iv)	Advertising	3,200
(v)	Heat and light	2,400

From the above information, you are required to prepare a Profit and Loss Statement in conformity with the Hotel and Catering E.D.C. recommendations on uniform accounting. Your statement should, therefore, show the following profit levels:

1. Gross profit
2. Net margin
3. Departmental operating profit
4. Hotel operating income
5. Hotel operating profit
6. Hotel net operating profit

Exhibit 24.3

Sandown Hotel

Trading , Profit and Loss Account for year ended 31 December 19-2

	Rooms	*Food*	*Bar*	*Total*
	£	£	£	£
Sales	30,000	30,000	10,000	70,000
less Cost of Sales	–	12,000	4,000	16,000
Gross Profit	30,000	18,000	6,000	54,000
less Wages	6,600	7,800	1,600	16,000
Staff Accommodation	1,800	2,000	600	4,400
Net Margin	21,600	8,200	3,800	33,600
less Dep. expenses	3,300	3,000	1,200	7,500
Departmental Operating Profit	18,300	5,000	2,600	26,100
Add Other Income				1,100
Hotel Operating Income				27,200
less Administration Costs		4,400		
Advertising		3,200		
Heat and Light		2,400	10,000	
less Staff Accommodation			4,400	5,600
Hotel Operating Profit				21,600
less Property Repairs			3,200	
Rates and Insurances			2,600	5,800
Hotel Net Operating Profit				£15,800

The basic objective is to assist hotels towards more profitable operation by:–

1. Encouraging wider adoption of methods which use accounting information for planning and control.
2. Adopting accounting records which will result in clear and understandable information produced in a uniform manner.
3. Translating of the system into large and small operations.
4. Recommending forms of presentation for management information.

The system would benefit the industry by providing:

1. Easily recognisable figures.
2. Straightforward comparison of figures.
3. The basis for preparation of inter-hotel/inter-company comparisons.

Many hoteliers are not using the system and the following are some of the reasons:

1. Lack of understanding.
2. Owners and managers have different priorities.
3. Many hotels do not employ a full-time accountant and are therefore not able to operate the system.

4. The cost of installing the system. This is not easy and would require the following:
   (*a*) Subsidiary books and ledgers to comply with the uniform layout enabling all records to be processed in a predetermined manner.
   (*b*) Standard departmentalisation for all members in the system.
   (*c*) The adoption of an accounting code and uniform accounting practices on valuation of fixed assets, stock, depreciation and apportionment of expenses to operated or sales departments.

Labour Costing

All employers paying wages and salaries must operate a P.A.Y.E. (Pay As You Earn) deduction system, whereby they deduct income tax and national insurance from the pay of their workers and hand the money over to the Inland Revenue on a regular basis. Very lowly paid workers may have to pay no tax or national insurance at all, the level at which tax and national insurance starts to be deductible is changed every year by the Chancellor of the Exchequer in Parliament. A relatively new provision, which came into operation in 1983, is that employers also have to operate a Statutory Sick Pay system for workers who are absent from work because of sickness.

Besides the national insurance which is paid by the employees, that is the amount deducted from their wages, employers also have to pay an *extra* amount of national insurance for each employee the amount of which is based on the amount earned by the employee. The rates applicable are changed every year by Parliament. This *extra* amount is suffered by the employer, it cannot be taken from the employee's wages.

Assume that for all employees the following totals of wages and salaries have been incurred for a particular week:

Gross Pay of all employees (i.e. before deductions)	£1,000
Income Tax deducted before wages/salaries paid	£200
National Insurance to be suffered by employees, and deducted before wages/salaries paid	£70
Net Wages/Salaries paid (£1,000 – £200 – £70)	£730
National Insurance to be suffered by the employer	£130
The week's wage costs are therefore:	£
Gross Pay	1,000
National Insurance to be suffered by employer	130
Week's wage costs	1,130

This could be expressed in a different form as:

	£	£
Amount actually paid to employees (Net Wages)		730
Deducted from employee's wages and paid to Inland Revenue:		
P.A.Y.E. Income Tax	200	
National Insurance (employee's portion)	70	270
Gross Wages		1,000
Add National Insurance for employees to be paid by the employer only		130
Week's wage costs		1,130

It can be seen that the total wage costs are £1,130, and it can be calculated using either of the methods above.

Labour Costing Records

Detailed labour costing is not a feature of the hotel and catering industry, especially in the commercial sector. Industrial firms with a detailed system for their selling product may extend this to the canteen service. Local authorities (re. school meals) and hospitals also operate detailed systems and may be able to give a direct labour cost for each meal produced.

The standard system of hotel accounts allocates labour costs to sales departments after the Gross Profit level to arrive at departmental operating profit. Many hotels and restaurants will have a weekly labour cost summary similar to Exhibit 24.4.

Exhibit 24.4

Fine Restaurant
Labour Cost Analysis
Week ending 9/2/19-2

	£	%	*Previous Yr %*
Sales	2,000	100	100
Kitchen	280	14	13
Waiting	160	8	9
Ancillary	100	5	6
	540	27	28

In absorption costing systems it should not be difficult to identify direct and indirect costs but with marginal costing a clear distinction between variable and fixed costs is more difficult (see Chapter 12).

The fact remains that in most restaurant operations food cost is the basis of pricing policy, and therefore labour is 'indirect' and will be absorbed by the gross profit %. If contribution pricing is adopted i.e. any activity which contributes to fixed costs should be operated, labour costs are often assumed to be 'fixed' when clearly a large proportion is 'variable', in particular casual labour employed part-time for peak season operations or for banqueting.

Research into Labour Costs

University research was carried out in the late 1960's in Greater London. It revealed the following:

(*a*) *Percentage of Turnover*

Staff meals were not included in the sample. The average labour costs were 25% of turnover in a sample of 90 firms. In a group of restaurants controlled by one firm the labour cost varied from 16% – 45% of turnover. This was caused by two factors: volume and stability of turnover (net sales) and the 'fixed' nature of the labour cost.

(*b*) *Labour a Fixed Cost?*

In a manufacturing concern variable costs are usually much greater than fixed labour cost. In most catering organisations the reverse is true and many treat labour as a fixed cost.

(*c*) *Accounting Records*

Most only operate records for P.A.Y.E. and national insurance. No further analysis of wages was available. Bonus rates apply in some organisations but minimum time rates in the latest Wages Order (Wages Council Acts 1959) are the usual calculations for gross pay.

Unlike manufacturing concerns all labour costs are included in the Profit and Loss Account.

There is no current evidence to suggest that attitudes have changed since the above research took place.

Exercises

24.1. Drawn below are 4 composite bar charts with unmarked sections on each bar. What are the eight missing descriptions?

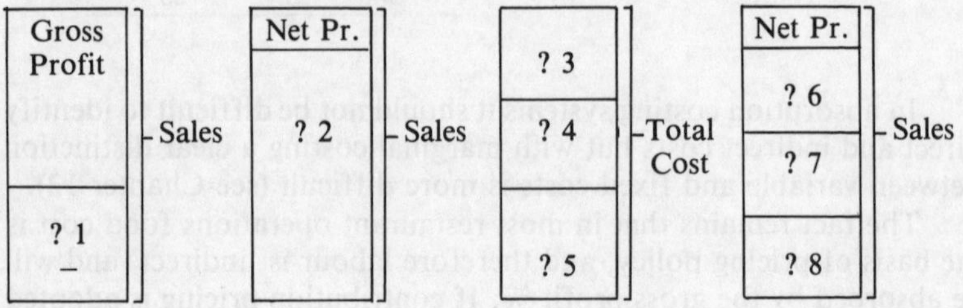

24.2X. Two restaurants A and B operate in very different ways giving different levels of service and quality of food. Both operate a bar but with very different results. Below is a summary of the trading results for a year:

	Rest. A	Rest. B
Food costs (% of sales)	50%	35%
Bar costs (% of sales)	40%	30%
Labour costs (whole estab)	£24,000	£21,000
Overheads (% of sales)	10%	15%
Food sales	£40,000	£40,000
Bar sales	£80,000	£20,000
Numbers of customers	100,000	8,000

You are required to:

(*a*) Present the information in a comparative statement which shows clearly the overall G.P.s of the two restaurants, the G.P.s after deduction of labour, and the net profits.

(*b*) Deduce from the figures the character and style of the two restaurants.

(*c*) Calculate the A.S.P. of the customers in the two establishments and the proportions of this average spend which is spent on food and drink in each establishment.

24.3. Complete on a separate sheet of paper, the following questions:

Sales = Material cost + ... (one item required)
Sales = Material cost + ... + ... + Net profit (two items)
Total Cost = ... + ... + ... (three items)
Sales = ... = Net Profit (one item).

24.4. A restaurant employs the following staff

(*a*) a manager at £7,800 per annum
(*b*) 4 chefs – total gross wages and N.I. contributions £360 per week
(*c*) 3 waiters total £228 per week
(*d*) staff meals are cost at £300 for a 4 week period.

Calculate the labour cost for a 4 week period in which £72 was paid out of petty cash for casual labour.

24.5X. A restaurant's weekly sales were £7,200. The wages for the week were £1,340 and the manager's salary is £13,520 per annum. Staff meals cost £200 per week. Calculate the labour cost as a percentage of sales.

24.6. The Grand Hotel's labour cost statement for last year was:

Dept.	£	%
Reception	5,000	12.5
Housekeeping	12,000	30
Bars	3,000	7.5
Restaurant	8,000	20
Kitchen	9,000	22.5
Other	3,000	7.5
	40,000	100%

The annual turnover was £160,000. This is expected to rise by 5% next year and due to increases in N.I. contributions and an expected new catering wages order the relationship between turnover and labour costs is expected to increase by 2½% over last years %.

Allocate the budgeted labour costs for next year to the above departments using

24.7X. A catering firm employs 5 staff. Their gross pay for week ending 9th December was £90, £16.10, £80, £70, £60.90, respectively.

Assume National Insurance Contributions to be 12% employer, 8% employee, 20% total. The Gross pay £16.10 was Statutory Sick Pay. Calculate the labour cost for the week taking into account staff meals of £20 and a National Insurance threshold of £35.

24.8. (*a*) Give six different items of expense incurred when a new member of staff is employed.

(*b*) The planned expenditure on wages for a banquet was £61.20 which was based on 40 man hours at £1.53 per hour.

As a result of a staffing error and due to a pay rate alteration the actual hours worked were 47 and the rate paid was £1.59.

You are required to:

(i) Calculate the total variance from the budget.

(ii) Show what part of the variance was attributed to the rate change and what part was attributed to the 'efficiency' aspect.

24.9. Prepare a Departmental Trading Account with Cash and percentage columns and a General Profit and Loss Account from the following:

		Rooms	*Restaurant*	*Bar*
Stocks 1st January 19-5		–	1,000	3,000
Stocks 31st December 19-5		–	2,000	2,000
Purchases		–	21,000	6,000
Sales		50,000	30,000	20,000
Returns Outwards		–	500	–
Carriage Inwards		–	500	–
Carriage Outwards	£ 150			
Salaries	£15,000			
Wages	£20,000			
Other Expense	£10,000			

Kitchen equipment costing £5,000 (to last 10 years. Scrap value nil).
Debtors £2,500 2% expected to be bad
China, glass and cutlery costing £4,000 has been valued at £3,700 on 31st December 19-5.

Comment on Gross Profit percentage of each Department.
Calculate and comment on the net profit percentage.

24.10X. (*a*) Design a suitable Departmental Trading Account for use in a 1st class restaurant. The analysis is needed to compare the trading results of food, drink (average margin 50%) and tobaccos. The layout must provide for both monthly and cumulative results and emphasise the different gross profit percentages of each type of selling activity i.e. department.

(*b*) The trading account provides two important accounting ratios i.e. Gross Profit Ratio and Rate of Turnover. Explain briefly the use of each ratio.

(*c*) List the above three departments in order (starting with the highest ratio) for both Gross Profit and Rate of Turnover. Briefly explain the reasons for your answers.

25

Marginal Costing

Learning Objectives

At the end of this chapter you should be able to:

25A Understand the concept of marginal costing as a 'contribution' to profit.

Marginal costing divides costs between those which are fixed and those which are variable. This was discussed in chapter 12 Costing Concepts. The main points are worth revision: –

Sales – Cost – Profit relationships

Costs can be classified as either fixed or variable in relation to sales. Many accountants argue that this classification is too difficult to apply in practice. Fixed costs are never truly fixed and variable costs do not vary in direct proportion to changes in sales. Some costs, for example telephone charges, are partly fixed and partly variable.

For simplicity we will assume that food and beverage costs are variable in proportion to sales, and labour and overheads are fixed.

The revenue account Exhibit 22.1 on page 263 can be redrafted as a *contribution statement*.

	£
Sales	30,000
less variable costs	12,000
=CONTRIBUTION	18,000
less Fixed Costs	10,800
=Net Profit	7,200

The *contribution* is the amount contributed to help to cover Fixed Costs and to provide a net profit. If the contribution is *greater* than Fixed Costs then there will be a Net Profit. If it is less than Fixed Costs there will be a Net Loss. Finally to state the obvious, if Contribution exactly equals Fixed Costs then there will neither be a profit nor a loss, this is said to be break-even.

The Contribution Concept Applied to Seasonal Establishments

Any activity which makes a positive contribution to Fixed Costs is worthwhile. Let us consider a catering organisation during the 'off' season in Exhibit 25.1.

Exhibit 25.1

The following is a 6 monthly revenue account of a catering operation during the 'off' season.

	£	£
Sales		10,000
Cost of Food and Beverages		4,000 A
Gross Profit		6,000
Labour – Fixed	1,800 B	
Variable	2,700 C	
Fixed Expenses	1,200 D	
Other Variable Expenses	1,300 E	7,000
Net Loss		1,000

It could be tempting for someone to speculate that it would be better to shut down the operation during the off-season, and consequently save money by not incurring a loss. Would this be true? Let us now reconstruct it as a Contribution Statement.

	£
Sales	10,000
less Variable Costs A + C + E	8,000
= CONTRIBUTION	2,000
less Fixed Costs B + D	3,000
Net Loss	1,000

We can see that a positive contribution of £2,000 is made towards Fixed Costs. Therefore the activity should be carried on.

What would have been the position of the activity had been shut down?

	£
Sales	Nil
less Variable Costs	Nil
CONTRIBUTION	Nil
less Fixed Costs B + D	3,000
Net Loss	3,000

The greater net loss comes about because Fixed Costs have to be paid, such items as Rent, Rates, Insurance etc, even though the activity is not taking place during the off-season.

Break-even Calculation

Suppose we wish to know at what point of activity the firm will break-even, i.e. at which point it makes neither profit nor loss. Above this level of activity we will make a profit, below it we will incur a loss.

The level at which neither profit not loss will be made will be where:

	Sales	=	Fixed Costs	+	Variable Costs
i.e.	S	=	F	+	V

In the case we have just considered in Exhibit 25.1 we were incurring a loss of £1,000. We want to know what sales will have to be to break-even. Thus we do not currently know the desired figure of Sales. As variable costs are also dependent on sales we do not know them either. The one figure which will not have altered from Exhibit 25.1 will be that of fixed costs. We know that variable costs (£8,000) are 80% of Sales (£10,000). We can therefore reconstruct the formula

$$S = F + V$$

which means $S = F + V\text{ (80\% of S)}$

From this it follows that F is 20% of S, i.e.

$$S = F\text{ (20\% of S)} + V\text{ (80\% of S)}$$

As we know that F is £3,000, therefore $S = \frac{100}{20} \times £3{,}000 = £15{,}000$

To check that we have got the correct answer:

$$S(£15{,}000) = F(£3{,}000) + V(80\%\text{ of S} = £12{,}000)$$

Therefore in Exhibit 25.1 the sales would have to be increased from £10,000 to £15,000 to get to the break-even point.

If we had known the selling price of each 'unit' of sales, and the variable costs of each unit, then we could calculate the contribution per unit. We could then have calculated the number of units to be sold to break even. The formula is:

$$\frac{\text{Fixed Costs}}{\text{Contribution Per Unit}} = \text{Break-even Point in Units}$$

If in Exhibit 25.1, the selling price per unit had been £5 and the variable costs £4 per unit, then the contribution would have been £1 per unit. The calculation is therefore:

$$\frac{£3{,}000}{£1} = 3{,}000\text{ units}$$

3,000 units × £5 selling price = £15,000, the same answer as shown by using the S = F + V formula.

The concept of contributions can be applied to any catering activity in the short term. Other examples are:

1. *Pricing Functions or Banquets*

   (To cover only the cost which will occur if the function takes place.) This contribution is clearly reducing the fixed costs appropriate to the facilities offered, which will be there with or without the operation of the function.

2. *Hotels offering special packages such as weekend breaks out of season.*

   It must be remembered that an organisation must cover all its costs, both fixed and variable, in the long term if it is to be profitable and remain in operation. The concept of contribution can therefore be used in pricing decisions for the short term only.

Contribution Pricing Examples

A resort hotel has facilities to use for dinner dances during the 'off' season.

The following information is available:

Maximum number of customers 200, cost of food and beverages per person £4, other variable costs including labour and music £400, fixed costs which apply to the facilities £14,600 p.a. or £40 per day/evening.

Calculate:

(*a*) The price per person ex. VAT to make a profit of £100 for the function.

(*b*) The break-even price.

(*c*) The price to contribute to half the fixed costs.

(*d*) The price to cover only the variable costs.

(*a*) Sales = Variable costs + Fixed costs + Net Profit

therefore Sales = Food 200 × £4 + other V.C. £400 + £40 + £100

i.e. Sales = £1,340 or expressed per customer as $\frac{£1,340}{200}$ = £6.70 per person

This can be checked as follows:

		£	£
Sales would be 200 × £6.70			1,340
Less	Food Cost (which are variable) 200 × £4	800	
	Other Variable costs	400	
	Fixed costs	40	1,240
Therefore profit would be			100

(*b*) Sales = Variable costs + Fixed costs
therefore Sales = £800 + £400 + £40
i.e. Sales = £1,240 or expressed per customer as $\frac{£1,240}{200}$ = £6.20 per person

This can be checked as follows:

	£	£
Sales would be		1,240
Less Food Cost	800	
Other Variable costs	400	
Fixed costs	40	1,240
Profit or loss (as there is neither profit/loss we have broken even)		Nil

(*c*) Sales = Variable costs + ½ Fixed costs
therefore Sales = £800 + £400 + £20
i.e. Sales = £1,220 or expressed per customer as $\frac{£1,220}{200}$ = £6.10 per

This can be checked as follows:

	£	£
Sales would be		1,220
Less Food costs	800	
Other Variable costs	400	
Fixed costs	40	1,240
Loss (this equals ½ fixed costs)		20

(*d*) Sales = Variable costs only
therefore Sales = £1,200 or expressed per customer as $\frac{£1,200}{200}$ = £6 per person

The dinner dances can be offered at prices over £6 ex. VAT to make a contribution to fixed costs. £6.20 is the break-even price when fixed costs will be covered. Prices over £6.20 will produce net profit.

The above calculations assume the maximum number of customers and fixed costs on a daily basis. Different calculations would be necessary if prices were based on weekly fixed costs and only say four bookings per week. Note that the price to contribute would still be £6 as in the above calculations. The calculations on a weekly basis of four bookings are worth illustration:

The price ex. VAT to cover the variable costs would be S = VC,
S = (800 × £4) + (400 × £4) = £4,800 i.e. $\frac{£4,800}{800}$ = £6 per person
Food other VC

The break-even price would be S = VC + FC = £4,800 + (7 × £40) = £5,080

i.e. $\frac{£5,080}{800}$ = £6.35 per person

It should be noted that at unit level the variable costs are the same per unit (i.e. they do not vary with sales) but the fixed costs per unit increase or decrease with sales. The variable costs were £6 per person in the above calculations whether the sales were 200 a day or 800 a week. The fixed costs per unit on the basis of a function per day were $\frac{£40}{200}$ which = £0.20, but on a weekly basis of 4 functions it is $\frac{£280}{800}$ = £0.35 per unit.

Exercises

25.1. The Seaton Hotel has a normal occupancy of 44,000 sleeper-nights per year, with the following trading results: –

	£
Sales	447,000
Cost of food	98,000
Labour Costs	111,000
Fixed Overhead Costs	51,000
Semi-Variable Overhead Costs	86,000
Variable Overhead Costs	39,000
	385,000
Net profit	62,000

A Tour Operator proposes to send off-season guests totalling 420 additional sleeper-nights at a charge of £7.35 per day. Apart from the cost of Food and Variable Costs, there would be an increase of £606 in Labour Costs, and £694 in Semi-Variable Costs.

(*a*) List the trading results per sleeper-night

(*b*) Prepare a statement to show what contribution would be made by the extra business. (nearest £)

(*c*) State whether the Tour Operator's proposal is financially acceptable.

25.2. An Industrial Catering Company has luncheon facilities for 3,000 customers during a five day week. They serve standard meals which have a variable cost of 30p. Fixed overheads are £270 per week. Contracts have been made with three local firms for their workers to be served with a daily lunch, five days per week, as follows:

Firm A	600 per week at 57½p each
Firm B	800 per week at 55p each
Firm C	1,000 per week at 50p each

The management forecast that demand for lunches from the general public would enable the dining room to operate at a full capacity. The weekly profit target is £400.

You are required to prepare a schedule showing the calculation of the lowest price at which meals could be offered to the general public and at the same time achieve the profit target.

(HCIMA)

25.3X. A restaurant has opened all the year in a seasonal resort. Assume the ON season to be 6 months.

The Revenue account for the year was:

Sales	100,000
Food Cost	40,000
Labour	30,000
Overheads	20,000
Profit	10,000

threequarters of the business takes place in the ON Season £10,000 of both labour and overheads are Fixed Cost on a pure time basis. Assume variable costs are in direct proportion to sales.

Should the restaurant open or close during the off season?

25.4. (*a*) What is contribution accounting?

(*b*) The following is a 6 monthly revenue account of a catering operation during the 'off season.

Sales	10,000
Cost of Food and Beverage	4,000
Gross Profit	6,000
Labour – fixed	2,000
variable	3,000
Allocation of Fixed Expenses of organisation	1,000
Other variable expenses	1,000
Loss	1,000

If the operation is discontinued the fixed expenses will still apply to the organisation.

Should the operation be closed during the off season?

(*c*) Assuming that variable expenses vary exactly with turnover, calculate the sales increase required to break even.

25.5. The Management of the "Excel Restaurant" are considering their pricing and costing policies for the coming financial year. Two alternative policies are being considered: –

1. To charge a price of £8 per meal; food costs would be 40%; fixed costs for the year £40,000.
2. By altering the décor, changing the style of the restaurant and providing a better quality meal, to charge a price of £12 per meal; food cost would be 36%; fixed costs for the year £70,000.

It is anticipated that the restaurant has the capacity to serve up to 18,000 customers a year (although at no time in the past has full occupancy been achieved).

You are required to: –

(*a*) From the above figures
 (i) calculate by formula the break-even point in numbers of customers of each policy.
 (ii) calculate by formula the number of customers, for each policy, at which a profit of £20,000 would be made.

(*b*) From the attached profit graph (which has been constructed from the figures above) and your answers in 1., suggest which of the two policies should be adopted giving reasons for your choice.

Note: the prices per meal given above are Ex-V.A.T. so that you may ignore V.A.T.

Profit Graph

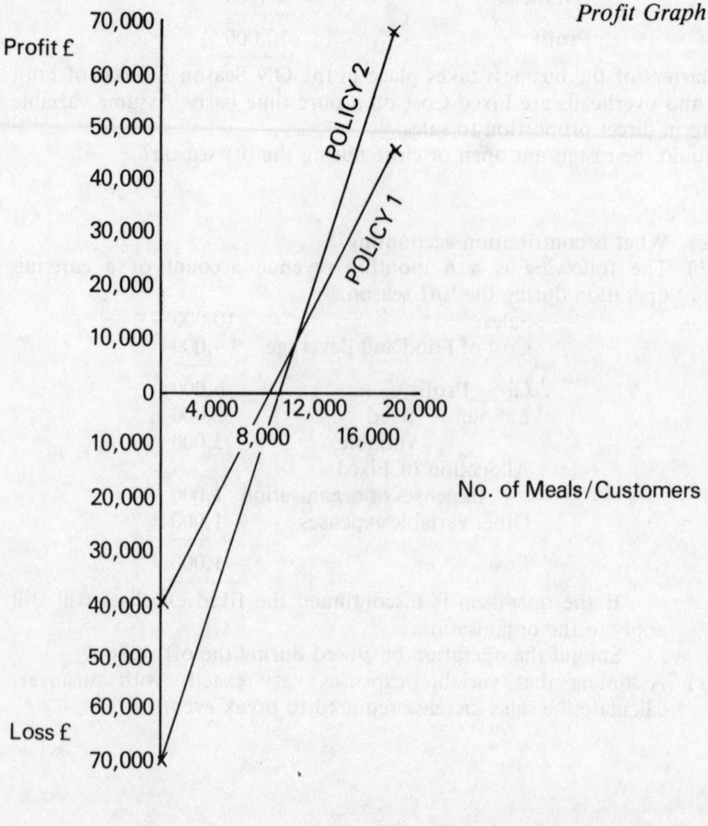

25.6. Briefly explain the use of contribution as a measure of profitability.

25.7X. The Cozy Restaurant has made a loss of £3,636 over the first six months of the year although it had been estimated that a profit of £10,000 would be made for the year.

Various proposals have been made to rectify the situation. You are required to evaluate and comment upon each of these proposals.

Figures for the six months show:

	£
Sales Income	100,000
Cost of Goods Used	60,000
Labour Cost	25,000
Overheads	18,636

The average spending is exactly £2 per customer. The full capacity of the restaurant is twice the occupancy which has been achieved.

However, labour costs have been carefully watched. £5,000 of this can be regarded as constant but the remainder is proportionate to the level of sales.

Of the other overheads £8,636 are fixed. This figure would be increased, however, if the restaurant was working above 75% capacity constantly, as additional plant would be required.

In choosing between the proposals taxation can be ignored.

Proposal 1. Spend £1,000 on advertising to increase sales.

Proposal 2. Introduce a scheme for bulk buying of goods used. It is estimated that this will reduce cost by 9% but fixed overheads will be increased by £1,000.

Proposal 3. To reduce prices by 15 per cent to achieve 100 per cent capacity utilisation.

Proposal 4. For the foreseeable future to plan only to break-even and to reduce variable costs other than cost of goods used to achieve this.

(HCIMA)

25.8X. As newly appointed manager of a restaurant you have been presented with the following estimated figures for the following year, which have been based on past performance: –

(i) between 30,000 and 40,000 customers will visit the restaurant;
(ii) the average amount spent by customers will be £4.20 per customer;
(iii) food costs will be between 30% and 40% of sales;
(iv) wages, which will cover the range of customers, will be £40,000;
(v) other fixed costs will amount to £35,000.

You are required to: –

(*a*) Estimate the range of net profit (or loss) which may be made for the year.
(*b*) Calculate the break-even point in numbers of customers
  (i) if food costs can be held at 30% of sales
  (ii) if food costs are 40% of sales.
(*c*) Comment briefly on the figures obtained in your answer to questions (*a*) and (*b*), above.

25.9X. An outside catering firm, which has just set up in business to produce and deliver meals to pensioners and other people in their homes, has estimated the following figures on the running of its operations: –

Foor cost per meal	£1.10
Other variable costs per meal	£0.30
Fixed costs per week	£504.00
Selling price per meal	£2.50

It is estimated that 700 meals a week can be sold.

(*a*) You are required to calculate the following, assuming that 700 meals will be sold: –
- (i) the variable cost per meal.
- (ii) the fixed cost per meal.
- (iii) the contribution per meal.
- (iv) the total net profit for a week.

(*b*) Also calculate: –
- (i) the sales income (to the nearest pound) needed to break even in a week.
- (ii) the number of meals needed to achieve a net profit of £400 per week.

25.10. The hotel in which you are employed as banqueting manager produced its final accounts on 31st December 19-4, from which it was calculated that labour costs accounted for 30% of total sales and overheads another 20%.

For the evening of 17th July 19-5, you have enquiries for three banqueting functions, the data in respect of which is as follows: –

1. Mr. Mercer's function.
   120 covers to be charged at £4 per cover for the meal. Wine sales are expected to be 70 bottles at an average selling price of £2 a bottle with a 50% gross profit margin. Total food costs £190.
2. Mr. Britton's function.
   100 covers to be charged at £5 per cover for the meal. Wine sales are expected to be 60 bottles at an average selling price of £3 a bottle with a 60% gross profit margin. Total food costs £230.
3. Mr. Franklin simply wishes to hire the banqueting suite at a charge of £200 and will make his own arrangements for food and drink.

Your general manager has laid down a rule that banqueting functions should be charged with labour and overhead costs in the same proportion to sales as revealed by the most recent final accounts.

You are required to draw up a statement to rank the functions in order of acceptability in accordance with: –

(*a*) the general manager's rule;
(*b*) the concept of "contribution".

26

Appreciation of Computers and Accountancy Information Systems.

Learning Objectives

At the end of this chapter you should be able to:

26A **Demonstrate a knowledge of computerised accounting systems.**

Modern Methods of Processing Data

Chapters 18 and 19 have been dealing mainly with the principles of double entry, and the book-keeping records have been in the form of the basic conventional system. However, it must not be thought that all the book-keeping and accountancy methods in use are necessarily the same as the one described in this book. What is important is that the main ends which the financial book-keeping records purport to serve remain the same, but it is the means by which the actual records are effected that can be altered. Just because a computer or mechanized system is used does not mean that the answers will change. The question 'What is the total of debtors?' should receive the same answer whether the firm uses bound books, loose-leaf ledgers, keyboard accounting machines, punched card equipment, or a computer. The final accounts should remain the same whichever system is in use. The changes take place in the means by which the information or data is gathered together and processed so as to give the answers, and the speed with which this is accomplished.

It would, however, be a mistake to think that a more advanced system would only give, more quickly, exactly the same answers as before and nothing else. The system should be designed so that besides the essential answers which much be given by any book-keeping system further desirable information is obtainable as a by-product. Any such information must stand up to the criticism of whether or not it is worth obtaining. If the cost of obtaining it is greater than the benefits which flow to the firm from having it, then clearly it is not worthwhile information. The system should therefore be designed so as to give worthwhile information and exclude information which fails to stand up to the test.

You may well ask why it is that so far you have been studying mainly the basic conventional double entry book-keeping system. Has it not all been a waste of time? The answer to that must be that all of the more modern methods have developed from the conventional system. The basic information obtainable from any other book-keeping method remains the same. This consists of the changes in assets and liabilities, and convenient collection points are established to aggregate expenses and revenue so that the changes in the capital can be calculated. Thus the double entry system is capable of being used by any type of firm. When a person first learns book-keeping, he does not know exactly which systems will be in use at firms that he will be in contact with during his working life. In five years time from now, a small firm using manual methods may use a computer, and the reverse could even be possible. A firm using one type of computer could in later years be using one of a completely different type. By understanding the ends towards which the double entry system is aimed, the student will therefore appreciate the ends towards which the other methods are aimed.

Probably one of the best ways to introduce modern methods is to trace their development from the conventional double entry system. The firm at which you are employed, or will be employed, would then be at some stage along this span of development. You should then be able to relate the firms book-keeping methods to what used to be done, and also to what may be done in your firm in the future.

It must always be borne in mind that, barring the legal needs which accounts fulfil, the costs of running the system should not exceed the benefits. To take an exaggerated example, a very small store could hardly be expected to use an expensive computer, as the costs of running it would far exceed any benefits which the firm might receive. Before advocating a more advanced system of book-keeping this test should always be applied.

The Development of Modern Methods

1. Bound Books

Up to the advent of the typewriter in 1866, bound volumes were universally used for book-keeping records. The accounts took the basic double entry form described in this book, but there was much manual copying of items that have now been eliminated from the present basic system. As carbon paper had not been invented, the sales invoices, debit and credit notes were copied into the sales and returns books before they were dispatched to customers and suppliers. Now, of course, copy sales invoices and debit and credit notes obtained by the use of carbon paper obviate any need for a copy to be made in the books. It is rather interesting to note that the purchases invoices were also usually copied into the purchases book, even though reference could easily be made to the purchases invoice received by the firm.

2. Loose-Leaf Ledgers and Carbon Paper

The typewriter and the consequent development of carbon paper led to the transition away from bound books to loose-leaf ledgers.

Typewriters could obviously be used more easily with loose sheets of paper, and with the use of carbon paper could give several copies of such things as invoices and debit and credit notes. Typed ledger accounts were also neater than hand-written records.

At first, the loose-leaf ledgers were kept in covers which could be opened and closed by operating a key. The loose sheets therefore had to be extracted and placed into the typewriter, then removed from the typewriter and replaced in the covers. Soon it was seen that continually extracting them and replacing them in the covers was a waste of time. The loose leaves, especially if they were somewhat sturdier and in the form of cards, could easily be kept in trays.

Experiments then began as to how one operation could produce several different records. This was done by designing special stationery with interleaved carbon or with a carbon backing on the sheets. This stationery was in the form of sets. For instance, one typing operation with a sales set might produce the following records:

Two sales invoices – one to be retained as a copy and the other sent to the customer.

An advice note for the customer.

Instructions to the warehouse to send the goods.

The use of carbon paper to produce multiple copies from a single entry was extended to produce systems for keeping the Sales and Purchases Ledgers, the Cash Book, and the Wages records. These systems often use a peg-board base to make sure that the papers line up – holes in the paper fitting over the pegs on the base board. When preparing the wages for example – the top sheet on which the initial writing is done will be the wages slip which goes into the employee's pay packet. The employer's pay record card will be next underneath and record the details of the pay, National Insurance and Income Tax. The final copy will form the accounting record put on file giving the details of the cash payment of wages to each employee. Normally three copies is a maximum and hence the term 'three in one' systems, since this method produces three separate records from one entry.

3. The Typewriter and the Adding Machine to Accounting Machines

Adding machines were in existence in the latter part of the nineteenth century. In 1901, an accounting machine was constructed in the United States which was a combination of the adding machine and the typewriter. Other machines were developed, some primarily being based on the adding machine while others were developed from the typewriter.

These machines were used eventually in combination with multi-copy carbon stationery much more sophisticated than the sales set already described. Different coloured paper for forms so that it was easy to distinguish between various records came more into use. One operation produced not only several records but also automatically calculated the new balance on the account after the entry was made, and also totalled up the amount of each type of entry made for control purposes. These machines were used not only for financial accounting records but for costing records as well. Very often they are specially designed for use by particular firms.

The mechanical accounting machines were improved by including electronic features which increased the speed of the equipment, and allowed much more information to be stored in the machine internally. The ledger cards could also contain a magnetic stripe on the edge or back which had information recorded on it in addition to the visibly printed front of the card. These electronic accounting machines were also known as Visible Record Computers (VRC).

4. *Punched Card Accounting Machines*

A class of accounting machine which worked in an entirely different way was also developed. This was the punched card machine developed in the United States by Dr. Hollerith in 1884.

This method of accounting was based on information which was recorded by the means of holes being punched into cards. The whole system can be summarised into:

1. Punching holes into cards to represent the information that is being dealt with.
2. Sorting the cards out into a required order.
3. Getting the machines to tabulate the information in printed form in a way desired by the firm.

To do this the firm needed three basic kinds of machines:

1. A punch
2. A sorter
3. A tabulator

However, the most important part of the system was the actual punched cards. These were all the same size with one corner cut off so that in a pile of cards it was easy to see if one was facing the wrong way. The card consisted of a number of columns across with ten positions running down the card.

Since the advent of the electronic computer, the punched card accounting machine has fallen into disuse.

5. *Computers*

For accounting work computers follow on logically from punched cards. Computers were first used for business purposes around the year 1952.

The first computers were quite large machines. As a rough illustration of the comparison with today, a machine that would fill up the whole of the space in a room could today have its work performed quicker and more efficiently by a machine that would easily fit on to the top of your desk.

A computer has five basic component parts:

(i) An input unit.
(ii) A store or memory unit.
(iii) An arithmetic unit.
(iv) An output unit.
(v) A control unit.

Using Computers to do Book-keeping and Accounts: An Introduction

Whatever was written about the use of computers in business would be out-of-date by the time that this book is printed and on sale. It is therefore pointless in a general textbook to be too specific about particular makes of computers. This book will therefore apply itself to a consideration of the general principles involved.

The larger computers, used by bigger firms, have very substantial memories and are called 'main-frame computers'. A 'mini-computer' has all the characteristics of a mainframe computer, but it is on a much smaller scale and will cost less than a main-frame computer. A 'micro-computer' is the smallest in the range of computers, and is based on micro-chips which are small electronic devices which enable the computer to be small in size. There is no clear dividing line between main-line and mini-computers. In addition there is very little practical difference between the smaller of the mini-computers and the larger of the micro-computers.

Main-frame computers cost a lot of money and take up a fair amount of space. This is not true of micro-computers which are relatively cheap and take up very little space. The time has now come when the production of micro-computers means that any business, except the very smallest, can afford to have and to use a computer *if it wants to do so*.

As the micro-computer is almost certainly the type of computer which most students will meet, whether at college or at home, then it is this type of computer with which this book will be concerned. At one time whenever discussion of a computer took place, then there used to be quite a fair amount of technical detail given as to how a computer worked. This stage in the development of computers has now passed, what people need to know is not so much exactly how it works, but instead they will want to know what the computer can do for them. Whilst it may be desirable to have a very general idea as to how a computer works, much more than that will not be needed by most users. After all, when you have a remote controlled television set you are not very much bothered how it functions, what you want is that when you press the button to put the TV set on BBC 1 then the TV set responds correctly.

This brings us to the view expressed by some students that if computers can perform book-keeping extremely well indeed then why should the student bother to learn book-keeping. After all, if he/she can be taught to press a few buttons then that is all that is needed. Using the instance in the last paragraph, when you pressed the button for BBC 1 you would know if instead you got Channel 4. On BBC 1 you were going to watch a pop music programme, instead if it went wrong you might see a political programme. Using a computer for book-keeping needs the ability to be able to see if the transactions being entered have been done properly. Normally if you feed the correct data into the computer in the prescribed manner then you will get the correct answers. However, if something has gone wrong and you do not know book-keeping properly then you are going to believe the book-keeping records produced on the computer. We all know the student who multiplies 25 by 14 on his pocket calculator and gets an answer of 13,360 and believes it. His basic knowledge of arithmetic should have told him that it cannot be more than a few hundred for the answer. Similar considerations apply when using computers.

Hardware

For small firms the typical micro-computer system will consist of four main types of equipment, or 'hardware' as it is called.

(i) The micro-computer itself. It will resemble a small typewriter with a keyboard, on which you can type instructions and data. Besides this it will have a 'memory' on which it can store the information, and it will also have a processing unit in which the calculations are performed.

(ii) A visual display unit, or VDU as it is usually referred to. This is rather like a television set. In fact most readers will know that personal computers often use your own ordinary television set to keep costs down. Any information which is inside the computer can be displayed on the VDU.

(iii) A printer. This will produce printed copies of the ledger accounts, journals, trial balance etc.

(iv) A disk drive. Only a limited amount of information can be held in a computer's memory. Also most micro-computers have this information wiped out when the machine is switched off. For business use a computer must keep a copy of everything that it is told. In micro-computers this information is usually kept stored on magnetic disks, called 'floppy disks' which will be described later.

The machine which enables us to record information on to the floppy disks is known as the disk drive. Anyone having a personal computer will probably use audio-cassettes with ordinary cassette recorders. These will not normally be very suitable for much in the way of business use.

Software

The computer has to be given instructions as to exactly what the user wants it to do. These instructions are called 'programs'. Notice the spelling of the word 'program' in computer language as compared with the word 'programme' in normal English usage. The collective name given to computer programs is 'software'.

The programs will vary, depending on exactly what it is that you want the computer to do, and they will also vary with different makes of computers. If you were sufficiently expert, and had enough time, you could write a set of programs for your computer. However, most software is written by computer experts, and for it to be a good program it should have been exhaustively tested before being put on to the market for sale.

The software is normally supplied on 'floppy disks'. These are plastic disks, which are flexible, thus the use of the word 'floppy'. They work in a similar manner as an audio-cassette, but they contain much more information and they can also record it much faster. Exactly how much information can be supplied on a floppy disk will depend on the type of disk drive in use.

Book-keeping Programs

There are in fact a large number of book-keeping programs available on the market. Each make of micro-computer will need a different program, or alterations made to it, as at present it is often impossible to use programs written for one make on another make without some form of alteration.

Even if you have the same make of micro-computer as the firm down the road you may well use a different program for the same book-keeping function. A firm with several branches would probably want a different program from that of a firm without branches. A firm which only had cash sales would want a different program from a firm which only had credit sales. A firm which supplied services only would want a different program from a firm which supplied goods only.

To start off, the program is 'loaded' into the computer. This is effected differently in different computers, but when the stage is complete the computer will have copied the program from the disk into its own memory. This will be done very quickly. Once that this is done, either the programme starts running automatically, or else the key marked 'run' on the computer keyboard has to be pressed. The title of the programme will be displayed on the VDU. The program shown on the screen will tell you when and how to feed in the data which is to be processed, e.g. entering credit sales. If would be impossible here to state how this should be done, for every program is different.

In an ordinary manual system of book-keeping the entering of credit sales would be in the Sales Journal and in the Sales Ledger accounts. Similarly credit purchases would be entered in the Purchases Journal and the Purchases Ledger. That would completely finish the book-keeping entries. With most book-keeping programs run on a computer it is possible to get automatic by-products of the data fed in for other reasons. If sales are known in detail, exactly which items have been sold, and how many of each item, and purchases are known, and how many of each item has been bought, then it is possible for the computer automatically to produce stock records, for every single item of stock.

In a firm dealing in quite a few types of goods a simple book-keeping system would not have shown how many of a particular item should be in stock at any time. The only way this could have been found out would have been for someone to actually go and count the items. In a computerised system the entering of items sold will not only be entered in the figures in the Sales Journal, but will also be automatically entered in the stock records as well. Similarly with items bought. Given the opening stock of every individual item, if the sales and purchases of each item is put into the stock records then the closing stock of each item on a particular day can be automatically produced by the computer. There will be actual physical stock checks from time to time to ensure that the computer system is working properly.

Wages Programs

Imagine the wages clerk of some decades ago manually calculating the wages of employees. He would first of all multiply the hours worked by the amount paid per hour, if work was done on a time basis, and make allowances for any overtime. This would give him the gross wages figure. From this he would need to deduct P.A.Y.E. income tax, by consulting a set of tax tables. Then he would deduct national insurance by consulting another set of tables. Any superannuation would then have to be worked out, also any further deductions. Once these had been deducted from the gross wages the net wages figure would be shown.

All of this would take a lot of time, and the room for errors was quite considerable. Now all that would be needed would be to enter the employee's works number into the computer and the number of hours worked. As the tax tables, national insurance tables, superannuation arrangements and other deduction details will already be in the computer, the computer will print out a pay slip giving full details of all the above items. Assuming that workers are paid in cash then it will also work out for the entire workforce how many £10 notes, £5 notes and coins are needed to make up the wage packets. This would all be done in a mere fraction of the time taken to do it manually.

Collection of Data

With manual accounting systems the information required is written into the system from original documents, such as orders received from customers or from issue tickets for stock records. The basic entry into the accounts may then be transferred or 'posted' to the other accounts involved which requires further written entries. This system may be improved as has been mentioned earlier by 'three in one' systems – which cut down on the amount of 'posting' and thus reduce both time and errors in the recording process.

Modern manual accounting systems attempt wherever possible to cut down on repetitive copying of entries into journals and use instead files of the original documents. Careful design of the stationery used for invoices and other documents also helps to reduce the time needed to maintain the records.

Computer Inputs

Where computers are used in the accounting process, the basic information instead of being hand written into the system needs to be entered into the processing by a means that the computer can accept. This can be through a number of methods which are briefly described.

Keyboard Systems

For most accounting transactions the information will be entered through a keyboard like a typewriter. The keyboard often has a screen (Visual Display Unit or VDU) attached which shows what has been entered on the keyboard. The operator thus enters the information onto the keyboard, and can check visually that the entry is correct.

The keyboard can be connected to equipment which will record the information entered. The method of recording will vary from system to system. The most common method of recording now is on to magnetic disks, or the smaller diskettes (floppy disks). Very large amounts of information can be recorded onto a single disk. Disks and diskettes are very convenient in size and cost and provide a fast, quiet and reliable means of recording data for transmission to the computer. Magnetic tape cassettes (standard audio cassettes) can also be used in much the same way as disks – but are not as widely used in practice except in small home computers.

For some purposes it may be desirable to record the data on to punched cards rather than magnetic disk. Some keyboards therefore produce a card – which can be read manually because of a printed interpretation on it. Cards can be sorted in different ways away from the computer and can act if necessary as a source document or record card.

Magnetic Ink Character Recognition (MICR)

It is possible for equipment to read information directly from a document, if that information is recorded in magnetised ink. The best known use of this method of collecting information for the computer is the standard bank cheque which contains magnetised ink characters on the front which allow the cheques to be sorted automatically between all the clearing banks.

Optical Recognition

Equipment can be obtained which will 'read' either marks on preprinted forms, or specially printed writing. Thus instead of feeding information through a keyboard it can be read directly thus saving time and cost. Perhaps the most widely seen use of this approach is in supermarket checkouts where a bar code (see Exhibit) on each product can be read by a special reader. The bar code contains full details of the product being sold. These types of system tend to be expensive and have problems with some input material.

Exhibit 26.1

0 20248 009533

A Bar Code.

Problems of Data Collection

Whatever method of data collection is used its accuracy and completeness is vital if a computer system is to work properly. There is a standard saying for computers – Garbage In Garbage Out (GIGO) which means that if you do not put the correct data into the computer you cannot possibly get the correct output when required. Great care has therefore to be taken to check the accuracy of the input. This may for example involve having two independent operators prepare input tapes from the original data. These will be compared automatically and only used if they agree. This is only one of a whole range of checks to make sure a system is accurate.

Mistakes are just as important in a manual system, but they can usually be traced more easily since a written record can be looked at directly. Once information is recorded onto magnetic disk it is much less visible and errors become harder to spot.

Coding Information

One special requirement when entering data into a computer system is to describe the input in a way that enables the computer to work efficiently. In a manual system words as well as numbers are used to describe the data being entered. A customer will be entered by name and the products he is ordering will be described in words, in addition to the quantities involved.

A computer system works much better if the information is transformed into numerical terms. Thus, instead of describing the customer as Mr. Jones, the computer will require a code number for Mr. Jones, say customer number 3562. Similarly it is necessary to have code numbers for the products rather than simply to use a name. To help people using information from the computer, usually the printout shows the customer name in addition to the number, but for working purposes the computer is only interested in the number.

Thus when information is being fed into the system it is necessary for the code numbers to be included. When a customer's order is received somebody will have to check that the goods ordered are correctly coded – not simply described in words. The accuracy of the coding is vital.

The simplest type of coding is to give a single consecutive number to each transaction. For example Sales Invoices might be numbered in consecutive order 1, 2, 3, 4, and so on. Each new customer could be allocated a number at the end of the list which is unique to him. This type of numbering is called a Sequence Code as it simply classifies things according to the sequence in which they arise. Sequence codes are commonly used and may be applied not only to customers, but also to suppliers and employees who are described by employee number as well as name and products which have a number code.

Sequence codes do not give much information other than a specific and unique number in the sequence. For accounting purposes it is usually important to classify the information in more detail. A logical coding system can be drawn up which allocates numbers in blocks which fit the accounting structure. If we want to code the account number then a Chart of Accounts should be drawn up and code numbers allocated to each part of the chart as shown: –

DESCRIPTION OF ACCOUNT	CODE NUMBER
ASSETS	100 – 299
LIABILITIES	300 – 499
CAPITAL	500 – 599
SALES REVENUES	600 – 699
EXPENSES	700 – 899
OTHER ITEMS	900 – 999

One block of numbers 100 – 299 is allocated to assets. Within this block individual asset accounts will be given a specific number e.g.

100 – 199	Fixed Assets	
	101	Land
	102	Buildings
	103	Plant and Machinery and so on
200 – 299	Current Assets	
	201	Bank Account
	202	Trade Debtors
	203	Stock in Trade and so on

Block Coding uses sequences to put items in order but by grouping things into a logical structure of blocks makes them easier to understand for someone working with the system.

A single block code usually does not contain enough information about a transaction. It is therefore common to find a series of codes grouped together. This Group Code will consist of fields or groups of numbers each describing separate aspects of the transaction. For example if a business buys a tyre to repair a car from the XYZ garage it will want to code –

Field 1 The suppliers code number
Field 2 The expense account involved

If the XYZ Garage were supplier number 4362 and the motor repair expense account number 852 then the invoice would be coded 4362852. The computer will then ensure that the invoice for the type is recorded as a credit to XYZ Garage personal account in the purchase ledger and a debit to the Motor Repair Account in the nominal ledger.

The number of fields is not limited and can be extended to contain as much information as is necessary for later analysis by the computer. If the information is not coded the computer cannot use it. However if the code gets very long there are more likely to be mistakes in the original coding process – which could outweigh the benefits.

To help make the code numbers easier for people to understand they are developed to have more meaning than a simple sequence code. This is often done for assigning numbers to products in the inventory. For example: In the sports shop at a ski-resort hotel:

The first digit describes the nature of the product:

1. Hats
2. Socks
3. Gloves
4. Trousers

The second digit describes the material from which the item is made:

1. Wool
2. Cotton
3. Nylon
4. Felt

The third digit may describe the colour of the product: –

1. Blue
2. Grey
3. Black
4. White

Thus a product with number 142 would be a grey felt hat.

This is called Faceted Coding and is designed to be more informative than sequential coding. It will generally be used as part of a Group Code. The crucial problem with coding is to try to eliminate errors. This can only be done by training people well in the first place and by using a well thought out coding system which is as simple as possible. Checks will have to be included in the system – both specific double checking the person doing the coding, and also getting the system to check itself by including check digits in the codes themselves.

It is beyond the scope of this book to describe exactly how checks are built into the system, but a couple of examples will give the reader a general idea of how they work. Suppose that a payroll is put on to the computer, and in error one employee is shown as working 250 hours in a week, obviously quite impossible. Included in the automatic check which will be thrown up by the computer is that no one can work more than (say) 100 hours per week. Also if a sales invoice works out as minus £280 then that will be shown up automatically by the check, as minus figures are impossible for sales.

When feeding numeric data into a computer, the following types of error can be made:

Error	Example
Transcription	12345 becomes 12545
Transposition	12345 becomes 12435
Double Transposition	12345 becomes 12543
Omission	12345 becomes 1345
Addition	12345 becomes 123745
Random	A combination of two or more of the above, or any other error.

Since people remember words more easily than numbers it is sometimes useful to combine words or letters with the numbers. A good example is the coding of flights from airports which include an abbreviated description of the airline with a specific flight number e.g. BA 192 British Airways flight number 192. People find this easier to remember and check than just five numbers.

Data Processing

Since there is an enormous difference between firms, both in terms of the work that they do and their size and organisation, there are correspondingly a very wide variety of methods of data processing for accounting purposes. Each organisation must decide which is the way it wants to keep its information, both with regard to cost and effectiveness. A very small firm will normally find that a simple manual recording system is adequate, whereas a large firm will need to handle a much higher volume of data and therefore require a computerised system. Because computers have become so much cheaper, and have become so versatile, they have effectively taken over from accounting machines and punched card equipment. The issue today therefore is whether the expense of a computer is justified or not to take over the manual accounting system.

Benefits of Computerisation

The benefits which can be gained from the computer, if it is properly used are: –

1. SPEED – Once the information has been fed into the machine it is handled very fast.
2. GOOD SERVICE – Because it is so fast all queries should be answered faster, and goods sent out sooner.
3. BETTER INFORMATION – Since it can handle huge amounts of data and process it in a short time – managers can be given better information at the right time.

4. VOLUME – Where there are large volumes of data to handle – the computer is much cheaper than other methods and indeed may be the only possible way of doing the work.

5. ACCURACY – Once correct data has been fed in, the computer is very accurate.

6. VERSATILE – Computers can be used over a very wide area of the organisation for many purposes – not only accounting. In addition they can deal with peak workloads with more flexibility than people – since the machine does not object to working overtime.

Problems with Computers

Computers can cause many problems to an organisation including: –

1. COST – Setting up an effective system – both for hardware and software is very expensive. This cost needs to be carefully justified by the benefits.

2. INTRODUCTORY PROBLEMS – When a computer is brought in it will require new ways of doing things which if not carefully managed can disrupt the whole business.

3. DEPENDENCE – Once the computer takes over the whole system depends on it. If it breaks down or is damaged or sabotaged – the firm can lose all its records very easily. Care must be taken to keep copies.

4. PEOPLE PROBLEMS – People can respond badly to the introduction of computers – resenting their impact on the work they have always done. They do not want to work in a dehumanised environment.

5. SYSTEMS ERRORS – The development of software can be difficult and involve error until properly sorted out. Because it is a very skilled job – this may cause many problems if properly trained people are not employed.

6. INFLEXIBLE – Once a system is introduced it must be followed. Computers will not generally allow people to change minor procedures in a way as they can with manual procedures.

Introducing a Computer

When thinking about introducing a computer therefore a business needs to conduct a feasibility study. This study is to assess the benefits and problems associated with whether or not to introduce a computer to take over from a manual procedure. Computers are not an automatic choice since they will only provide a benefit if they are introduced with great care. This will be expensive and may not be justified in some small businesses. However the availability of good ready designed software packages to do standard accounting work on ledgers, analysis, wages and stock records – is continually increasing. This together with the reducing cost of the hardware means that the benefits of computers are extending to more and more organisations.

Non-Computerised Book-keeping Methods: Advantages and Disadvantages

It has already been stated that only a feasibility study can determine whether or not it is advantageous for a computerised system to be introduced or not. It is a matter for each organisation, with its own unique set-up to determine this, only someone with an inside knowledge of the organisation can manage to carry out such a study.

However, it is possible to say that a great deal of the original mechanical means of carrying out book-keeping has been rendered obsolete, and the more recent advances in micro-computer technology have made obsolescence the case with most firms. Where mechanical means, bought largely before computers on their present scale had arrived, are still in use then one advantage is that the money was spent several or more years ago and that nothing else needs to be spent, which would not be true if a computerised system was to be bought. The old system may possibly give all the information that could be used by the firm, but with some other firms a computer system could be used to give extra *cost-effective* information.

Manual methods have the great advantage of flexibility, and there can be no bother about the machinery or computer developing faults. Whether it would be cheaper or not only a feasibility study could decide. One can hardly imagine that a small fish and chip shop for instance could make really profitable use of a computer. On the other hand it would be difficult to imagine a firm with, say, 200 people, not being able to make good use of a computer. These are generalisations only, the author has no doubt that individual cases could give a different answer when all the facts were properly known. The three-in-one system also has the benefit three different entries being made with one writing action.

Exercises

26.1. The sports shop of the Ski Hotel also sells shoes which are made by ABC Ltd. The manufacturer produces shoes in half-sizes as follows: –

	Size Ranges
Mens	6½ to 9½
Boys	2 to 6
Ladies	3 to 8
Girls	1 to 6

An eight-digit code is used to identify shoes. Reading from left to right, it is made up as follows:

Digit one shows whether the shoes are mens, boys, ladies or girls. The numbers in use are mens 1, boys 2, ladies 3, girls 4.

Digit two shows the situation concerning laces. No laces is given number 0, short black laces 1, long black laces, 2 short brown laces 3, long brown laces 4, short white laces 5, long white laces 6.

Digit three shows the colour. Black 1, Dark Brown 2, Tan 3, White 4, Blue 5, Green 6, Yellow 7.

Digit four shows the material of the upper part of the shoes. Leather 1, Synthetic 2, Canvas 3, Suede 4.

Digit five shows the material of the sole. Leather 1, Rubber 2, Synthetic 3.

Digit six shows whether any guarantee is given to purchaser as to period of use during which shoes can be returned if worn out. No guarantee 0, three months 1, six months 2, one year 3.

Digits seven and eight show size. Size one is shown as 10, size one and a half as 15, size two as 20, size two and a half as 25, and so on.

Examples of codes are:
Code 10433085 is a pair of mens shoes, no laces, white canvas, synthetic sole, no guarantee given, size 8½.

Code 43211240 is a pair of girls shoes, short brown laces, dark brown leather uppers with leather soles, six months guarantee, size four.

(a) You are required to give the code numbers which would apply to:
  (i) Boys shoes, with long black laces, black in colour, synthetic uppers, leather soles, six months guarantee, size 5.
  (ii) Ladies shoes, no laces, yellow, leather uppers and soles, no guarantee, size 6½.
  (iii) Mens tan shoes, leather sole, synthetic uppers, short brown laces, three months guarantee, size 9½.
  (iv) Girls blue shoes, size 3½, no laces, suede uppers and leather soles, no guarantee.

(b) State exactly what kind of shoes are denoted by the following code numbers:
  (i) 31123045
  (ii) 26432060
  (iii) 10223085
  (iv) 40612320

(c) If red shoes were added to the product range, what do you think would happen to the code?

(d) What would you suggest should happen to the code numbers if the range of footwear was extended to boots for men and for boys?

(e) What other information do you think would be desirable for ladies shoes not already given in the code?

(f) If the exact system of coding was adhered to, and the company extended its men's shoe range up to size 12, what problems would result?

26.2. What kinds of errors are these:

(i) 56789 shown in error as 5679
(ii) 56789 shown in error as 56987
(iii) 56789 shown in error as 56879
(iv) 56789 shown in error as 567899
(v) 56789 shown in error as 56779
(vi) 56789 shown in error as 658976

Answers to Exercises

3.1 (a) A,B,C. (b) D,E,F,G,H.

3.2 30, 15, 5, 90, 75, 55.

3.4 Delivery note, bin card, goods received, goods received note.

4.1 Capital a, c, d, f, j, l. Revenue – b, e, g, h, i, k.

4.3 (a) £2, (b) 60%.

4.5 (a) £0.73, (b) £3.16.

4.6 (a) £1.11, (b) £3.20, (e) 68%.

4.8 (a) 67½% (b) Above target.

4.10 (b) Each item in order 7.128 + 0.04 + 0.088 + 0.45 + 0.08 + 0.24 + 0.04 + 0.026 + 0.021 = 8.113 (c) 8.113 (d) 0.676 (e) 2.25.

5.3 Payment Totals: Stationery 1.34, Post 19.80, Sundry 1.92, Travel 3.25, Ledger 3.78. Balance carried forward 4.91.

5.5 (a) 72.02% (b) 80% (c) 38.46%.

5.6 (a) Sales 700 – VAT 91.30 = 608.70 – Food Cost 253.40 = G.P. 355.30. G.P. as % Sales 58.37% (b) £9.92.

5.10 (a) July (b) May, June, July, August (c) September.

11.1 Closing stock 22 × 1.40 = £30.80.

11.2 Closing stocks: FIFO 7 × 90p = £6.30: LIFO 5 × 70p + 2 × 90p = £5.30.

11.4 (a) (i) 6 × £13 = £78 (ii) 6 × £10 = £60 (iii) 6 × £12.50 = £75.
(b) Trading Accounts show gross profits (i) FIFO 340 (ii) LIFO 322 (iii) AVCO 337.

12.1 (a) £2.40 (b) £0.96 (c) £0.24 (d) 80% (e) 1.20 + 0.96 + 0.24 = 2.40

12.2 Sales 2,400 – Food Costs 1,200 = Gross Profit 1,200 – Labour and Overheads 1,000 = Net Profit 200.

12.3 (a) Selling Price 2.40 – Food Costs 1.20 – Labour and Overhead 0.50* = Contribution per unit 0.70 (*Total Cost 1,000 so 500 variable = 0.50 per unit).

(b) Sales 2,400 – Variable Costs 1,700 = Contribution 700 – Fixed Costs 500 = Net Profit 200.

(c) As fixed costs constant at 500 therefore contribution must be 1,000 if net profit is to be 500. This means extra £300 contribution compared with (b). With 1,000 meals price of each one needs increasing by 0.30 to give selling price £2.70.

12.4 (a) (i) 1,250 covers or £5,000 (ii) Margin of Safety 2,500 covers – 1,250 covers = 1,250 covers or £5,000.

12.6 (a) per text (b) Entrance and toilet measurements ignored. Bar and Cellar £351 × 250/750 = £117: Restaurant £351 × 500/750 = £234.

13.1 Overall G.P. weighted by sales mix A 0.1 × 0.5 = 0.05 + B 0.4 × 0.6 = 0.24 + C 0.2 × 0.65 = 0.13 + D 0.3 × 0.7 = 0.21 = Total 0.63. This means that overall gross profit will be 63%. Fixed expenses £33,000 so gross profit should be £33,000 + £30,000 = £63,000. This is target and as overall gross profit is 63% this means that sales of 100% should be £63,000 × 100/63 = £100,000. Sales 100,000 – Food and Beverages 37,000 = G.P. 63,000 – Fixed Costs 33,000 = Net Profit 30,000. Exlusive Sales 10,000 covers × £10 each = £100,000. Including VAT £100 × 115/100 = £11.50 per cover. Exclusive price per course, total £11.50 divided by sales mix A × 0.1 = £1.15 : B × 0.4 = £4.60: C × 0.2 = £2.30: D × 0.3 = £3.45.

13.2 (i) Total Sales 247.50 + 38.00 + 299.25 + 11.25 + 18.80 = 614.80 Gross Profits 160.875 + 26.60 + 185.535 + 5.85 + 13.16 = 392.02 Gross Profit % 392.02/614.80 × 100/1 = 63.76%.

(ii) Total customers 50 TH + 57 ALC = 107
Average spend per person 614.80 ÷ 107 = £5.75 appox.

(iii) Sales mix T.H. 247.50/614.80 = 40.26%; similarly Starters 6.18%: Main Course 48.67%: Sweets 1.83%: Coffee 3.06%.

13.3 Food as % Sales: Main 40% × 55% = 22%: Starters/Sweets 36% × 25% = 9%: Wine 30% × 20% = 6%. Total 22 + 9 + 6 = 37%. Sales is 100% – Food Cost 37% = 63% Gross Profit. It is known that net profit is to be 725 which + Fixed Expenses 4,000 = Gross Profit £4,725.

As G.P. % is 63% Sales will be £4,725 × 100/63 = £7,500 Food & Beverage Costs are £7,500 – £4,725 = £2,775. Selling Price per meal £7,500 ÷ 1,000 covers = £7.50. Dish prices : Main £7.50 × Mix 55% = £4.125: Starters/Sweets £7.50 × 25% = £1.875: Wine £7.50 × 20% = £1.50.

13.6 (a) Turnover 1,000 − Food Costs 300 (40% × 750) − Beverage Costs 162.50 (65% × 250) = New Gross Profit 537.50.

(b) Turnover 1,700 − Food Costs 510 (1,275 × 40%) − Beverage Costs 276.25 (425 × 65%) = New Gross Profit 913.75.

(c) Food Sales 1,700 × 70% = 1,190 therefore costs = 1,190 × 40% = 476.00: Beverage Sales 1,700 × 30% = 510 therefore costs = 510 × 65% = 331.50. Food Costs would rise to 476.00 + 331.50 = 807.50. Therefore Gross Profit would fall 807.50 − 786.25 = 21.25.

(d) Food Costs would be 1,190 × 50% = 595 + Beverage Costs 510 × 55% = 280.50 = total 875.50. Gross Profit 1,700 − 875.50 = 824.50.

14.1 10 cases × 12 = 120 bottles for 216 = 1.80 each Selling price ex VAT 1.80 × 100/30 = 6.00. Including VAT it will be 6.00 + 15% = 6.90.

14.2 (a) 403.65 − VAT 52.65 = 60 bottles per 351.00. 1 bottle 351 ÷ 60 = 5.85 ex VAT.

(b) Cost per measure 5.85 ÷ 32 = 0.183

(c) S.P. per measure ex VAT 0.183 × 100/40 = 0.4575

(d) S.P. per measure incl. VAT 0.4575 × 1.15 = 0.53.

14.3 (a) Cost 9.2 × £3.1 = 28.52. Value of bones 1.7 × 0.10 = 0.17 Weight 9.2 − bones 1.7 = 7.5 kg. Therefore usable meat cost (28.52 − 0.17) ÷ 7.5 = £3.78 per kg.

(b) Served meat weighs 7.5kg × 60% = 4.5 kg. Cost per kilo (28.52 − 0.17) ÷ 4.5 = £6.30.

15.1 (a) Sales ? = Food Costs 89.60 + Labour 146.05 + Net Profit 15%. Therefore 85% Sales = 89.60 + 146.05. Therefore Sales 235.65 × 100/85 = 277.24. Per cover ÷ 50 = 5.55 rounded.

(b) Sales (50 × 5.55) 277.50 − 235.65 = Net Profit 41.65.

15.2 (a) per text. (b) Banquet price (Sales) = Food 200 + labour 150 + overheads 100 + 10% Sales. Therefore 90% Sales = 200 + 150 + 100 = 450. Sales therefore 450 × 100/90 = 500 or £5 each guest.

15.4 Expected number of sales = 400 × 70% × 250 = 70,000. Total costs food 70,000 × 0.80 = 56,000 + labour & overheads 35,000 = 91,000. Per guest 91,000 × 70,000 = 1.30 ex VAT per unit. Subsidy per meal 1.30 − 0.75 = 0.55.

15.6 Overheads (Rooms) £172,000 × Room area/Total area = 172,000 × 12,600/15,700 = 138,040 (rounded). Total Costs Rooms Dept: Wages 148,000 + Direct Expenses 123,000 + Overheads 138,040 = 409,040. Total Costs + Net Profit (20% Sales) = Sales, therefore Total Costs = 80% Sales. Room Revenue 409,040 × 100/80 = 511,300.
Average occupancy = 630 × 60% = 378 sleeper nights. Per year 378 × 52 = 19,656. Charge per sleeper night 511,300 × 19,656 = £26 (rounded). Per week £26 × 7 = £182.

15.7 Departmental profits: Rooms 3,920, Restaurant 880.

15.9 Rooms £12,300: Restaurant £3,150: Bar £1,500.

15.14 (a) per text. (b) (i) Variable 4,341 × 1.96 = 8,508 + Fixed 5,296 = 13,804 + Net Profit (22/78 × 13,804) 3,893 = Selling price ex VAT 17,697;
Per cover 17,697 ÷ 4.341 = £4.08 (rounded).
(ii) To breakeven 13,804 × 4,341 = £3.18 (rounded).
(iii) 1.96 variable + contribution 0.14 = 2.10.

16.1 per text.

16.2 (a) 35.21 + 10% Service 3.52 = 38.73 + VAT 15% 5.81 = 44.54.
(b) Account 22.43 + Service 2.80 = 25.23 + VAT 3.78 = 29.01.

16.5 Per text.

17.1 (a) 10,700, (b) 23,100, (c) 4,300, (d) 3,150, (e) 25,500, (f) 51,400.

17.3 Assets (i) (iii) (iv) (vi): Liabilities (ii) (v).

17.5 Wrong Assets: Loan, creditors. Wrong Liabilities: Stock, Debtors.

17.7 5,400.

17.9 Assets 5,500 + 5,700 + 8,800 + 4,950 + 1,250 = Total 26,200. Capital 23,750 + Creditors 2,450.

17.11

(*a*)	− Cash, − Creditors	(*e*)	+ Cash, + Loan
(*b*)	− Bank, + Fixtures	(*f*)	+ Bank, − Debtors
(*c*)	+ Stock, + Creditors	(*g*)	− Stock, − Creditors
(*d*)	+ Cash, + Capital	(*h*)	+ Premises, − Bank.

17.13 Fixtures 4,500 + Motor vehicle 4,200 + Stock 5,720 + Debtors 3,000 + bank 5,450 + Cash 400 = Total 23,270. Capital 18,900 + Loan 2,000 + Creditors 2,370.

18.1

	Debited	*Credited*		*Debited*	*Credited*
(a)	Office Machinery	D. Isaacs Ltd.	(b)	C. Jones	Capital
(c)	Cash	N. Fox	(d)	Loan: P. Exeter	Bank
(e)	D. Isaacs Ltd.	Office Machinery	(f)	Bank	N. Lyn
(g)	Motor Van	Cash			

18.3 Cash Dr 2,000 & 75 & 100, Cr 1,800, Bank Dr 1,800 & 500, Cr 950 & 58 & 100, Capital Cr 2,000, Office furniture Dr 120, Cr 62, Betta Built Dr 62 & 58, Cr 120, Motor van Dr 950, Evans & Sons Cr 560, Works machinery Dr 560, Cr 75, J. Smith (Loan) Cr 500.

18.4 Cash Dr 500 & 400 & 200; Cr 350 & 50: Bank Dr 10,000 & 1,000 & 350 & 1,000 & 1,800; Cr 3,000 & 2,000: Phillips Garages Dr 2,000; Cr 3,600: R. Jones Dr 3,000; Cr 1,000 & 1,800 & 200: J. Smith, Dr 200; Cr 700: Loan J. Hawkins Cr 400: Loan H. Thompson Cr 1,000: Motor van Dr 3,000 & 3,600: Cr 3,000: Office equipment Dr 700 & 50; Cr 200: Capital Cr 10,000 & 500.

18.7 Totals – Cash Dr 597 Cr 173, Capital Cr 500, Purchases Dr 299, Sales Cr 97, Returns outwards Cr 47, E. Morgan Dr 116, Cr 116, A. Moses Dr 19 Cr 98, A. Knight Dr 55 Cr 55.

18.8 Totals – Cash Dr 1,028 Cr 955, Bank Dr 1,000 Cr 710, Purchases Dr 133, S. Holmes Dr 78 Cr 78, Capital Cr 1,000, Motor van Dr 500, Sales Cr 126, D. Moore Dr 98, Returns outwards Cr 18, Fixtures Dr 150, Kingston Equipt Co Dr 150 Cr 150, Watson (Loan) Cr 100.

18.10 Totals – Bank Dr 2,005, Cr 450, Capital Cr 2,000, Purchases Dr 289, Mills Dr 23 Cr 175, Fixtures Dr 150, Cash Dr 275 Cr 203, S. Wong Cr 114, Rent Dr 15, Stationery Dr 27, Returns outwards Cr 23, Rent received Cr 5, U. Henry Dr 77, Sales Cr 352, Motor van Dr 300, Wages Dr 117, Drawings Dr 44.

18.12 *Trial Balance* – Drs: Cash 215, Purchases 459, Rent 30, Bank 96, Hughes 129, Spencer 26, Carriage 23; Crs: Capital 250, Sales 348, Mendez 130, Booth 186, Lowe 64. Totals: 978.

18.13 *Trial Balance* – Drs: Purchases 360, Bank 361, Cash 73, Wages 28, Lindo 74, Shop fixtures 50, Motor van 400, Elliot 35; Crs: King Loan 60, Braham 134, Henriques 52, Capital 800, Sales 291, Returns outwards 44. Totals: 1,381.

19.1 *Trading:* Purchases 14,629 *less* Closing stock 7,245 Cr Sales 18,462, Dr Gross profit 11,078. *Profit and Loss:* Dr Salaries 2,150, Motor expenses 520, Rent and rates 670, Insurance 111, General 105, Net profit 7,522. *Assets:* Premises 1,500, Motors 1,200, Stock 7,245, Debtors 1,950, Bank 1,654, Cash 40. Totals: 13,589. *Balance Sheet* – Capital 5,424, *add* Net profit 7,522, *less* Drawings 895, 12,051. *Liabilities:* Creditors 1,538.

19.2 *Trading:* Dr Purchases 23,803, *less* Stock 12,291, Gross profit 17,282, Cr Sales 28,794. *Profit and Loss:* Dr Salaries 3,164, Rent 854, Lighting 422, Insurance 105, Motor expenses 1,133, Trade expenses 506, Net profit 11,098.

Balance Sheet: Assets: Buildings 50,000, Fixtures 1,000, Motors 5,500, Stock 12,291, Debtors 3,166, Bank 3,847. Totals: 75,804.

– Capital: 65,900, *add* Net profit 11,098, *less* Drawings 2,400, Creditors 1,206.

19.5 Trading, Dr: Opening stock 2,368 + Purchases 11,874 – Returns out 322 + Carriage in 310 – Closing stock 2,946 = Cost of goods sold 11,284. Gross profit 7,111; Cr Sales 18,600 – Returns in 205. Profit and Loss: Dr: Salaries 3,862, Rent 304, Carriage out 200, Insurance 78, Motor Expenses 664, Office expenses 216, Lighting 166, General 314, Net profit 1,307. Cr: Gross profit 7,111. Balance sheet: Fixed assets, Premises 5,000, Fixtures 350, Motor 1,800. Current assets, Stock 2,946, Debtors 3,896, Bank 482, Totals 14,474. Capital: Balance 12,636 + Net profit 1,307, less Drawings 1,200 = 12,743. Current liabilities, Creditors 1,731.

19.7 STRAIGHT LINE 4,000 − 700 = 3,300 − 700 = 2,600 − 700 = 1,900 − 700 = 1,200 − 700 = 500.
REDUCING BALANCE 4,000 − 1,600 = 2,400 − 960 = 1,400 − 576 = 864 − 346 = 518 − 207 = 311.

19.8 STRAIGHT LINE 12,500 − 1,845 = 10,655 − 1,845 = 8,810 − 1,845 = 6,965 − 1,845 = 5,120.
REDUCING BALANCE 12,500 − 2,500 = 10,000 − 2,000 = 8,000 − 1,600 = 6,400 − 1,280 = 5,120.

19.11 (*a*) Old Method: Motor van account 4,000 − 800 = 3,200 Balance − 640 = 2,560 Balance − 512 = 2,048 Balance − 410 = 1,638 Balance.
Modern Method: Motor delivery van kept at cost 4,000. Separate provision for depreciation account: Year (1) 800 + Year (2) 640 = Balance 1,440 + Year (3), 512 = Balance 1,952 + Year (4) 410 = Balance 2,362.
(*b*) per book.

19.13 D. Fung's account: Dr Balance b/fwd 200, Cr Cash 150, Bad debts 50. C. Manley's account: Dr Balance b/fwd 120, Cr Cash 36, Bad debts 84. Bad debts: D. Fung 50, C. Manley 84, Cr Transfer to Profit & Loss 134.

19.14 (*a*) Provision for bad debts 19-7: Dr balance c/d 1,186, Cr Profit & Loss 1,186. 19-8 Dr Profit & Loss 186, Cr Balance c/d 1,000. (*b*) Profit & Loss 19-7 Dr 1,186 & 140, 19-8 Cr 186. (*c*) 19-7, Debtors 11,860 − Provision 1,186 = 10,674, 19-8, Debtors 10,000 − Provision 1,000 = 9,000.

19.17 (*a*) Motor expenses: Dr Paid 744, Accrued c/d 28, Cr Profit & Loss 772; (*b*) Insurance: Dr Paid 420, Cr Profit & Loss 385, Prepaid c/d 35; (*c*) Rent: Dr Paid 1,800, Accrued c/d 490, Cr Accrued b/f 250, Profit & Loss 2,040; (*d*) Rates: Dr Prepaid b/d 220, Paid 950, Cr Profit & Loss 880, Prepaid c/d 290; (*e*) Rent received: Dr owing b/f 180, Profit & Loss 580, Cr Received 550, Owing c/d 210.

19.19 Rates account: Dr In advance b/d 150, Cash (May) 400, (Nov) 400, Total 950. Cr Profit & Loss 750, In advance c/d 200.

19.21 Trading: Dr Opening stock 10,000 + Purchases 15,000 − Purchase returns 620 − Closing stock 12,000 = Cost of goods sold 12,380, Gross profit 27,120. Cr Sales 40,000 − Sales returns 500. Profit & Loss: Dr Wages 13,500, Staff Meals 1,000, Rates 550, Telephone 122, Bad debts 20, Provision for bad debts 18. Depreciation − Fittings 400, Van 600, Net Profit 10,910. Cr Gross profit 27,120.

19.22 Trading: Dr. Opening Stock 3,910 + Purchases 62,100 − Returns Out 307 + Carriage In 215 − Closing Stock 7,475 = Cost of Goods Sold 58,443, Gross Profit c/d 71,907. Cr: Sales 130,900 − Returns In 550. Profit & Loss A/c: Dr: Wages 42,810, Carriage Out 309, Motor Expenses 1,630, Rent & Rates 2,865, Telephone 490, Insurance 387, Office Expenses 1,377, Sundries 284, Depreciation Motors 1,200, Office Equipment 1,600, Net Profit 18,955. Balance Sheet: Fixed Assets, Motor Van 6,000 − Depreciation 3,100 = 2,900, Office Equipt. 8,000 − Depn. 3,350 = 4,650, Current Assets, Stock 7,475, Debtors 12,300, Prepayments 510, Bank 23,115, Cash 295. Capital, Balance 25,955 + Net Profit 18,955 − Drawings 8,420 = 36,490. Loan 5,000, Current Liabilities: Creditors 9,370, Expenses Owing 385. Totals 51,245.

21.2 ROL (1,000 × ½) + 50 = 500 + 50 = 550.

22.2 Balance end of April 2,000: May Nil: June 6,000 overdraft: July 7,000 overdraft.

22.3 (*a*) per text. (*b*) March-May loss 1,825 (16.59%): June-August profit 2,988 (7.76%): Sept-Nov profit 7,800 (11.82%): Dec-Feb 1,062 profit (3.86%): Total profit 10,025 (7.01%).

22.5 Balances end of July 26,525: August 32,124: September 34,672.

22.6 (*a*) Receipts: Shares 100,000 + Sales 117,500 − Payments Labour 36,000, Overheads 19,000, Purchases 52,000, Fixed assets 97,000 = Final balance 13,500. Net Profit in Profit & Loss is 12,000. Balance Sheet: Fixed Assets 97,000 − 5,000, Stock 8,000, Debtors 2,500, Cash 13,500 − Creditors 4,000 = Working Capital 20,000 Share Capital 100,000 + Profit & Loss 12,000.

(*b*) Various.

22.8 (*a*) Sources: Balance b/f 1,300 + Equipment Sale 200 + Debtors 7,000 less New Equipment 1,600, Creditors 5,500, Expenses 1,000, Drawings 520, Final balance 120 overdrawn.

(*b*) Gross Profit 2,300, Net Profit 1,000.

(*c*) Fixed Assets 5,200 − 2,100, Stock 2,000, Debtors 1,000 − Creditors 1,500 − Overheads owing 120 = Working Capital 1,380. Total 4,480. Capital 4,000 + Net Profit 1,000 − Drawings 520.

23.1

			Variance	
	Budget %	Actual %	£	%
Sales	100	100	350A	6A
Materials	38	47	400A	17A
Gross Profit	62	53	750A	19A
Labour	28	30	40A	2A
Overheads	16	18	90A	9A
Net Profit	18	5	880A	77A

Main reasons: 6% less Sales: Large increase in Materials.

23.2 *1 Portion dish A*

1. 250g of x at £2 kg =	0.50	2. 2000 dishes of A					
200g of y at £1 kg =	0.20	x	SQ 500	AQ 510	SP £2	AP £1.90
		y	400	390	£1	£1.20
Standard cost of A	0.70					

	x	*y*
Price Variances	500 × .1 = 51F	390 × 0.2 = 78A
Usage Variances	£2 × 10 = 20A	£1 × 10 = 10F

Reconciliation 2000 × 0.7 = £1400 Standard cost

– Favourable 51 + 10 = 61

– Adverse 78 + 20 = 98

1437 Actual cost

23.3 (i)

		Fixed		Flexible		Actual
		£		£		£
Sales	£2×10,000 =	20,000	£2×9000 =	£18,000	£2.2×9000	19,800
Cost	£3×2000 =	6,000	£3×1800 =	5400	£2.8×2000	5600
Gross Profit	£1.4×10000	14,000	1.4×9000	12,600		14200

(ii) a) AQ × Diff. in P 9000 × .2 = 1800 (F)
b) STGP/UNIT × Diff. in Q £1.4 × 1000 = 1400 (A)
c) AQ × Diff. in P 2000 × .2 = 400 (F)
d) SP × Diff. in Q £3 × 200 = 600 (A)

(iii) Fixed Budgeted Gross Profit 14,000 + Fav. Variances: Sales Price 1,800 + Cost Price 400 − Adverse Variances: Sales Volume 1,400 − Cost Usage 600 = Actual Gross Profit 14,200.

24.1 1 Food Cost: 2 Total Cost: 3 Material Cost: 4 Overhead Costs: 5 Labour Cost: 6 Material Cost: 7 Overhead Cost: 8 Labour Cost.

24.3 Gross Profit: Labour cost + overheads + net profit; Material cost + labour cost + overhead cost: Total cost.

24.4 Manager 600 + Chefs 1,440 + Waiters 912 + Staff Meals 300 + Casual labour 72 = Total 3,324.

24.6 Budgeted sales 160,000 × 1.5 = £168.000

Labour costs last year $\frac{40,000}{160,000} = 25\%$: Next year $25\% \times 2\frac{1}{2}\% = 27\frac{1}{2}\%$

Budgeted labour costs next year − 168,000 × 0.275 = £46,200

Allocated reception 5775, housekeeping 13860, Bars 3465, restaurant 9240, kitchen 10,395, other 3465 total 46,200.

24.8 (*a*) Text. (*b*) (i) Actual (47 × 1.59) 74.73 − Budget (40 × 1.53) 61.20 = Variance 13.53 (ii) Rate change (47 × 0.06) 2.82 + Efficiency (7 × 1.53) 10.71 = 13.53.

24.9 Gross Profits: Rooms 50,000, Restaurant 10,000, Bar 13,000, less Carriage 150, Salaries 15,000, Wages 20,000, Other 10,000, Bad Debts 50, Deprecetion, kitchen 500, China 300, Net Profit 27,000.

25.1 (*a*) In order 10.16 less 2.23: 2.52: 1.16: 1.95: 0.89: = net profit 1.41.
(*b*) Extra business: Sales 3,087 less Food 937, Variable 374, Labour 606, Semi-Variable 694 = Contribution 476.
(*c*) Yes, because positive contribution made.

25.2 Profit from contracts A 345 + B 440 + C 500 = 1,285 − Food 720 − Fixed 270 = Net Profit 295. Extra profit required from 600 more meals 105. Therefore Food Cost 600 × 30p = 180 + Profit yet to be made 105 = Revenue to earn from 600 more meals 285. Charge per meal 285 ÷ 600 = 47.5p per meal.

25.4 (*a*) text. (*b*) Sales 10,000 − Variable: Food 4,000 − Labour 3,000 − Other 1,000 = Contribution 2,000. As a contribution is made the operation should be kept OPEN during the off-season (*c*) 5,000.

25.5 (*a*) (i) Policy 1 Contribution per unit 4.80 therefore B/E point is 40,000 ÷ 4.80 = 8,333 customers. Policy 2 B/E 70,000 ÷ 7.68 = 9,115 customers. (ii) Policy 1 = (40,000 + 20,000) ÷ 4.80 = 12,500 customers. Policy 2 = (70,000 + 20,000) ÷ 7.68 = 11,719 customers.

(*b*) See your lecturer.

25.10 Contributions: Mercer 360, Britton 378, Franklin 200. Net Profits: Mercer 50, Britton 38, Franklin 100.

(*a*) Ranking 1. Franklin 2. Mercer 3. Britton.

(*b*) Ranking 1. Britton 2. Mercer 3. Franklin.

26.1 (*a*) (i) 22121250 (ii) 30711065 (iii) 13321195 (iv) 40541035.

(*b*) (i) Ladies black shoes, short black laces, synthetic uppers, synthetic soles, no guarantee, size 4½.

(ii) Boy's white shoes, long white laces, canvas uppers, rubber soles, no guarantee, size 6.

(iii) Men's dark brown shoes, no laces, synthetic uppers, synthetic soles, no guarantee, size 8½.

(iv) Girl's green shoes, no laces, leather uppers, rubber soles, one year guarantee, size 2.

(*c*) Digit three range will be given number 8 for red colour.

(*d*) Digit one range will be extended as men's boots 5, boy's boots 6, ladies' boots 7, girl's boots 8.

(*e*) Probably useful to know whether they are high-heel, medium heel or flat heel.

(*f*) Digits 7 and 8 cover size. Size 9½ is 95 and there is no room left in range of digits 7 and 8. Would either have to extend to a nine digit system or completely alter present system. Otherwise size ten (10) would be completely indistinguishable from size one (10), size 10½ could not be accommodated.

26.2 (i) Omission (ii) Double Transposition
(ii) Transposition (iv) Addition
(v) Transcription (vi) Random.

Index